WARFARE, RAIDING AND DEFENCE
IN EARLY MEDIEVAL BRITAIN

WARFARE, RAIDING AND DEFENCE
IN EARLY MEDIEVAL BRITAIN

DR ERIK GRIGG

ROBERT HALE

First published in 2018 by Robert Hale, an imprint of
The Crowood Press Ltd, Ramsbury, Marlborough,
Wiltshire SN8 2HR

www.crowood.com

© Dr Erik Grigg 2018

All rights reserved. No part of this publication may be reproduced or transmitted in any form or by any means, electronic or mechanical, including photocopy, recording or any information storage and retrieval system, without permission in writing from the publishers.

British Library Cataloguing-in-Publication Data
A catalogue record for this book is available from the British Library.

ISBN 978 0 7198 2678 8

The right of Dr Erik Grigg to be identified as author of this work has been asserted by him in accordance with the Copyright, Designs and Patents Act 1988.

Typeset by Jean Cussons Typesetting, Diss, Norfolk

Printed and bound in India by Parksons Graphics

Contents

About this Book   6
Acknowledgements   7

1. Information and Methodology   8
2. The Archaeological Evidence   47
3. Analysing the Earthworks   63
4. Written Evidence   84
5. Across the World: Raiding and Dykes from other Periods and Places   107
6. Raiding: The Epitome of Early Medieval Warfare   113
7. Conclusions   137

Appendix I: The Dykes Listed and Measured   141
Appendix II: The Dykes Described   155
Endnotes   204
Index   221

About this Book

This book examines how small-scale raiding characterized early medieval warfare in the period AD400–850 (it is a common misconception that the medieval period in Britain started in 1066, when in fact it began at the end of Roman rule). The early medieval period has traditionally been called the 'Dark Ages', but I tend to avoid using this term. 'Dark Ages' suggests an impenetrable time, one more likely to be inhabited by wizards and dragons than a period of normal human beings. I feel this is unfair on the people who lived in that time. The correct term for the period between the classical civilizations (in Britain's case the Roman Empire) and the modern period is the Middle Ages or the medieval period. For this reason I prefer the term 'early medieval' for the centuries immediately after the end of Roman rule.

While it is common knowledge that towards the end of the early medieval period the Vikings raided their enemies, what is less well known is how the Britain they encountered was already a product of raiding and the measures designed to prevent it. Across Britain, there are over 100 early medieval dykes, some of the largest archaeological monuments in this country; in total, they stretch for over 250 miles (400km). They were built to counter the raiding that shaped early medieval Britain. They vary in size from just 100m in length to the famous Offa's Dyke, which is at least 59 miles (95km) long. They are a symptom of the endemic low-intensity warfare and frequent small-scale forays into neighbouring territories that shaped this period. This book sets out to explain the planning and execution of these raids and how the dykes functioned.

The research behind this book is partly based on a thesis submitted to the University of Manchester for the degree of Doctor of Philosophy in the Faculty of Humanities in 2015.

Acknowledgements

The author would like to thank the numerous academics and archaeologists without whom this work would never have been completed, including Nick Higham, Paul Fouracre, Martin Ryan, Charles Insley, Tim Malim, Alexander Stilwell, Andrew Noble, Jay Alcock-Brown, Antony Lee, Peter Williams and Margaret Worthington. Thanks are also extended to the many county archaeologists and SMR/HER officers who have answered my multitude of questions.

Particular thanks go to my family (especially my wife, Nicky, my parents and my children James and Helena), who have put up with numerous muddy treks across boggy fields to look at lumps in the ground. The older dog in the pictures is our much-missed Tofus, who sadly passed away during the writing of this book; the puppy is Luna, who is doing her best to replace him while we do our best to replace the slippers she destroys.

All photographs and diagrams in this study are the author's, unless otherwise stated.

CHAPTER 1

Introduction and Methodology

Early medieval warfare was carried out on a much smaller scale than most people probably imagine. It was rarely big set-piece battles with kings directing groups of soldiers across an open field. It was a lot more petty and shabby than that (despite the boasting of the poets to the contrary). Warlords, greedy bullies with a fondness for treasure, would gather bands of warriors and raid neighbouring territories. They would be after cattle, slaves and gold. They would burn down enemy homes and hack down those who got in their way. Most of the population, though, did not live by war, but off the land. Sometimes they would take their tools and dig dykes across the routeways that these marauders swept down. When the alarm was raised, the farmers would gather their spears and man these earthworks, hoping to scare the raiders away. Sometimes it would work, sometimes it did not and the defenders (or raiders) would be massacred. The dykes survive as clues to this lost world of medieval conflict.

This book covers the very early medieval period in Britain, that is, between AD400 (roughly the end of Roman rule) to AD850 (when Viking raids became more serious attempts to take over the country). It is the world of the Anglo-Saxons and Picts, but anyone looking for 'facts' will be sorely disappointed as all we have is a patchwork of scattered evidence. To make any sense of warfare in this period we need the skills of a historian to sift through the written sources, archaeological expertise to analyse the physical remains and the help of re-enactors who can offer practical solutions to how weapons were made and wielded.

Though images of knights or marauding Vikings capture the imagination, the study of warfare is not popular amongst many academics and many have underplayed the role of violence in the past, or made inaccurate assumptions about its nature. One scholar dismissed those who defined castles as defensive structures as members of the 'rape-and-pillage' school of history and whilst it is that true castles performed other roles as centres of administration, symbols of power and homes for the families of the elite, to ignore their military role because it is 'simplistic' or 'reeks of testosterone' is very short-sighted.[1] Whilst writing this book I attended an academic conference where a scholar basically dismissed anyone who thought castles were about war as a sexist, misogynist dinosaur. The tendency to underplay the role of violence in the narrative of the past is particularly prevalent amongst scholars of early medieval Britain. In recent decades, the Anglo-Saxon 'Invasion' has been dismissed as a peaceful change in culture. One of the most influential books on Vikings in the twentieth century suggested that accounts of their attacks were exaggerated by monks who had reason to paint the pagan men of the north in the worst possible light and Vikings are increasingly portrayed as traders, not raiders.[2]

With the hostile Anglo-Saxon takeover of lowland Britain being dismissed and Vikings reduced to market traders, the early medieval period is becoming safe, tranquil and, to be honest, a bit boring. The reluctance of the post-Vietnam generation of archaeologists to ascribe a military purpose to any defensive earthwork or buried weapon has been termed 'the pacification of the past'.[3] Today, however, many historians and archaeologists are returning to the notion that war, raiding and slavery were fundamental parts of the shaping of prehistoric, early historic and medieval societies. I hope to prove that low-intensity warfare characterized this period and dykes are one manifestation of that phenomenon:

> There was in Mercia in fairly recent times a certain vigorous king called Offa, who terrified all the neighbouring kings and provinces around him, and who had a great dyke built between Wales and Mercia from sea to sea.
> (Taken from Asser's *Life of King Alfred* written about AD900.[4])

Across Britain, there are numerous long earthworks, some of which stretch for miles across the landscape. Unfortunately, this tantalizingly enigmatic reference to an eighth-century Mercian king building an earthwork along the Welsh border is one of the few early medieval clues as to who built them. Even in this quote, it is not clear why it was dug, though the author seems to imply that this king built it because he was 'vigorous' and wanted to terrify his neighbours.

Despite having numerous ramblers following them across the landscape every year, we know surprisingly little about dykes. The quote above suggests that Offa probably ordered that one to be built, but we cannot be sure who ordered the building of the rest, or, more importantly, why. Furthermore, while we suspect that there was a rash of dyke building in the early medieval period, we are also uncertain which dykes are definitely early medieval (and which are not). This book is partly based on my PhD thesis on early medieval earthworks (dykes), a subject I chose because I felt that a comprehensive study of early medieval dykes was long overdue. As my study reached a conclusion, it became apparent how most of the dykes had a military function. If that was the case, it meant that warfare was far more endemic than many had thought and that these earthworks can help us to reconstruct some of the mechanics of such conflicts. By placing warfare (in particular raiding) back into the narrative, we can see how it helped to mould early medieval Britain.

My interest in this period of history started at a very early age. In 1982, my parents bought me a copy of Michael Wood's *In Search of the Dark Ages*, a book that tied into a television series I had avidly watched the previous year.[5] Despite being just fourteen, my copy was read and reread many times over. I had been particularly interested in the King Arthur episode and that shadowy period just after the end of Roman rule in Britain. It seemed incredible to me that we knew so little about how the country I lived in, England, and the language I spoke, English, had come into being.

The following Easter, my father and I went on a camping trip to Dorset to visit some ancient monuments that had interested him as a young man. In a small bookshop, I picked up a copy of *Exploring Ancient Dorset*, a guide to that county's key archaeological monuments.[6] What fascinated me was the dykes of the early medieval period (or Dark Ages, as was the term more commonly used in those days), which seemed to guard Dorset against the Anglo-Saxons of Wessex. We visited one, Bokerley Dyke, and strode along the mysterious grass-covered bank. Later, we drove to Wareham, where, in the walls of Lady St Mary's church, pre-Anglo-Saxon names could be seen carved into the stones in the walls. I was at that age an avid fan of the writing of J.R.R. Tolkien and was captivated by the way in which he would add layers of history to a landscape and his characters would slowly realize that they strode through the remains of lost kingdoms and empires. Here, I thought, in Dorset – underneath modern England – was a lost world, a 'Welsh' kingdom protected by vast earthworks. These dykes were literally the biggest pieces of evidence as to what had happened. They were not scraps of pot or garbled accounts written (and rewritten) long after the events, but clues in our landscape. If I could decode them, then I could cast light on this murky period.

During my time at school and as an undergraduate I had to study the Tudors, the twentieth century and the English Civil War, periods where there are so many surviving documents that it seemed to be more like journalism than history. The Dark Ages, the early medieval period, was what I wanted to study. I knew that it would take an interdisciplinary approach. I would need to understand the landscape, unravel the documents, decode the place names and piece together the archaeology. Long after I graduated, I studied Latin and Brythonic languages (like Cornish), joined an archaeology group, read the works of landscape historians, analysed early medieval texts and avidly devoured hundreds of archaeological reports. When I was able to take a Master's degree at the University of Manchester, working with early medieval specialists, I found out that nobody had made a comprehensive study of early medieval dykes. I could not believe my luck; most aspects of this period had been studied and reappraised on multiple occasions, but this subject seemed almost untouched. Sure, great archaeologists and historians had discussed individual dykes or even a few nearby earthworks, but nobody had seriously gathered together all the evidence and pondered what their construction meant for this period. I applied to do a PhD thesis at Manchester and, luckily, my request was accepted.

This book is the outcome of that study. In it, I attempt to establish how many dykes date to the early medieval period and calculate how many people were needed to build them. I collate all the available evidence (including archaeological and written) in order to hypothesize why these dykes were built and what functions they fulfilled. This book analyses what Fox calls 'travelling, running or linear earthworks', but as these are rather clumsy terms, the term 'dykes' is used throughout.[7] This work is limited to the period AD400 (roughly the end of Roman rule in Britain) to 850 (just before Viking raids became invasions), in order to exclude Roman defences and those structures built by, or to counter, the Vikings.

The study mainly covers Wales, England and lowland Scotland where the dykes are located; the highlands and islands of Scotland do not seem to contain any. This book helps us to understand how dyke building fitted into the wider changes that transformed Britain south of the Forth–Clyde line in the period 400–850. At the start, lowland Britain was part of the Roman Empire; it fragmented into tribal groupings and then towards the end of the period large kingdoms emerged, some of which spoke a Germanic language brought by invaders from across the North Sea.

While this work contains evidence obtained by archaeologists, it is not written by one. Linking archaeological evidence with written evidence is always problematic, but if historians do not study periods where archaeology provides the bulk of the evidence, they potentially surrender the chance to marry an analysis of early medieval texts with the physical remains from the period.

CHANGING ATTITUDES TO EARLY MEDIEVAL WARFARE

Let us examine the changing attitudes of historians to early medieval warfare in a little more detail. Up until about thirty years ago, scholars discussing this period would often mention warfare without specifying how it worked in any detail. The Anglo-Saxons simply 'invaded' Britain, conflicts were 'wars', battles were just 'battles' and it was presumed that it was sufficient to describe kingdoms fighting each other with little or no discussion of the logistics of how that happened. There was also a move to airbrush war out of the narrative. As well as the trend to classify Vikings more as traders than raiders, attitudes to the Anglo-Saxon invasion began to change. With it no longer seen as a mass invasion where hordes of Germanic warriors either murdered the natives in a genocidal war or swept them aside into Wales, scholars rightly began to ask if many Britons could simply have adopted Anglo-Saxon culture. Others took this idea further until it began to be argued that hardly any or even no Anglo-Saxon crossed the North Sea in the fifth century.[8] Such a hypothesis requires large swathes of archaeological, linguistic and historical evidence to be dismissed or radically reinterpreted in ways most scholars would not accept and has been described as simple 'silliness'.[9]

In terms of dyke studies, one example may suffice of how the study of these earthworks changed from a simplistic view of warfare, through a pacification process to a more nuanced view involving raiding. Initially, the Cambridgeshire Dykes were seen as defences erected during times of war, though it was not known when they were built. In the 1920s and 1930s, archaeologists excavating Bran Ditch in Cambridgeshire found the remains of over fifty bodies, most of which showed clear signs that they had met a violent end. They assumed they were from a Viking massacre, though later writers have classified them as executed criminals from the period 900–1080. A frenzied act of mass butchery became a deliberate and considered judicial process. Muir cast doubt on whether Cambridgeshire Dykes ever worked as military structures, though admitted that they might break up a cavalry charge.[10] More recently, attitudes have changed, and the Cambridgeshire Dykes have again been seen as defensive solutions to military attack.

The problem scholars often had with warfare was that they simply did not understand how early medieval people fought and the odd references to battles in sources like *The Anglo-Saxon Chronicle* did little to help. However, not all scholars followed this trend of removing the role of conflict from their theories. In 1987, a conference at Oxford on Anglo-Saxon warfare was held, looking at many various aspects of how conflicts were fought, evidence of weapon injuries from cemeteries, the weapons used and the logistics of fighting wars.[11] Almost a decade later a collection of papers looking at early medieval violence across Western Europe, its causes and nature, was published under the editorship of Guy Halsall.[12] Academic studies can only go so far and the growth of experimental archaeology (recreating the past in a physical form, such as making replica swords) and the growth of re-enacting gave new insights into how early medieval weapons worked in practice. Underwood's 1999 book discussed the archaeological and written evidence and then he examined how to make and wield the weaponry.[13] Although no substitute for the real thing, it is now possible to watch re-enactors using weapons of the same weight and design in mock battles, bringing back to life the noise and chaos of early medieval fighting.

In more recent studies, fighting and warfare have become integral to the story of how Roman Britain became early medieval England, Scotland and Wales. Scientific advances mean that it is much easier to differentiate between victims of battle (or massacres) and murder victims. Historians are far more willing to accept the role raiding played in undermining Roman authority and conflict is now integral to the narrative of how lowland Britain became Anglo-Saxon England. Cattle raids are seen as an important way in which early medieval leaders gained wealth; slave raiding is seen as having a similar function and, like cattle raiding, could destroy communities as well as help to create new elites. Warlords who engaged in raiding are now seen as the founders of early medieval kingdoms and raiding by and between kings is seen as a mechanism whereby such rulers reinforced their power. Now no study of the Vikings is complete without a long discussion about how warriors were trained, weapons made and an examination of how raiding worked in practice. In 2007, the Landscapes of Defence Project hosted a conference at University College London specifically on 'Landscapes of Defence in the Viking Age'. Whilst at the conference, I noticed how continental academics had no problem with the idea that an earthwork could have a military function.[14]

The footsteps of marching war bands, the scars of battle on the bodies of warriors and most other evidence of early medieval warfare have long since faded away, but the dykes built to counter those raids still survive. Their size, location and distribution are among the few clues as to how and where early medieval conflict occurred. Now that war and raiding are again seen as an important part of the tapestry of early medieval history, before we turn to studying dykes in depth I feel it will be helpful first to see how scholars have classified, discussed and reappraised this least understood aspect of early medieval warfare.

THE DEVELOPMENT OF DYKE STUDIES

'I would maintain that, on a subject of such bewildering confusion as that of our ancient dykes and earthworks, any reasonable hypothesis that enables us to group together a certain number of these boundary lines, can hardly fail to be of service.'[15] Guest's 1849 call for a systematic study of the dykes of Britain went largely unheeded, but an examination of how previous scholars have studied dykes might help us to understand how they work as well as formulate future research strategies. Early medieval dykes can attract some bizarre theories; Pitt Rivers once postulated that Bokerley Dyke and Grim's Dyke acted as a giant funnel for herding deer from the New Forest to Cranborne Chase Forest, a claim so unlikely that even he dropped it almost immediately.[16]

An analysis of, say, modern cars that merely concentrated on Ferraris and Bugattis would be considered fatally flawed, yet most studies of early medieval dykes have focused on the more famous and larger ones. As dykes are physical features, most discussions have been by archaeologists, who have focused on the size, length and fabric of a dyke rather than on their role in early medieval society. This book addresses the whole issue of why there was such a rash of dyke building and what that tells us about the processes at work.

After Asser's brief mention of Offa's Dyke, it was not until the rise of antiquarianism in the eighteenth century that descriptions of most of these earthworks were published. While some antiquarians probably exaggerated the size of earthworks, we must be cautious of dismissing outright the descriptions of the dykes from before they suffered the ravages of the Agricultural Revolution. Some scholars went beyond merely describing the dykes and tried, often erroneously (with hindsight), to link them with known historical events like the Belgic invasions mentioned by Caesar or Caesar's own invasion. Among these early, rather speculative descriptions, the work of the Wiltshire historian Sir Richard Colt Hoare (1758–1838) stands out, not only in terms of the quality of his survey work, but also his ability to differentiate between features of different dates, for example by realizing that the central section of Wansdyke was actually a Roman road.

The rise of modern archaeology in the nineteenth century led to great strides being made; Augustus Henry Lane Fox (1827–1900) was the first to excavate dykes in a systematic manner. In 1875, he used excavation evidence to demonstrate that the flint mines at Cissbury in Sussex predated the Iron Age hill fort because a portion of the rampart overlay a mineshaft. This conclusion that newer features are to be found on top of older ones seems obvious to modern readers, but this reasoning was a massive step forward that led to later scholars developing dating by stratigraphy.

In 1879, Fox excavated the Danevirke in Denmark with a colleague using a spade borrowed from a nearby cottage, but despite these ad hoc methods and his inability to date securely the monument, he was able to detect modifications made to the dyke. In 1890, Fox inherited a large estate based on Cranborne Chase, an area full of archaeological sites, allowing him to indulge further his passion for archaeology, though it also entailed him adopting the name Pitt Rivers; modern scholars usually refer to him by this later moniker. Pitt Rivers (as we shall now call him) carried out further excavations at Bokerley Dyke (which he called Bokerly Dyke) and Wansdyke between 1888 and 1891, but age prevented a planned excavation at Offa's Dyke. He was a military man, a General, whose studies of the development of the rifle (for example, how new models usually innovate slightly on older designs) influenced his thinking about changes in archaeological artefacts over time. He unsurprisingly saw dykes as military structures built by successive waves of invaders.

After Pitt Rivers, works on dykes took something of a step backwards for the next three decades. In 1913, Godsal wrote a study encompassing many of the more famous dykes. However, it contained no new survey of the earthworks or archaeological evidence, but was full of rather crude notions of race that sound quite offensive to modern ears.[17]

Arguably the most famous figure in twentieth-century dyke studies was Sir Cyril Fox. His fieldwork was thorough and the plans he produced were far in advance of anything previously seen, but he also analysed the monuments, attempting to link them with known historical events. He started studying the dykes in Cambridgeshire, which he postulated were built by the East Angles (the Anglo-Saxons who inhabited Norfolk and Suffolk) in the early medieval period. He spent the years 1925–32 carrying out an intensive survey of Offa's Dyke and Wat's Dyke, which was collected into a single volume in 1955.[18] He concluded that Offa's Dyke was a single structure designed to mark the Anglo-Welsh border and ran from sea to sea with the gaps (for example, in Herefordshire) being where thick woodland made an earthwork unnecessary. Though he concurred that it looked military, he thought it was an agreed boundary often set back from the actual frontier to allow the Welsh access to resources like the River Wye. Inspired by his rigorous fieldwork, in 1946 Fox, along with O'Neil and Grimes, produced an excellent guide to surveying dykes.[19] In 1958, Fox and his second wife, Aileen, wrote a work on Wansdyke that dismissed the idea that Wansdyke reached the Bristol Channel and concluded that it was in fact two separate monuments built at different periods by the West Saxons.[20] Fox's fieldwork methods have greatly influenced scholars up until the present.

Despite being employed by the Ordnance Survey, Osbert Crawford's 1953 book also went beyond merely surveying dykes and is the first work systematically to compare British dykes with examples from the Continent.[21] The study was a reaction to Major and Burrow's book on Wansdyke, which Crawford (rightly) considered full of inaccuracies.[22] Crawford noted how many of the British dykes seemed to bar thoroughfares and that overseas dykes or walls varied in their purposes, some being military structures, others customs barriers, while some combined the two purposes. Unlike many who have written on the subject, Crawford did not limit his analysis to the major dykes; in one article he looked at how the names of mythical giants had become associated with the relatively obscure dykes of Cornwall.[23] His analysis was unfortunately largely limited to describing dykes as either military-political (with no clarification of what that meant in practice), or in respect of the coastal dykes (like Dane's Dyke at Flamborough Head or the Cornish dykes) calling them beach heads. He also made no attempt to group what he termed defensive linear earthworks by period (probably because of the lack of dating evidence); in his list of them given as an appendix to his field archaeology guide he includes prehistoric and Anglo-Saxon dykes together with undated earthworks. These shortcomings are easy to criticize now, but at the time Crawford's work was exceptional.

Since the days of Fox, there have been major scientific advances in archaeology by which scholars can test previous assumptions, such as whether areas of primeval woodland explain possible gaps in a dyke. The technique of examining soil samples for pollen so that we can understand the flora of historic landscapes has a long history. It was rarely used on dykes prior to C. Crampton's 1966 study of dykes in Wales, which was the first to date various earthworks using pollen and soil samples from under the banks.[24] Heathland and peat developed in the uplands from the

Bronze Age onwards. Crampton, in a brilliant piece of insight that was decades ahead of its time, felt that the amount of clay and silt weathered into the peaty podzol was a good indicator of the age of the ground and so could be used to date the banks that overlay such soils. An analysis of mollusca (snails or beetles) from archaeological deposits can also tell us if a dyke originally passed through open, marshy, dry or wooded areas. A series of excavations carried out by H. Stephen Green on Wansdyke in the late 1960s provided the first opportunity to combine snail and pollen analysis to dyke studies.[25] While the evidence for snails was largely inconclusive, the pollen samples (analysed by G.W. Dimbleby) suggested that central parts of the eastern half of Wansdyke passed through pasture. Now at last historians knew what kind of landscapes the builders of the dykes worked in.

Today we have even more scientific tools that we can use to analyse dykes. The emergence of radiocarbon dating, dendrochronology and Optically Stimulated Luminescence (the limitations of which are discussed in detail later) has further helped us to date organic material. We can now see features below the ground surface using geophysical surveying techniques (resistivity and ground-penetrating radar), which can help to locate sections of dykes long since ploughed flat, though this technique is often useless through the tarmac of modern roads that sometimes cross earthworks.

Another recent advance is Light Detection and Recognition (LIDAR), in which highly accurate images of the ground are taken using lasers mounted on low-flying planes. This technique allows us to make aerial photographs that not only reveal surface remains in open country, but also the ground surface in wooded areas so that even overgrown sections of earthworks are now detectable. If a dyke has been completely flattened, though (like the Black Ditches of Suffolk), LIDAR is of little use. Where LIDAR data are available (for example, Gilling Wood Dyke in Yorkshire, Danes Dyke, Giant's Grave in Cornwall and Heronbridge), it is possible to see if medieval ridge and furrow respect the dyke and presumably therefore post-date it.

These new tools require new skills. Green's study of the pollen at Wansdyke demonstrated the need for dedicated experts to analyse the results of these new scientific techniques and recent advances in technology have increased the need for qualified specialists to interpret the plethora of technical data. Large and well-funded studies now produce much greater amounts of information not only using pollen and snail analysis, but also geophysics and radiocarbon dating. A 1996 study carried out by the Archaeological Field Unit of Cambridgeshire County Council that examined the four Cambridgeshire Dykes involved careful excavation and the application of the full range of modern scientific techniques.[26] The study helped to clarify the dating of the dykes, the construction methods, past environmental conditions and possible evidence of maintenance.

The age range suggested by the stratification and the radiocarbon dates (AD330–700) are frustratingly still too wide to link them with specific political events. Unfortunately, the archaeologists were unable to dig the tarmac roads that overlay the ancient thoroughfares through the dykes, so it was impossible to prove or disprove that gaps originally existed to allow the movement of goods and people through the dykes.

Despite the numerous advances in the science of archaeology in the last century, the methodologies used in the study of dykes have often not significantly changed. Scholars have often just concentrated on trying to prove that dykes were either longer or shorter than previous studies suggested, with endless discussions about whether certain hedgerows marked the course of the lost sections of dykes or were later features. In 1977, Frank Noble's MPhil thesis rejected Fox's view that impassable forest in Herefordshire was the cause of gaps in Offa's Dyke, instead suggesting that there was little undergrowth under the canopy of mature woodland in medieval Britain as there were more mammals.[27] Noble also proposed that many hedges that Fox claimed were hypothetical lost sections of the earthwork were actually later agricultural features. He unfortunately died soon after producing his thesis, though his pioneering work did lead to the creation of the Offa's Dyke long-distance footpath and there was a posthumous publication of parts of his work. In Fox's day, Offa's Dyke was thought to consist of 80 miles (130km) of constructed earthwork, but, thanks partly to Noble, more recent authors have concluded that it consists of the main earthwork, which is less than 62 miles (100km) in length, and disconnected banks that may or may not have been built as part of the same scheme.

The study of Offa's Dyke was continued by David Hill (later aided by Margaret Worthington), using students from the Extra Mural Department of the University of Manchester to complete a comprehensive survey of Offa's Dyke and test-dig some sections.[28] Rather than seeing it as an Anglo-Welsh border (especially as neither England nor Wales was united in Offa's day), they noted how the only portion of the dyke that was not in question, the central section, approximated to the Mercian–Powys border. They excavated many of the hypothetical gateways on Offa's Dyke, mainly where modern roads, paths and tracks cut through the dyke, and also pioneered the use of resistivity surveys to locate sections of earthworks ploughed flat by agriculture. When they excavated the ditch at the hypothetical gateway sites, they found no evidence for causeways. They decided that the dyke was defensible, rather than defended, and that it was not permanently manned like Hadrian's Wall, merely patrolled with local defenders called up in times of trouble. They thought that it was designed to prevent raids from the Welsh kingdom of Powys. Their model of a military infrastructure behind the dyke of warning beacons and defended villages unfortunately relied more on conjecture than concrete evidence.

Ever since Asser's assertion that Offa's Dyke reached from sea to sea, the debates about the lengths of certain dykes have raged, especially over Wansdyke. Collinson claimed that Wansdyke was 80 miles (129km) long; Pitt Rivers estimated it to be just 60 miles (97km) long; Major and Burrows suggested it was 74 miles (119km) long; while Fox's maps show only about 24 miles (39km) of built dyke. While the debates about the extent of individual dykes are important (for example, if Offa's Dyke did not reach from sea to sea, it is more likely to mark the Mercian–Powys border than the Anglo-Welsh divide), recently historians have begun to go a little further by actually analysing dykes. They have sought to explore the wider cultural, psychological and/or political reasons for both dyke construction and the consequences of their existence. As far back as 1981, Richard Muir postulated that the Cambridgeshire Dykes might have no practical purpose, but were merely enormous and empty displays of royal power.[29]

Since the 1980s, scholars studying Roman frontier defences (limes) have begun to interpret them as zones of interaction rather than watertight barriers.[30] At the same time, scholars of early medieval fortifications have increasingly been inclined towards the view that rulers invested in earthworks less to ward off invaders than to unify their kingdoms. Rulers promoted the idea that the neighbouring kingdom or tribe was 'the enemy', then imposed their power over their own people by enforced labour service building fortifications against their enemy.

Perhaps earthworks could also reduce conflict as well as divide people. In 1999, Nicholas Boldrini postulated that the two branches of the Roman Ridge in South Yorkshire might mark not a border, but an attempt to create a 'liminal' space, perhaps in which to parley.[31] Liminal is a popular buzzword amongst some historians and archaeologists, but it simply means border or transitional areas not under the secure control of anyone. Such developments reflect the post-processualist movement in archaeology, which views variations in material culture as less reflective of the innate differences between tribes than as attempts to construct regional identities among rather cosmopolitan groups of people. Groups used fashion and other aspects of culture to form an identity. In early medieval terms, it would mean that people were not naturally or innately Anglo-Saxons or Britons (or on a smaller scale Mercians or the people of Powys), but that these cultural identities were forged and moulded by leaders with agendas.

Theories that espouse symbolic rather than practical uses for dykes have become popular. Damian Tyler has proposed that Offa's Dyke was less a practical military structure than a symbol of Offa's imperial pretensions and an attempt to copy what the Romans had done on their northern British frontier; it was part of a state-building exercise by which Offa portrayed himself as the protector of all the English.[32] Similar reasoning has been put forward for Wansdyke; Andrews Reynolds suggested that it was an attempt by the new kingdom of Wessex to define itself against the powerful Mercian kingdom to the north, while Draper argued that on a smaller scale East Wansdyke stimulated the creation of the shire of Wiltshire.[33]

Some still argue a potential military use for dykes. For Stuart Laycock, however, some dykes, like the Cambridgeshire Dykes and Wansdyke, did not mark the border between British and English kingdoms, but were earlier cultural divides built as the country collapsed into tribal warfare in the period between the final years of Roman rule and the arrival of the Saxons.[34] He argued that they marked the fragmentation of Britain along much older tribal lines during and after the end of Roman rule in a similar way to the situation in Yugoslavia in the 1990s. Some recent scholars have been less certain about why the dykes were built and have examined various hypotheses, but come to no concrete conclusions. One of the authors of the Cambridgeshire report who went on to analyse the Welsh Border dykes, Tim Malim, has argued that they helped kings to control trade and also the movement of people in and out of their kingdoms, prevented raiding and displayed the power of the crown.[35]

The trend of analysing motives rather than measuring the length of dykes has led to the most wide-ranging analysis of the cultural, social and political reasons behind dyke building carried out by Paolo Squatriti of the University of Michigan.[36] His studies have covered some of the major early medieval dykes from across Europe, various Bulgarian earthworks including the Great Fence of Thrace (Erkesia), Offa's Dyke and the Danevirke, even Charlemagne's attempt to dig a canal between the Danube and the Main. It is worth examining his ideas in some detail.

Like Tyler and Reynolds, Squatriti postulates more symbolic and political roles for dyke building: the act of building the earthwork is as important (or possibly even more so) than how the final structure was utilized on a daily basis. He dismissed utilitarian functions for dykes, such as their use as a fighting platform (as the kingdoms did not have the manpower to garrison them), or being a border marker so that travellers would know where the edge of the kingdom lay (as they have gaps). He pointed out several problems with the idea that dykes were just political boundary markers: they are unnecessarily large; later cultural or administrative boundaries rarely follow them; medieval kingdoms did not have sharp borders; and, finally, expansionist kingdoms like Mercia had little reason to fossilize their boundaries. He proposed that they were just theatrical features intended to enhance the prestige of kings and, in turn, their kingdoms. Such theatricality was particularly apt when kings had only recently established themselves and wished to demonstrate both internally and externally that they had control over their territory, in particular over debatable borderlands. The diggers knew they served little utilitarian purposes, but showed their loyalty to the ruler by accepting false military reasons given by the kings for constructing the earthworks. People in border areas recently incorporated into the kingdom were required to do the digging as a labour service to their ruler; it was the easiest way a king could extract value from a people in an economy where monetary taxation was unusual (as coinage was rare) and it incorporated them in the power structures of the kingdom.

Squatriti's suppositions contain weaknesses, however, some of which he acknowledged. He was unable to explain why, for example, if these earthworks were built to glorify individual kings, the name of the ruler who ordered them was so rarely remembered. Specialists in the Bulgarian earthworks offer a very different scenario, noting how the dykes functioned militarily on a practical level and how forts replaced linear earthworks as the main type of defence.[37] Without a comprehensive gazetteer of all dykes, his study was limited to the better known and largest examples. He freely admitted to me when I contacted him that the smaller dykes in Britain may have had a military function, as his idea about earthworks being non-practical exercises in the theatre of kingship only applies to the larger examples. Additionally, although he mentioned local people maintaining and sometimes rebuilding dykes, he did not explain why they did this if the dyke had no obvious practical use for them. The borders of the early medieval kingdoms did not just move, they were amorphous zones with debatable marches, as Squatriti himself acknowledges. This would mean that any king using the building of an earthwork to unite his kingdom would have an obvious dilemma when deciding where to construct it. If he built a dyke near the core of his kingdom, it would seem to exclude the marches and undermine his claims to a larger territory; if he built it near the fringes of his control, he would provoke neighbouring rulers and expose the workers to attack. Surely a successful, warlike, predatory expansionist king would probably be more interested in expanding his kingdom than marking limits.

Some recent works on the dykes of the Welsh borders and Cambridgeshire have suggested that dykes served a military purpose.[38] In 2012, Mark Bell published a study of dykes that attempted to list all the Dark Age dykes in Britain.[39] His list of dykes contained some of the earthworks mentioned in this book, though he seems unaware of many others, especially in Wales and northern Britain (Park Pale, Tor Dyke, Bank Slack and Broomhead Dyke in Yorkshire, for example). Bell also accidentally included numerous prehistoric earthworks that I have not included in this study (as they are not relevant to the study of early medieval earthworks). Bell concluded that the builders of these earthworks probably designed them to control raiding; it is reassuring that he, independently of this study, reached the similar conclusion, though this book makes the case in far greater depth and using far more sophisticated methods of analysis.

DEFINING TERMS

Before proceeding further, we need to set some parameters and define terms. There does seem to have been a propensity for building dykes in this period that appear to be related to raiding, so it is through those earthworks that this book examines warfare. To extend it to cover more of later medieval Britain would have made the scope unmanageable. First, we need to define some historical terms. There is no simple term for this period without concocting a rather clumsy phrase (like 'post-Roman and pre-Viking period'), or using the term 'Anglo-Saxon', which is incongruous across some parts of Britain such as Wales. I avoid the term 'Dark Age', as it makes the times sound more like Middle Earth than a real historical period and carries the connotation that it is somehow uncivilized and degenerate compared with Roman times. While the Romans may have had cities and engineering, their bloodlust in the arena and willingness ruthlessly to crush those who opposed them hardly makes them civilized in my book. I therefore use the term 'early medieval' for simplicity's sake to define the period from 400 to 850. While most historians would still class it as early medieval, the period from 850 to 1066 is here termed 'Viking', as although this is inaccurate (technically it should only apply to Scandinavian raiders and therefore is not applicable to the natives or peaceful settlers of Scandinavian origin), it is readily understood by most people. The period after 1066 to 1485 is simply referred to as 'later medieval'.

Some have used rather clumsy terms for these earthworks, like 'travelling, running or linear earthworks', but I use the term 'dykes'. Defining what is and what is not an early medieval dyke is problematic, as any definition may prejudge the conclusions. Earthworks designed to keep animals fenced in (or out) are excluded, as are those that enclose settlements (hill forts and *burhs*, for example) and drainage dykes. Luckily, the word 'dyke' (which goes back to the Old English language that was formed in the early medieval period) and the Welsh equivalent, *clawdd*, are not narrow terms, but can mean just a bank, a ditch or a combination of the two. Usually one cannot have a bank without a ditch from which the material is quarried, but if one is absent due to later damage, the terms dyke or clawdd are still apposite. Therefore, this study includes earthworks that contain one or both of those features and does not define a settlement, a drain-water, or have an agricultural purpose.

As well as drainage dykes and hedges, there are other earthworks frequently mistaken for early medieval dykes that we must take particular care to exclude. The first are head dykes, which are usually late medieval features that divided the settled, fertile, arable, lowland areas from less fertile, upland, rough grazing and so prevented animals eating crops. The second group are later medieval earthworks found around private woods and game parks (often called park pales or woodbanks). The third type of earthwork to exclude is roads; some dykes look very similar to Roman roads and vice versa, which has caused confusion among scholars. We must also rule out border markers, these are often on the same alignment (or contiguous) with administrative borders. With parish boundaries and dykes, the word 'contiguous' is used to denote that the dyke and the parish boundary are on the same line; the word 'follows' used by other studies might imply that we could be certain which of the two came first. In the next section, we shall sift out these red herrings.

A Hundred is a traditional subdivision of a county; in areas where the Vikings settled they are called *wapentakes* and in Wales, *Cantrefs*. The number traditionally refers to the number of warriors an area could provide in time of war. Some have assumed that they mark an area that was once a subkingdom, clan or subtribe later absorbed into a larger political unit, usually a kingdom.

'RED HERRINGS'

In order to study early medieval warfare, I first had to catalogue the earthworks I thought were defensive dykes (*see* Appendix I: The Dykes Listed and Measured). The main difficulty was the lack of reliable data, as previous lists of dykes are incomplete, out of date and poorly referenced.[40] I therefore began by establishing a comprehensive list, or gazetteer, of dykes, which includes those that are probably from this period, those mistakenly assumed to be of an early medieval date, those that possibly are from the period and older dykes possibly reused during the early medieval period. Obviously, such a list can never be comprehensive, as new dating evidence may arise and I may have missed smaller dykes destroyed, for example, by later agricultural activity.

The entries in Appendix II 'The Dykes Described' are edited versions of much longer discussions I wrote about each individual dyke (in my house there are box files for the dykes of each county containing photocopies of hundreds of archaeological reports and folders on my computer giving detailed descriptions of each earthwork). Most dykes were visited whilst researching this book and that fieldwork helped to answer many questions. The fieldwork involved working out how long the earthwork was, measuring the banks/ditches, looking for signs of gateways, establishing how far a person patrolling the dyke could have seen and how easily the dyke could be spotted from a distance. Some of the dykes are longer or shorter on the ground than was claimed by older written accounts (especially older antiquarian descriptions) and online aerial photographic databases coupled with fieldwork helped to resolve these discrepancies. Before I give that list, I need to give some reasoning behind it.

I first sifted out any earthworks built for peaceful purposes and concentrated just on those dykes built to counter early medieval raiding, making sure that those left were designed with war in mind. Second, by considering other possible explanations for the dykes, I made sure that the theory of the military stop line against raiders was the most plausible theory for why so many of this type of earthwork were built in the early medieval period.

It is possible to mistake a dyke for a natural feature. Bwlch Aeddan near Guislfield in Powys, for example, may look like a ploughed-out dyke, but it is probably a natural feature. Head dykes (which were usually built in the later medieval period onwards) can look similar to early medieval dykes; these are boundaries built to make the change between arable land and rough grazing uplands. Joseph Train in 1824 erroneously postulated that a series of head dykes in Dumfriesshire and Galloway was a single early medieval earthwork called Deil's Dyke.[41] Head dykes have a distinct form that can be easily distinguished through observations in the field. They run parallel with contour lines at the head of valleys, are usually found where there is a change in land quality and their ditches (which are smaller than other early medieval dykes) usually face towards the uplands to keep free-roving livestock out of arable fields. Tor Dyke in Yorkshire superficially resembles a head dyke, but as the ditch is downhill of the bank and about 3m deep and 6m wide, this earthwork is quite clearly very different.

There are wood boundaries and park pales that have been confused with early medieval dykes, but it is possible to distinguish the two. Wood and park boundaries usually enclose a discrete area (even if it is no longer a wood or a park). Some have no ditch as they were constructed from stones found on the surface or from stacked turf; others have ditches that face inwards, although these are usually quite small. Scholars have postulated that some of the earthworks listed in the Appendixes are park or wood boundaries like Minchinhampton Bulwarks in Gloucestershire and there are written records dated 1276–1306 of a private wood in the vicinity of that earthwork.[42] Foxfield near the East Hampshire Dykes is called a *haga*, or game reserve, in the late Saxon Meon Charters, but the nearby dykes seem far too big to be mere park boundaries and do not surround a discrete area.[43] The northern section of the Catrail earthwork in the Scottish Borders is possibly a sixteenth-century 'woodbank' – as it lies across a change in soil quality it could indeed mark the edge of a wood. Senghenydd Dyke in Glamorgan, another earthwork included in the Appendixes, encloses a part of the Aber valley including the two villages of Senghenydd and Abertridwr; this is a thirteenth-century private hunting estate.

Some early medieval dykes have been erroneously classified as roads in the past (the Catrail in the Scottish Borders, Rowe Ditch in Herefordshire, Roman Rig in Yorkshire and the Giant's Hedge in Cornwall), but they are obviously very different structures and look quite different when excavated. Early medieval dykes consist of an earth bank and a ditch that cuts a valley or a ridge, Roman roads usually have a metalled surface between two drainage ditches, medieval causeways are usually found crossing marshy areas and medieval hollow ways usually consist of a sunken roadway with no associated banks. Later road builders certainly reused sections of a few dykes, but only very short stretches. While early medieval dykes were not roads, some ancient thoroughfares have been erroneously classified as dykes. Recent excavations of Brent Ditch, an earthwork often thought of as part of the Cambridgeshire Dykes, have found no evidence of a bank, suggesting it was not a dyke but a hollow way.

Some dykes that enclose peninsulas have been confused with forts. Earthworks built to defend the approaches to a transitory encampment like the one the Vikings dug near Reading (Coombe Bank) in 871–2 are very similar. Though there is no written evidence that Heronbridge in Cheshire was ever an Anglo-Saxon *burh* (a defended town or fort), the archaeologists who carried out the recent excavations at the dyke consider it a fort. There is no evidence of early medieval gateways in the earthwork or signs of occupation at the site apart from some burials, so I define it as a dyke. Park Pale in Yorkshire could also be a fort, but again there is no evidence of gateways, occupation or written evidence to support the idea.

Some historians have claimed that early medieval dykes are actually trade barriers; if so, this means they were not stop lines against raiders as I think. For most of this period, though, there is insufficient evidence of inland trade to prove that the primary stimulus for the construction of such large earthworks was to control commerce. Apart from the Roman coins found at Bokerley Dyke that predate the earthwork in its final form, no excavation has found small denomination coins (which we would expect to be dropped occasionally if tolls were being collected at the dykes) or evidence of gateways, let alone ones with attached buildings for customs officials at any early medieval dyke. In fact, no medieval coins have been recorded at any dyke and no early medieval trade centres, which were called *emporia* or wics by Anglo-Saxons (like Ipswich, productive sites like Cottam in Yorkshire, or coastal trading sites like Meols in the Wirral) were located in the vicinity of any dyke. Like Roman frontier works, a dyke could have also acted as a trade barrier as an ancillary purpose, but there was not enough trade to stimulate the boom in dyke building. Perhaps the rise of trade that we see reflected in the growth of the minting of coins in the late seventh century onwards could even have hastened the end of dykes that blocked trade routes.

It is possible that a dyke built for a ritual reason can superficially look like a defensive structure. Ritual activity is hard to define, but includes any repetitive action including religious and ceremonial functions. Many earthworks are named after supernatural figures, but this may be due to the original builders being long forgotten rather than the actual structures being associated with gods or religion. There are three types of ritual activity that are possibly associated with dykes: delimiting a sacred space, a meeting place and a site for execution. These three are discussed in turn in this section.

Dykes that cut off peninsulas of land could hypothetically demark an area designated for a ritual purpose, but apart from Ponter's Ball in Somerset, which does seem to block a causeway giving access to Glastonbury, the areas enclosed by such earthworks (like Dane's Dyke in Yorkshire or the dykes of Cornwall) contain no significant religious sites apart from the occasional humdrum parish church.

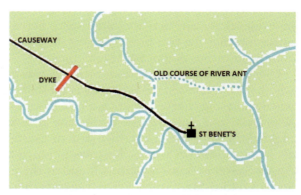

Horning Dyke showing how it could have defined a peninsula containing an abbey.

The case for two other earthworks delimiting religious sites like Ponter's Ball (one in Cornwall and another in Norfolk) is more compelling, but still not conclusive. In Norfolk, the Horning earthwork once cut the causeway that gave access to St Benet's Abbey. Prehistoric finds were made in the vicinity, including a Bronze Age hoard of metalwork found in 1980, so it is possible that the monks redug an earlier dyke (probably blocking access to an older sacred place) as a boundary marker or a defence for the monastery.[44] The monastery was probably established by Wulfric in the time of Cnut; a story of it being founded by a pre-Viking Anglo-Saxon called Suneman is probably a later fabrication. A Cornish example at Stepper Point near Padstow is equally problematic. Medieval documents from the Priory of Bodmin and a 1694 map indicate that a chapel to St Sampson (a Byzantine saint not to be confused with the Welsh St Samson) once stood on the headland defined by the Stepper Point earthwork.[45] It is impossible to prove whether these dykes were defensive structures later reused for ritual reasons, or ritual earthworks later reused for a military purpose.

One possible non-military ritual function for an earthwork is as a meeting place. When writing about the Roman Rig in Yorkshire, Nick Boldrini concluded that the area defined by the two northern branches might be significant, rather than thinking of the dyke as just separating two distinct territories as others have done. Boldrini suggests the two branches created a 'liminal space', but what this meant in practice or what functions the builders carried out between the two branches he did not explore in any of his published articles, merely hinting that it might have served as a demilitarized zone for parleying and negotiation. As well as being insufficiently developed, the argument has other flaws: for half of its length, the earthwork is a single dyke, so it did not delimit a space; there are no gateways into the hypothetical 'delimited' space; there is no evidence for any activity in the space between the branches; and it is uncertain that the two branches ever met, so they do not define an area and the branches do not face each other.

One possible ritual function for dykes was as a place to execute those who had transgressed the laws and as we shall discuss in more detail later when analysing charters, there is a possible reference to a gallows on East Wansdyke and a possible execution site at Bran Ditch.[46] The propensity of Anglo-Saxons to reuse earlier structures, such as the high-status burials inserted into prehistoric barrows in north Wiltshire and the possible Anglo-Saxon execution victims found at the prehistoric Aves Ditch and South Oxfordshire Grim's Ditch, suggests that such graves are unrelated to the original purpose or date of the earthwork.[47] It is possible that dykes had meanings now lost to us and perhaps these were associated with power, punishment and execution. Equally, it could be that the ditches of dykes were convenient holes for bodies and banks were prominent places for execution (whether gallows for hanging or a block on which a person was beheaded), or for the display of the dead. If dykes were a focus for ritual, there is simply not enough evidence to suggest that it was anything but infrequent and unrelated to their primary functions as stop lines against raiders.

Scholars have often thought of some dykes as tidemarks in the Anglo-Saxon conquest of England and that the authors of Welsh law codes used Offa's Dyke to divide the Welsh from the foreigners to the east.[48] Stuart Laycock has concluded that earlier conflict between purely British kingdoms (before the Anglo-Saxon invasion, in whatever form that took, was in full swing) was the primary stimulus for early medieval dykes in the immediate post-Roman period. While this is entirely feasible, the dating evidence does suggest that kingdoms that identified themselves as Anglo-Saxon were firmly established when many, if not most, of the dykes were constructed in Britain. Offa's Dyke, Heronbridge and the Cambridgeshire Dykes were probably not built by people who identified themselves as Britons. So, if most post-date the British civil wars of the immediate post-Roman period, do they mark stages in the Anglo-Saxon takeover of lowland Britain? The dykes on the Welsh borders do seem to separate two groups with very distinctive and mutually antagonistic cultures, British/Welsh and Anglo-Saxon. While they are rarely contiguous with the national border, on a large-scale map Offa's Dyke and some lesser works like Wat's Dyke, Upper Short Ditch and Lower Short Ditch lie fairly close to the Anglo-Welsh border; Wat's Dyke seems to mark the western edge of 'hides', the typically Anglo-Saxon method of land organization. We should remember that we are looking at over 100 dykes and most clearly do not fit the theory of Anglo-British/Welsh frontiers. Perhaps these four dykes on the Welsh border, which possibly do mark a national frontier, were more about keeping people apart, like the Berlin Wall, than keeping armies out, like the Maginot Line.

As stated in the introduction, there is a debate as to whether the Anglo-Saxon settlement involved a mass migration of Germanic migrants into lowland Briton, or if it was more of a change in culture. That said, the most Anglicized parts of Britain lay on the east of the island, whilst those areas that either never fell under Anglo-Saxon control or did so very belatedly (Wales, Cumbria and Cornwall) lay on the west side. Although most historians see the Anglo-Saxon settlement as a far more piecemeal and haphazard process than a simple wave moving from east to west, probability would suggest that dykes that mark an Anglo-British divide are more likely to run north–south, but many, like Wansdyke, run west–east.

In Wales and the border areas, there are dykes that clearly make no sense as an Anglo-Welsh divide. The dykes of south Wales like Cefn Morfydd and Bwlch y Clawdd seem to divide the Welsh uplands from the equally Welsh lowland plains, while dykes like Clawdd Mawr in Dyfedd and Vervil Dyke near Bridgend were surely too far west to be Anglo-Welsh divides. The attacks of the West Saxons may have stimulated the Cornish to build their dykes, but we would expect them to run roughly parallel to the River Tamar if they were designed to mark a cultural, linguistic or ethnic divide, which they manifestly do not. Some dykes could mark stages in the invasion or acculturalization process, for example the Cambridgeshire Dykes could represent a border between the territory of the East Angles and areas to the west that were still under the control of British rulers.

A good example of how linking dykes to Anglo-British divisions is often unconvincing and problematic is the western border of Kent. While the Feasten Dyke in Kent and the Surrey–Kent dyke may have marked a fourth-century border between the Germanic kingdom of Kent and Britons to the west, they might just as easily have marked the later Kentish–Mercian border. Early medieval sources suggest that the western border of the kingdom of Kent fluctuated and Kentish kings often ruled much of Surrey. This therefore suggests that the modern correlation between a dyke and the border of the county of Kent is possibly coincidental.

Scholars have suggested that the Grey Ditch in Derbyshire was an early medieval Anglo-British divide, claiming that Anglo-Saxon graves and place names are found predominantly south of the earthwork, while Celtic place names are to the north.[49] Unfortunately, Paul Brotherton has identified a series of Celtic place names south of the earthwork in the 'Anglo-Saxon' zone, such as Mouldridge Grange, Crich, Pentrich, and Chevin near Belper.[50] It has been suggested that Tor Dyke was the boundary between the early medieval British kingdom of Craven to the south and Anglian settlements to the north.[51] Although Craven is Brythonic (the root of the name, craf, means either garlic, a reference to wild garlic in the area, or scrape, referring to the limestone scars), the first reference to this name being applied to this area is in the *Domesday Book*; it is entirely possible it was never a kingdom. Fleming suggests that like the

Swaledale dykes and Scot's Dyke, it marks the eastern edge of the early medieval British kingdom of Rheged; while Craven could be a district or subkingdom of Rheged, we have little idea about the organization or even the extent of either.[52] Even if they divided kingdoms, it does not mean that they were not military.

Borders can be amorphous zones or narrow lines drawn by political leaders to define the edge of a territory; they can mark an area of separation or of contact and they can be artificial or utilize natural features such as rivers or forests. There is a suggestion that for much of the early medieval period political borders were zones, rather than lines, with kingdoms having heartlands where the king's lands and kin were concentrated, surrounded by frontier zones from which they extracted tribute.

While it is possible that Offa's Dyke and Wat's Dyke fulfilled the role of an ethnic, linguistic or cultural divide, we cannot be certain that this was their primary purpose and most early medieval dykes are probably too short or in the wrong location to have served as Anglo-British divides. With closer dating of the dykes and a better understanding of the process whereby lowland Britain became English we may be able to match dykes with this process, but at present that is not possible. Linear features can define nations without that being their prime purpose; for example, Scottish and Cornish people often define themselves with reference to Hadrian's Wall and the River Tamar respectively, but the former structure is totally unrelated to the creation of Scotland, while the latter is entirely natural. The theory that British dykes were distinctively more sophisticated is also probably false, as Offa's and Wat's (built by the Anglo-Saxon Mercians) both have V-shaped ditches and marker banks. It seems that most dykes are not tide marks in the Anglo-Saxon conquest.

The boundary clauses in early medieval charters do suggest that by the end of the period covered by this book there existed clearly defined administrative areas. An estate boundary earthwork can be mistaken for a dyke. Luckily for us, borders are relatively stable in the English landscape and even when they become redundant, for example when they cease to mark the edge of a kingdom, they tend to become reutilized as parochial or county boundaries; Anglo-Saxon estates, for example, often became parishes. Marker dykes defining estates need only to be large enough to define a line in the landscape, rather than form a barrier to movement.

The best example of an estate marker dyke is Aelfrith's Dyke in Oxfordshire and the associated earthworks Old Dyke and Short Dyke. They are recorded as estate boundaries in Anglo-Saxon charters (S 828 dated 956, S 829 dated 965, S 603 dated 956 and S 758 dated 968) and lie extremely close to modern parochial boundaries. They are small in scale: the ditch at 0.57m deep and 1.7m wide is similar in scale to those found round many modern fields.[53] Perhaps disputes about ownership of the land in this fertile agricultural area prompted people to dig an earthwork to mark the limits of the estates. The idea that this area was one where there were land disputes is perhaps bolstered by the fact that these charters are considered to be of dubious authenticity, suggesting that people were tampering with documents to gain advantage.

Dividing border markers from defensive dykes by size is possible, but problematic. When the Clwyd-Powys Archaeological Trust (CPAT) tried to split dykes in their Short Dykes project into those that were simply defensive (larger earthworks situated on defensible positions) and those designed as boundary markers (slighter earthworks contiguous with probable borders), they found no clear-cut divide.[54] Aelfrith's Ditch, Bica's Dyke in Oxfordshire, Calver Dyke in Derbyshire, Fullinga Dyke in Surrey and Clawdd Seri in Gwynedd all have ditches that are clearly much smaller than the average (0.45–1m deep) and all but Calver are cited in charters as borders. Fullinga Dyke could have been a tribal boundary, as the name seems to relate to the Fullingas, a folk group of Anglo-Saxons who lived in north-west Surrey and gave their name to Fulham.

The Hayling Wood Dyke in East Hampshire is small in scale, follows a tortuous course and passes Marlands Farm (the name possibly means 'border lands' farm), so is perhaps also more likely to be an estate boundary ditch than to have had a military purpose. Hill suggested Whitford Dyke was a medieval border marker dyke, as it consisted of a low bank between two small ditches with the inhabitants on the two sides digging a ditch and throwing the earth in the centre to form the central bank. Long Mynd has a similar structure and so may be a border marker; Bwlch yr Afan in Powys has a central ditch flanked by two small banks, so may be a slight variant on this style. It is noticeable that the views forward from these dykes are not particularly good and unlike most early medieval dykes, they do not face down a clearly defined slope; these features of border markers aid the fieldworker to distinguish them from defensive dykes.

There are two earthworks in Cornwall (the Giant's Grave and the Giant's Hedge) that scholars have suggested delimited subkingdoms and so could be border markers. If the Giant's Grave did extend north parallel to the course of the modern A30, as has been suggested, it would delimit the Penwith peninsula, which contains a *lys* place name, Lesingey (suggesting a court or early medieval administrative centre), and the old Penzance market cross possibly recorded a tenth-century king, Ricatus.[55] Unfortunately, this reading of the inscription is probably an error and like the Giant's Hedge it only delimits a fraction of a local Hundred, which historians assume preserves the outline of earlier subkingdoms. There is no *lys* place name in the area delimited by the Giant's Hedge and both earthworks are ignored by parish boundaries. If these two dykes did delimit tiny subkingdoms, it seems unusual that they could afford to 'wall' their borders.

Attempts to match better documented kingdoms with dykes have been equally unconvincing. Peter Blair postulated that the rulers of Northumbria built Grey Ditch and the Roman Rig as a defence against Mercia, while

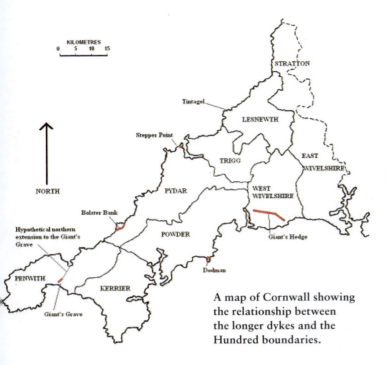

A map of Cornwall showing the relationship between the longer dykes and the Hundred boundaries.

other scholars have included Nico Ditch in the list of Northumbrian–Mercian border dykes; Roman Rig is probably prehistoric and Grey Ditch faces *towards* Northumbria.[56]

For two dykes, Offa's Dyke and Wansdyke, their sheer length makes it far more likely that they were border markers than stop lines, though they could have fulfilled both roles. When drawn on a map of England and Wales, Offa's Dyke does seem to define the western border of Mercia if not of England itself. Just the central section of Offa's Dyke covers 75 per cent of a line drawn along the Anglo-Welsh border from the River Dee to the River Wye and more than half (53 per cent) of the distance from the Dee to the River Severn. Perhaps it marks the culmination of the process whereby the smaller territories of Anglo-Saxon kin groups and tribes coalesced into larger kingdoms. Offa's Dyke is oddly not specifically called a boundary by any early medieval source, nor is it quoted in any land dispute, while references to it as a border in Welsh law codes post-date Offa by many centuries. Perhaps West and East Wansdyke were discontinuous parts of a similar attempt to mark the border of a major Anglo-Saxon kingdom, in this case Wessex. Andrew Reynolds is adamant that the two earthworks are related, that both were built by the West Saxons and define Wessex; every other recent study is either far more circumspect or flatly disagrees.[57] The northern border of Wessex from the Bristol Channel to the western edge of Surrey would have been 90 miles (145km) long, but the two Wansdykes (assuming they are both West Saxon earthworks) cover less than a quarter of this distance (23 per cent); I think that they can hardly be said to 'define' Wessex.

If we accept the argument that borders in England have a great longevity (often due to their reuse for different purposes), it is surprising how rarely early medieval dykes are contiguous with medieval and/or modern administrative borders. Only a quarter of the length of all early medieval dykes is contiguous with parish boundaries, roughly the same proportion as for the Roman and prehistoric dykes I have studied. The percentage of early medieval dykes contiguous with diocese, county and national boundaries is negligible. Even in areas where there is some correlation it is probably coincidental. In Cambridgeshire, the dykes cut across the grain of the geology of the region, as do parish boundaries in order to give all villages access to different types of land (fen, land suitable for arable cultivation and heathland). As they are convenient markers in an otherwise flat, feature-

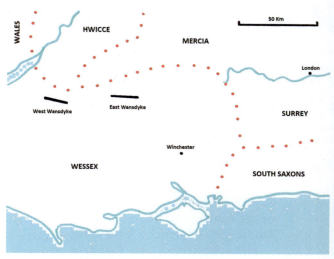

West and East Wansdyke in relation to the possible borders of Anglo-Saxon kingdoms.

less landscape, it is unsurprising that those who laid out the parochial boundaries utilized the dykes, but this does not mean that this was their original purpose. Lower Short Ditch is completely contiguous with parish boundaries, but the Anglo-Welsh border cuts perpendicularly across the centre of the dyke, completely ignoring it. Both parish boundaries and Anglo-Saxon estates bisect East and West Wansdyke, seemingly ignoring the existence of the earthworks; the Roman road 'linking' the two halves by contrast is consistently contiguous with parish boundaries. There are some possibly early medieval dykes (notably Aelfrith's Ditch, Bica's Dyke, Clawdd Seri and Fullinga Dyke) that may have originally been boundary markers, but the vast majority of early medieval dykes were probably defensive structures. When people used (or rather reused) early medieval dykes as borders or estate markers, which is surprisingly rare, it is probably because they were convenient landmarks whose original purpose had become redundant.

A popular theory among recent writers who have discussed early medieval dykes is that they did not serve a practical utilitarian purpose, but a largely symbolic one (though equally useful), of helping to forge a nation. The theory holds that dykes are symptoms of the rise of kingdoms and their construction was a way that a king could exert power over his subjects and make a statement in the landscape. If this holds true for most early medieval earthworks, my thesis that they are stop lines against raids is false, but is there any evidence for the nation-building theory? Most historians and archaeologists think that early medieval kingdoms were not simple blocks of territories as often crudely portrayed in historical atlases, but social constructs. They were formed from disparate groups, given an origin story and a single cultural identity by their rulers; they were manmade, not natural. The assertion and definition of the extent of these new political entities was part of their creation, that is, their borders and extent made and defined them. The very act of digging a dyke could have bonded the kingdom together and might have been a way for the king to extract labour service from his subjects. By building long, linear frontier markers, early medieval kings were emulating the Romans and giving their reign a quasi-imperial image. Although most early medieval dykes are quite small, the Devil's Ditch in Cambridgeshire is monumental in scale and perhaps a demonstration of royal might by the East Anglian rulers, whom we know from the treasures found at Sutton Hoo were not averse to displaying power. If this theory holds true, we should perhaps expect rulers to boast about dykes, name these structures after themselves or their kingdom, and the earthworks should be imposing features on the landscape and fringe a kingdom.

The evidence for this theory is strongest in the case of Offa's Dyke, which is why recent authors have frequently applied these ideas to this earthwork. Ian Bapty, for example, has criticized the simplistic idea that we can find the one simple way that the dyke 'worked', suggesting that Offa was not building a defended frontier, but was trying to overawe his opponents by the sheer monumentality of the structure.[58] This earthwork certainly seems monumental in scale and the fact that there is no evidence of recutting of the ditch suggests that the building of the dyke was more important than its maintenance. The reference to it reaching from sea to sea in Asser could be an echo of a Mercian boast and is one of the few direct references to dykes in early medieval texts. Mercians who claimed descent from the Anglo-Saxons could have been seen as pagan, illiterate usurpers, while the Britons were the inheritors of Roman Latin Christian culture and legitimacy. By building a monumental earthwork, Offa challenged that opinion by emulating the Roman frontier works and giving the Britons the status of barbarians beyond the pale, much as the Picts had been during Roman rule. The name Mercia derives from the Old English word for a border and, in the same way as the idea of the frontier defined Americans in the nineteenth century, this notion of being frontiersmen could have prompted the Mercians to mark the Anglo-Welsh divide with a monumental earthwork.[59] Paolo Squatriti postulated that Offa built the huge earthwork to demonstrate his mastery over the land as well as the people; it was a way of altering the flora to create a biodiverse barrier separating the highland Welsh from the agricultural lands of Mercia.[60]

This all sounds highly plausible for Offa's Dyke (even though it still could have also hampered raids), but the theory does not work for any other earthwork. Could Wansdyke have been built to unify the kingdom of Wessex? The evidence is less persuasive than it is for Offa's Dyke. Andrew Reynolds, among others, claims that the rulers of Wessex built Wansdyke to promote themselves and unify their kingdom, noting how the royal family of Wessex claimed descent from the god Woden, who gives his name to the earthwork.[61] Unfortunately, most Anglo-Saxon royal families trace themselves back to Woden and neither *The Anglo-Saxon*

Chronicle nor Asser's biography of Alfred (two documents designed to laud West Saxon kings) mentions the earthwork. It is very odd that when the West Saxon kings inaugurated *The Anglo-Saxon Chronicle*, they felt no need to thread Wansdyke into the narrative of the founding of Wessex; many different versions of this document survive and events are recorded near the dyke, like the battles at Woden's Barrow in 592 and 715. The two sections of Wansdyke were also constructed using different techniques, suggesting that they were never part of a single scheme.

Though this theory of earthworks as manifestations of growing royal power sounds far more sophisticated and seductive than simplistically proposing that the dykes were mere fighting platforms, there is little evidence to support it. Most early medieval dykes were surely too short to have added to the prestige of a king and even Paolo Squatriti, one of the leading proponents of this theory, does not think it a likely explanation for the smaller dykes (personal communication).

Archaeologists have not found inscribed stones near any dyke declaring who built it and none of the charters (that incidentally are usually issued by kings) that mention dykes give any hint that they reinforced the power of kings. Even the structure of the dykes does little to support this theory. As well as no stone inscriptions, the dykes did not have monumental gates designed to overawe people entering the dominion of a king who ordered their construction. None of the dykes seems to have been located in particularly prominent positions to advertise them (though there are good views from them) and there is some evidence that turf was used on some dykes to stabilize the bank, which would have camouflaged them.[62] Nor do the names given to most dykes support this theory; aside from a single remark in Asser, there is no written evidence associating any of the dykes with any known ruler. As there is little correlation between dykes and administrative borders, they probably never lay along frontiers.

If these dykes were built to bring lasting glory to their builder or the kingdom they defined, all but Offa's failed and even with that earthwork, the evidence to support this theory is, at best, very thin. Rather than representing the labour of an entire kingdom, calculations for this study suggest that the inhabitants of just a few villages could have built most of the dykes (more of this later). They were short in length and sliced across routeways; they were primarily designed to stop hostile people accessing territory, not to sew together tribes into kingdoms.

As the focus of this book is on warfare and in particular the small-scale raiding that characterized this period, I have tended to stress how dykes helped to counter raids, but they may have had multiple functions, even if defence was their prime focus. Those roles can include controlling trade, preventing cattle theft and being a symbolic boundary marker between kingdoms. An earthwork may also fulfil multiple functions, even if this was not what the designer intended; a dyke built solely for the glorification of a king may also have served as a reminder of the subjugation of a newly conquered border area as well as a defensive structure. While the building of similar monuments across Britain suggests a common factor or factors at work, humans make decisions based on numerous assumptions. A king who decides to build an earthwork for his own glory may tell his nobles that it is necessary to stabilize the kingdom, then persuade the peasants to dig the ditch by talk of the dyke preventing raids from outside the kingdom. Despite variations in early medieval dykes, the uniformity of the basic structure (a single large ditch downhill of a single large bank with no discernible gateways), suggests that most served a similar primary function, which was military, though it is possible that a few of the earthworks mentioned here had other functions.

So, the most plausible theory for the primary purpose of these dykes is defensive and even if we dismiss the earthworks that may not have been built to counter raids (Bwlch Aeddan, Brent Ditch, Horning Dyke and Aelfrith's Dyke, for example), we are left with over 100 dykes whose primary function seems to be cutting routeways to stop raids. Even Offa's Dyke may have helped to counter raids as well as unifying Mercia, adding to the imperial pretentions of the Mercian kings.

THE CLASSIFYING OF DYKE TYPES

The analysis of dykes I have carried out allows me to propose a typological model of early medieval dykes that may help to identify new examples. While some early medieval dykes are very long, most are short, less than 1.9 miles (3km) in length. They generally have a single ditch and bank, about 2m in depth/height and 6–8m wide. This is larger in scale than similar features on prehistoric or later medieval dykes and big enough to deter most attacks if they were manned. Many have berms, but there is no evidence they had gateways or palisades; the longer examples often had revetments, marker banks and sometimes ankle-breakers in the base of their generally V-shaped ditches. For those who are not aware what these terms mean: a berm is a level space between the bank and the ditch; a revetment is a retaining wall made of timber or stone in the front of the bank designed to hold it up; while an ankle-breaker is a smaller slot or trench in the bottom of a ditch.[63] They generally do not, or only partially, run on the same alignment as administrative borders like parish boundaries. They usually face downhill, cut ridges and their terminals are generally located by rivers. They cluster around the fringes of Mercia and though there are numerous possible examples from other parts of the country, few occur in northern Britain or west Wales. They seem to date from the first half of the seventh century, though at least one example, Offa's Dyke, dates from the late eighth.

Whilst most early medieval cultural artefacts (pottery, brooches, shield bosses, knives, axes and swords) have been catalogued and categorized, dykes have not. I hope to rectify that here. Early medieval dykes can be categorized into different subtypes based on their size, features and location in the landscape, although it should be noted that though there are certain characteristics exclusive to certain groups of dykes, many fit in more than one category. By definition, all of the multiple dykes (type F) and large dykes (G) also have characteristics that fit into one of the other categories (A–E). Offa's Dyke, for example, clearly falls into both category A (sinuous) and G (large), but if it is coupled with Wat's Dyke or some of the dykes of Powys it could also fit into category F (multiple); therefore, Offa's Dyke

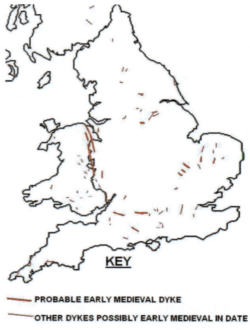

A simplified map of the dykes of Britain.

is a large sinuous dyke possibly in a multiple group. The Devil's Ditch in Cambridgeshire is a large route-blocking dyke in a multiple group, while the Crookham Common earthworks are not large, merely route-blocking dykes in a multiple group. A table classifying all the earthworks is given after the descriptions of the various types.

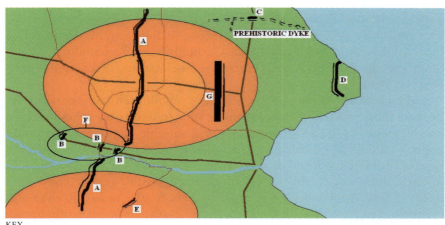

KEY
A: SINUOUS DYKES
B: ROUTE-BLOCKING DYKES
C: REUSED PREHISTORIC DYKE
D: PENINSULA DYKE
E: MARKER BOUNDARY DYKE
F: MULTIPLE (THREE ROUTE-BLOCKING DYKES IN A GROUP)
G: LARGE DYKE

A hypothetical landscape showing the different types of dykes.

Type A – Sinuous

Early medieval dykes in this category include Offa's Dyke, Wat's Dyke, Crugyn Bank in Powys, Fleam Dyke in Cambridgeshire, Fossditch in Norfolk, East and West Wansdyke and Bokerley Dyke in Dorset.

These dykes snake across the landscape, often for many miles, and seem to be best described by the word 'sinuous', a term scholars have already applied to sections of dykes. Fox used the terms 'travelling, running or linear', which are apt in describing the rambling route of many dykes. though travelling does unfortunately imply a start point and a destination for the earthwork. Though some, like Wat's and Offa's, have sections with a straight alignment, the sinuous dykes have multiple slight changes of directions, but not the abrupt dog-leg sections reminiscent of prehistoric dykes like Hug's Ditch.

Type B – Route-Blocking Dykes

Most early medieval dykes are route-blockers, which is unsurprising as blocking roads used by raiders seems to be their primary function. The Grey Ditch in Derbyshire, Rowe Ditch in Herefordshire, the Cambridgeshire Dykes and various dykes in Wales (mainly Powys), such as Clawdd Mawr near Llanfyllin, Crugyn Bank, Giant's Grave, Short Ditch and Upper Short Ditch, fall into this category.

These dykes seem to cut (and the lack of gateway evidence suggests 'cut' rather than 'control') routeways like Roman roads, ancient ridgeways and valley routeways. In Cambridgeshire, for example, the dykes cut a corridor of chalk grassland along which the Icknield Way travels, between the Fens to the west and the clay to the east. These dykes often end at steep slopes or waterways.

Type C – Reused Prehistoric

The early medieval dykes in this category include various examples in East Anglia (such as Devil's Ditch Garboldisham, Bichamditch, Launditch and the Black Ditches), Harrow-Pinner Grim's Dyke and Combs Ditch in Dorset.

Early medieval people possibly reused or rebuilt prehistoric earthworks because there was insufficient labour or time to build new dykes, or there just happened to be an existing one of a suitable alignment that could easily be redug. They are more often contiguous with parish boundaries than other early medieval dykes.

There does seem to be a concentration of possible reused prehistoric dykes in East Anglia. We know that the East Angles reused Roman and prehistoric enclosures when building churches, though whether that practice influenced the reuse of prehistoric dykes or vice versa is difficult to prove. Often the extremities of the East Anglian dykes are difficult to locate (a typical characteristic of prehistoric dykes, as they are generally smaller and by definition more eroded than their early medieval counterparts), but where probable Roman roads cut these dykes, the banks are more substantial.

There are reasons why these dykes seem larger in the sections nearer to where a Roman road cut the bank. Roman engineers may have punched a hole through a dyke and piled the earth on either side, but fieldwork has revealed that the sections that look heightened go on for a considerable distance on either side of the road, suggesting something else happened. Sometimes Roman roads have slight deviations in their course as they pass through a dyke; perhaps later workers imperfectly reconnected the Roman road after early medieval inhabitants had extended an existing prehistoric dyke to cut the route. What probably happened is that early medieval people reconnected the sections of a prehistoric dyke cut by a Roman road; they then built up the banks near the newly blocked routeway, so that raiders whose path was blocked would be discouraged from trying to outflank the roadblock.

Type D – Peninsula

Park Pale and Dane's Dyke in Yorkshire and all the Cornish dykes (Bolster Bank, Dodman, Giant's Grave, Giant's Hedge and Stepper Point) potentially fall into this category.

These dykes face towards the mainland and define peninsulas of land; they are surrounded on the other three sides by rivers, estuaries, marshes, the sea or a combination of these features. There are examples of Anglo-Saxon forts that consist of a bank and ditch that cut off a peninsula of land (Burpham in West Sussex, for example), which could cause confusion with this class of dyke. This present study has tried to eliminate such enclosures by dismissing anything that has an obvious gateway or signs of permanent occupation, but there is no sharp dividing line between a temporary fort and a dyke hastily thrown up across a narrow neck of land. While this study defines Heronbridge and Coombe Bank near Reading as dykes, a perfectly viable case can be made for them being forts, or at least bridgeheads protected by a dyke.

Iron-Age coastal forts like Treryn Dinas and Trevelgue Head in Cornwall share some of the characteristics of these dykes, but these prehistoric cliff castles are often multivallate, that is, they have multiple banks, whereas early medieval dykes usually have a single bank and ditch.

Type E – Marker Boundaries

The early medieval dykes Aelfrith's Dyke and Bica's Dyke in Oxfordshire fall into this category. All of these dykes have unusually small ditches (0.45–1m deep), small banks and are contiguous with administrative boundaries along their entire length. Charters usually cite these types of earthworks as estate boundaries.

Type F – Multiples

The dykes in this category include the Aberford Dykes and the dykes in Swaledale (both groups in Yorkshire), most of the dykes of the Welsh borders, the Cambridgeshire Dykes and those on Crookham Common. It is noticeable that many early medieval dykes are grouped in parallel lines facing in the same direction, so if a raider circumvents one, he faces another.

Type G – Large

Though there is no clear dividing line between these dykes and the rest, some were built on a monumentally larger scale. Early medieval dykes definitely in this category are Offa's Dyke, Devil's Ditch and Wat's Dyke, while there is some justification for adding East Wansdyke, Fleam Dyke, West Wansdyke, Bokerley Dyke, Becca Banks, Fossditch and Bran Ditch.

The larger dykes often have marker banks (unsurprisingly, considering their length; they need to be planned across a huge landscape) and more often display sophisticated engineering techniques (revetments and ankle-breakers), though these features are not unknown among smaller earthworks.

THE LIST OF DYKES

The following table summarizes the possible date, the typology and possible purpose for the earthworks mentioned in this book.

Dykes in Order that they appear in Appendix II	Date and Classification, if Early Medieval
Bardon Mill Dyke	Possible early medieval route-blocking (Type B) stop-line dyke
King's Wicket	Probable later medieval stock enclosure
Black Dyke	Possible sinuous route-blocking reused prehistoric (Type ABC) stop-line dyke
Catrail (Picts' Work Ditch)	Possible early medieval sinuous route-blocking (Type AB) stop-line dyke
Catrail proper	Possible early medieval sinuous route-blocking (Type AB) stop-line dyke
Deil's Dyke	Later medieval earthwork
Wallace's Trench	Possible early medieval sinuous route-blocking (Type AB) stop-line dyke
Heriot's Dyke (Haerfields)	Possible early medieval sinuous route-blocking (Type AB) stop-line dyke
Heriot's Dyke (Greenlaw)	Possible early medieval route-blocking (Type B) stop-line dyke
Military Way	Possible early medieval sinuous route-blocking (Type AB) stop-line dyke, later reused as a road
Grim's Ditch (Leeds)	Probable prehistoric dyke
Becca Banks	Probable early medieval sinuous route-blocking multiple large (Type ABFG) stop-line dyke
South Dyke	Probable prehistoric dyke
The Rein	Probable early medieval sinuous route-blocking multiple (Type ABF) stop-line dyke or sinuous marker (Type AE) boundary dyke

INTRODUCTION AND METHODOLOGY

Dykes in Order that they appear in Appendix II	Date and Classification, if Early Medieval
Bank Slack	Possible early medieval sinuous route-blocking (Type AB) stop-line dyke
Bar Dyke	Possible early medieval route-blocking (Type B) stop-line dyke
Broomhead Dyke	Possible early medieval route-blocking (Type B) stop-line dyke
Dane's Dyke	Possible early medieval peninsula (Type D) refuge dyke
Gilling Wood Dyke	Possible early medieval sinuous route-blocking or sinuous boundary marker (Type AB or AE) stop-line or boundary dyke
Nico Ditch	Possible early medieval sinuous route-blocking (Type AB) stop-line dyke
Park Pale	Possible early medieval peninsula (Type D) refuge dyke
Roman Rig	Probable prehistoric dyke
Rudgate Dyke	Probable early medieval route-blocking (Type B) stop-line dyke
Scot's Dyke	Possible reused prehistoric sinuous route-blocking (Type AB) stop-line dyke
Swaledale western group	Possible early medieval route-blocking multiple (Type BF) stop-line dyke
Swaledale middle group north	Possible early medieval route-blocking multiple (Type BF) stop-line dyke
Swaledale Hodic	Possible early medieval route-blocking multiple (Type BF) stop-line dyke
Swaledale Ruedic	Possible early medieval route-blocking multiple (Type BF) stop-line dyke
Swaledale southern	Possible early medieval route-blocking multiple (Type BF) stop-line dyke
Tor Dyke	Possible early medieval sinuous route-blocking (Type AB) stop-line dyke
Calver Dyke	Possible early medieval peninsula (Type D) refuge dyke or marker (Type E) boundary dyke
Grey Ditch	Probable early medieval route-blocking (Type B) stop-line dyke
Aberbechan Dyke	Possible early medieval or prehistoric sinuous route-blocking (Type AB) stop-line dyke
Abernaint Dyke	Later-medieval head dyke
Bedd Eiddil Dyke	Possible early medieval route-blocking (Type B) stop-line dyke
Bwlch Aeddan Dyke	Natural feature
Bwlch y Cibau Dyke (north)	Possible reused prehistoric route-blocking (Type B) stop-line dyke
Bwlch y Cibau Dyke (west)	Possible early medieval route-blocking (Type B) stop-line dyke
Bwlch y Clawdd	Possible early medieval route-blocking (Type B) stop-line dyke
Bwlch yr Afan Dyke	Possible early medieval marker (Type E) boundary dyke
Clawddtrawscae	Possible early medieval route-blocking (Type B) stop-line dyke
Tyla-Glas	Possible early medieval route-blocking (Type B) stop-line dyke
Cefn Eglwysilan and Tywn Hywel Dykes	Possible early medieval route-blocking (Type B) stop-line dyke
Cefn Morfydd Dyke	Possible early medieval route-blocking (Type B) stop-line dyke
Cefn-y-Crug Dyke	Possible early medieval route-blocking multiple (Type BF) stop-line dyke
Clawdd Llesg	Possible early medieval route-blocking (Type B) stop-line dyke
Clawdd Mawr (Dyfed)	Possible early medieval sinuous route-blocking (Type AB) stop-line dyke
Clawdd Mawr (Foel)	Later medieval head dyke
Clawdd Mawr Glyncorrwg/ Bwlch Garw	Possible early medieval route-blocking (Type B) stop-line dyke

Continued on next page

Dykes in Order that they appear in Appendix II	Date and Classification, if Early Medieval
Clawdd Mawr (Llanfyllin)	Possible early medieval sinuous route-blocking (Type AB) stop-line dyke
Clawdd Seri	Possible early medieval marker (Type E) boundary dyke
Cowlod Dyke	Possible early medieval route-blocking (Type B) stop-line dyke
Crugyn Bank (inc. Two Tumps)	Probable early medieval sinuous route-blocking multiple (Type ABF) stop-line dyke
Ffos Toncenglau	Possible early medieval route-blocking (Type B) stop-line dyke
Fron Hill Dyke	Possible early medieval route-blocking multiple (Type BF) stop-line dyke
Giant's Grave	Probable early medieval route-blocking multiple (Type BF) stop-line dyke
Heronbridge	Probable early medieval peninsula (Type D) refuge dyke or fort
Lower Short Ditch	Possible early medieval route-blocking multiple (Type BF) stop-line dyke
Pen y Clawdd Dyke	Possible early medieval route-blocking multiple (Type BF) stop-line dyke
Red Hill Cross Dyke	Possible early medieval route-blocking (Type B) stop-line dyke
Senghenydd Dyke	Probable thirteenth-century park boundary
Shepherd's Well	Possible early medieval route-blocking multiple (Type BF) stop-line dyke
Short Ditch	Probable early medieval route-blocking multiple (Type BF) stop-line dyke
Tor Clawdd Dyke	Possible early medieval sinuous route-blocking (Type AB) stop-line dyke
Ty Newydd Dyke	Possible early medieval route-blocking (Type B) stop-line dyke
Upper Short Ditch	Probable early medieval route-blocking multiple (Type BF) stop-line dyke
Vervil Dyke	Possible early medieval route-blocking (Type B) stop-line dyke
Wantyn Dyke (northern)	Possible early medieval route-blocking multiple (Type BF) stop-line dyke
Wantyn Dyke (southern section or Upper Wantyn Dyke)	Probable prehistoric or later medieval field system
Beachley Bank	Possible early medieval peninsula (Type D) refuge dyke
Offa's Dyke (central section)	Probable early medieval sinuous large (Type AG, though in places part of a multiple system, therefore AFG) route-blocking dyke that may have acted as an ethnic divide to promote the power of a king
Offa's Dyke in Herefordshire	Possible early medieval route-blocking (Type B) stop-line dyke
Offa's Dyke in the Wye – English Bicknor	Possible early medieval sinuous route-blocking (Type AB) stop-line dyke
Offa's Dyke in the Wye – St Briavel's	Possible prehistoric dyke or possibly an early medieval sinuous route-blocking (Type AB) stop-line dyke
Rowe Ditch	Probable early medieval route-blocking multiple (Type BF) stop-line dyke
Wat's Dyke	Probable early medieval sinuous route-blocking multiple large (Type ABFG) stop-line dyke
Whitford Dyke	Probable prehistoric dyke
Devil's Mouth Dyke	Probable prehistoric dyke
King Lud's	Probable prehistoric dyke
Foulding Dykes	Probable prehistoric dyke
Minchinhampton Bulwarks	Possible early medieval sinuous route-blocking (Type AB) stop-line dyke

INTRODUCTION AND METHODOLOGY 41

Dykes in Order that they appear in Appendix II	Date and Classification, if Early Medieval
Bran Ditch	Probable early medieval route-blocking multiple large (Type BFG) stop-line dyke
Brent Ditch	Probable prehistoric road
Devil's Ditch	Probable early medieval route-blocking multiple large (Type BFG) stop-line dyke
Fleam Dyke	Probable early medieval sinuous route-blocking multiple large (Type ABFG) stop-line dyke
High Dyke	Possible early medieval peninsula (Type D) refuge dyke
Miles Ditches	Probable prehistoric dyke
Worstead Street	Roman road
Bichamditch	Possible route-blocking rebuilt prehistoric (Type BC) stop-line dyke
Bunns' Bank	Possible early medieval sinuous route-blocking (Type AB) stop-line dyke
Double Banks	Probable twelfth-century park boundary
Devil's Ditch Garboldisham	Probable rebuilt prehistoric route-blocking (Type AB) stop-line dyke
Fossditch	Probable early medieval sinuous route-blocking large (Type ABG) stop-line dyke
Horning	Possible prehistoric dyke or early medieval peninsula (Type D) refuge dyke or ritual enclosure
Launditch	Possible sinuous rebuilt prehistoric route-blocking (Type ABC) stop-line dyke
Panworth Ditch	Possible sinuous route-blocking (Type AB) stop-line dyke
Black Ditches Suffolk	Possible rebuilt prehistoric (Type C) stop-line dyke
Buckinghamshire–Hertfordshire Grim's Ditch	Probable prehistoric dyke
Pear Wood	Probable early medieval route-blocking (Type B) stop-line dyke
Harrow-Pinner Grim's Dyke	Probable sinuous reused prehistoric route-blocking (Type ABC) stop-line dyke
Aelfrith's Dyke	Probable early medieval marker (Type E) boundary dyke
Aves Ditch	Probable prehistoric dyke
Berks Downs Grim's Ditch	Probable prehistoric dyke
Bica's Dyke	Probable early medieval marker (Type E) boundary dyke
Black Ditch, Snelsmore Common	Possible prehistoric dyke or possible early medieval route-blocking multiple (Type BF) stop-line dyke
Bury's Bank	Probable early medieval route-blocking multiple (Type BF) stop-line dyke
Crookham Common earthworks	Possible early medieval route-blocking multiple (Type BF) stop-line dykes
Grim's Bank Padworth	Possible early medieval sinuous route-blocking (Type AB) stop-line dyke
Hug's Ditch	Probable prehistoric dyke
Reading – Coombe Bank	Probable Viking defensive dyke
Reading – Oxford Road South Oxfordshire	Probable prehistoric dyke
Grim's Ditch	Probable prehistoric dyke
Western extension Wansdyke	Probable disconnected later medieval field boundaries
West Wansdyke	Probable early medieval sinuous route-blocking large (Type ABG) stop-line dyke
Bathampton section	Probable disconnected prehistoric and later medieval field boundaries

Continued on next page

Dykes in Order that they appear in Appendix II	Date and Classification, if Early Medieval
Central section	Roman road
East Wansdyke	Probable early medieval sinuous route-blocking large (Type ABG) stop-line dyke
Bedwyn Dyke	Possible early medieval sinuous route-blocking (Type AB) stop-line dyke
Mount Prosperous Dyke	Possible early medieval route-blocking (Type B) stop-line dyke
Inkpen Dyke	Possible early medieval route-blocking (Type B) stop-line dyke
Bolster Bank	Possible early medieval sinuous peninsula (Type AD) refuge dyke
Dodman	Possible early medieval peninsula (Type D) refuge dyke
Giant's Grave	Possible early medieval peninsula (Type D) refuge dyke
Giant's Hedge	Possible early medieval sinuous peninsula (Type AD) refuge dyke
Stepper Point	Possible early medieval peninsula (Type D) refuge dyke
New Ditch	Possible early medieval route-blocking (Type B) stop-line dyke
Ponter's Ball	Possible early medieval route-blocking or possible route-blocking peninsula (Type B or BD) stop-line dyke
Battery Banks	Possible early medieval sinuous route-blocking (Type AB) stop-line dyke
Bokerley Dyke	Probable early medieval sinuous route-blocking large (Type ABG) stop-line dyke
Combs Ditch	Probable sinuous rebuilt prehistoric route-blocking (Type ABC) stop-line dyke
Devil's Ditch Doles Wood	Possible early medieval sinuous route-blocking large (Type ABG) stop-line dyke
Devil's Ditch Pepper Hills Firs	Possible early medieval sinuous route-blocking large (Type ABG) stop-line dyke
Devil's Ditch Wonston	Possible early medieval route-blocking (Type B) stop-line dyke
East Tisted-Colemore	Possible early medieval route-blocking (Type B) stop-line dyke
Tisted Cross-Valley Dyke (N)	Probable prehistoric dyke
Tisted Cross-Valley Dyke (S)	Probable prehistoric dyke
Froxfield Short Dyke A	Possible early medieval route-blocking (Type B) stop-line dyke
Froxfield Short Dyke B	Possible early medieval route-blocking (Type B) stop-line dyke
Froxfield Short Dyke C	Possible early medieval route-blocking (Type B) stop-line dyke
Froxfield Short Dyke D	Possible early medieval route-blocking (Type B) stop-line dyke
Froxfield Long Dyke	Possible early medieval sinuous route-blocking (Type AB) stop-line dyke
Hayling Wood Dyke (including branch)	Possible prehistoric dyke or possible early medieval sinuous route-blocking (Type AB) stop-line dyke
Festaen Dic (Hartley Witney)	Possible early medieval route-blocking (Type B) stop-line dyke
Faesten Dyke (Kent)	Possible prehistoric dyke or possible early medieval sinuous route-blocking (Type AB) stop-line dyke
Fullinga Dyke	Possible prehistoric dyke or possible early medieval sinuous marker (Type AE) boundary dyke
Riddlesdown Dyke	Probable prehistoric dyke
Surrey–Kent Dyke	Possible early medieval route-blocking (Type B) stop-line dyke

While roads, later medieval park boundaries and the odd natural feature have been mistaken for early medieval earthworks, there are about 100 possible early medieval dykes from the period AD400–850 that were probably used to prevent raiders moving along routeways. There are also a dozen built to provide a refuge by blocking access to a peninsula.

HOW I ANALYSED THE EARTHWORKS

With the red herrings eliminated, the dykes catalogued, catagorized and mapped, we can move on to analysing them. Once I had worked out how big all the dykes were, I could analyse the data. Calculating how many people were needed to build the dykes gives us estimates of the amount of labour available to early medieval rulers like Offa.

Some have used early medieval administrative documents to do this (like the *Tribal Hidage* and *Burghal Hidage*, documents discussed in detail later), while others have produced estimates by dividing the volume of earth moved by the amount of soil a man can shift in a set period of time. These different methods have produced very different results: Tyler used the latter to calculate that just 10,000 men could have built Offa's Dyke in sixty-eight days, while Hill used the former to estimate that 125,000 Mercians took two years to build the earthwork.[64] If the higher estimates were accurate, it would mean that early medieval kingdoms had the administrative ability to mobilize a large percentage of the population, but the *Tribal Hidage* is not direct evidence of how many people built the dykes and Tyler's estimate of the earth-moving capacity of an early medieval worker was in my mind insufficiently researched.

Taking this into account, I therefore decided to make an accurate estimate of the volume of earth moved to build the dykes and then calculated a plausible figure of the amount of earth a man can move in a fixed amount of time. The dimensions of the dykes given in Appendix I formed a basis for then calculating the volume of earth moved by the builders of the dykes. Various estimates of how much earth a person can move, including some from the modern building trade, records of nineteenth-century navvies and experiments by archaeologists using replica medieval equipment were used to work out how much earth an early medieval worker could move. This gives far more robust figures than those in previous works. By showing that most were built by 100 or so people, it clearly reveals that dykes could be short-term solutions taken by relatively small groups of communities.

After working out where and how big the dykes are, the second major issue tackled was trying to date the earthworks. Since Pitt Rivers' excavation of Dane's Dyke, it has been obvious that dykes rarely produce effective artefactual dating evidence. Few written records exist; early medieval and prehistoric dykes are often confused as both come from periods where there are few, if any, contemporary coins to help with dating. As there are no forts or watchtowers along dykes from both these periods, there is also no occupation debris.

Despite this, dating an earthwork is possible, although it is often a matter of educated guesswork. Seeing if dykes overlay or cut Roman or even prehistoric archaeology was employed in this study to identify which dykes could be early medieval. Fox concluded that because Offa's Dyke cuts through Roman deposits, it logically must be post-Roman in date.[65]

While such stratigraphic evidence of dykes slicing through earlier features that can be dated is useful, it does not give an absolute date for an earthwork. As with dateable coins or pottery sherds found under the bank of a dyke, this method only tells us that the earthwork post-dates these finds (a *terminus post quem* date), but not by how much.

It would be tedious to discuss at length the logic I used to ascribe a date to each dyke, so the following example is given to demonstrate the reasoning involved. The common assumption among scholars is that Bokerley Dyke dates from around the end of Roman rule in Britain because Pitt Rivers found late Roman coins while excavating it. As it cuts across a Roman settlement next to a major road (where no doubt there was monetary trade with passing travellers), the coins could have entered the ground long before the earthwork was built, possibly making the dyke much later in date. It is unlikely that the Roman authorities would have sanctioned a dyke slicing across a road, especially as there is evidence that sites in Wiltshire continued to import pottery from Dorset, presumably using this route, into the fifth century.[66] Therefore, the dyke is early medieval.

The introduction of radiocarbon dating, dendrochronology and Optically Stimulated Luminescence has drastically improved the accuracy of dating archaeological features. Rather than the relative dating of stratification, archaeologists can now date organic material without reference to what is below or above. However, the banks of dykes are generally made of earth and not of the kind of organic material that can easily be scientifically dated, so these techniques are of limited use. A plateau in radiocarbon calibration right in the middle of the period under examination (AD 450–530) makes close dating even more difficult.[67] Unfortunately, organic remains taken from the ditch fill will always post-date the digging of the ditch (as they fell in it after it was dug) and organic material from under a bank could predate the construction by centuries. Unless we find organic material within the bank, we are not directly dating the building of the dyke and even then the matter hypothetically could have come from the ground surface and so predate the construction of the earthwork. Archaeologists who studied the Cambridgeshire Dykes in the 1990s took great care to overcome these difficulties. They made sure that samples from the ditch of Fleam Dyke were from the primary and secondary fills of the first phase (as the dyke was remodelled soon after it was dug, these samples probably date from soon after construction) and their bank samples were taken from the upcast from the primary ditch.[68] As no known prehistoric or Roman features existed in the immediate area, the samples were unlikely to be from an older settlement.

Such methods still only give a range of probable dates and some scholars do not always exercise appropriate caution when using such scientific data. Headlines were rather prematurely written when a single radiocarbon date from the remains of a fire found beneath the bank of Wat's

Dyke suggested that the dyke was much older than previously thought, only for another radiocarbon date eight years later to suggest it was much younger.[69] It should be noted that three different scientific dating procedures applied to the ramparts of a hill fort at Finavon in Scotland, a very similar structure to the bank of an early medieval rampart, gave very different results.[70] Radiocarbon dating suggested that the hill fort was 800–410BC (recently recalculated as 1000–100BC), archaeomagnetic sampling gave dates between 180–90BC, while thermoluminescence dating gave a figure of AD570–710. Another problem is that these earthworks were sometimes reused. If an early medieval ruler extended an Iron-Age dyke to block a Roman routeway, an excavation near the road may lead us to assume incorrectly an early medieval date for the whole dyke, while an excavation further away would suggest an Iron-Age dyke.

However, we must not dismiss scientific data just because they do not fit our theories, a trap many famous pre-historians fell into when radiocarbon dating was first introduced and the dates did not fit existing chronologies before they later hurriedly back-tracked. The figures given with the different dating methods often give a false sense of accuracy, but they are not absolute dates. We cannot date any dyke accurately enough to link it to an event or even the relatively short reigns of early medieval kings (which is why I have avoided linking individual earthworks with specific events or people). When taken as an aggregate, all the Optically Stimulated Luminescence and radiocarbon dates provide a date range for the probable peak of dyke building in early medieval Britain.

While it is probably unwise to try to link individual dykes with events in early medieval sources, some have even criticized any attempt to link archaeological with written evidence, suggesting that we should treat early medieval archaeology as prehistoric. This would mean ignoring all the written evidence. The sources for the early medieval period (usually written long after events) often dramatize and simplify events in a way that contrasts with the more nuanced approach of modern scholars, but to ignore written sources when there is so little other information about dykes is foolish. Even if a medieval source needs careful examination because it exaggerates, simplifies, has an obvious agenda or the surviving copy post-dates the events, it still can give us background information about the period. Early medieval references to dykes are rare and this near silence is something that any hypothesis about dyke building needs to acknowledge. My theory that they are short-lived reactions to intermittent raiding explains why there are so few written records. The most common medieval references to dykes come from charters. While they did not record the date of the construction of the earthwork, if a dyke is recorded in one the earthwork must predate the document (a *terminus ante quem* date), though how much older it is we cannot be certain.

A brief examination was made of British dykes from other periods and similar earthworks from abroad. Such studies gave interesting insights into the methods employed by scholars working in similar fields. Books about Chinese walls and dykes quote detailed contemporary descriptions of how the dykes were used and how much manpower was employed to build them.[71] Some scholars wonder if British dykes were once topped off with palisades, but studies of Danish dykes demonstrate that if a wooden palisade was originally constructed, there should be some physical evidence of it.[72]

Proving or disproving a military purpose for dykes is difficult. As we have seen, some historians like Fox and Squatriti have even argued that a ruler may build a symbolic barrier in a military style to demonstrate that he is fulfilling his duty to protect his subjects. If early medieval dykes had been garrisoned in the same way as, say, Hadrian's Wall, we would have found archaeological evidence for accommodation for the troops, forts built along their length or perhaps signs of occupation at the Iron-Age forts incorporated into such earthworks as Wat's Dyke and Wansdyke. These dykes were not garrisoned, but they were probably best defensible lines set back from the frontier and possibly patrolled by scouts who could summon local levies to man the earthwork during times of war. In the next section, we shall see the archaeological evidence of conflict at dykes.

CHAPTER 2

The Archaeological Evidence

FINDS FROM DYKES

As well as residual finds (things that predate the earthwork and get incorporated into the bank) and radiocarbon/Optically Stimulated Luminescence dating, there are some actual early medieval finds from a few of these dykes. However, apart for a cow pelvis and half a loom weight, almost all are weapons or were found with burials whose skeletal remains suggested a violent death. Unfortunately, such finds could be evidence of later secondary functions, such as people using abandoned dykes as a convenient location for furnished graves (burials with grave goods), as somewhere to bury victims of war, or a place where the condemned could be both executed and buried. The contamination of a structure with earlier or later deposits makes it necessary to know the context of each excavated artefact and discoveries made without proper records (for example, casual finds of weaponry from the entrance of rabbit holes, or records of eighteenth-century excavations by enthusiastic antiquaries) are used with caution. As well as the artefacts, archaeologists have also obtained pollen evidence that can tell us what kind of landscape dykes were dug through. Here we shall examine the archaeological and scientific evidence for the military use of dykes before looking at early medieval warfare in general.

Ironically, by far the most common archaeological evidence from medieval dykes is residual sherds of Roman and prehistoric pottery, but while these give a useful terminus post quem date for the earthworks (that is, they tell us that the earthwork post-dates the pottery), they do not tell us why the dykes were dug. Equally, burials cut by earthworks, for example the late-Roman burials from Bokerley Dyke in Dorset that Hawkes noted that the dyke truncated, can help with dating, but cannot tell us why it was constructed.[1] Early medieval finds might be rarer, but they are more useful. The table gives a list of all the possible early medieval finds from the dykes. Finds that predate the earthworks such as the Roman coins and pottery sherds from under the bank of the Devil's Ditch are not included. Note that many of these finds were rather poorly recorded by antiquaries.

The most common early medieval finds (as can be seen from the table on page 48) are quite clearly weapons or bodies; note how no early medieval coins have been found at any dyke. The spurs, stirrups and bridle bits

Possible Early Medieval Finds from Dykes

Dyke	Human remains	Weapons	Other finds
South Dyke (Aberford)			Cow pelvis bone and late Saxon sherds
Heronbridge	200 bodies displaying sword injuries		
Grey Ditch		Swords and spears	Spurs and bridle bits
Offa's Dyke (Buttington)	400 skulls		
Wat's Dyke			Broken loom weight
Beachley Bank		Lance head	
Bran Ditch	50 bodies including a baby, most beheaded	Knife	Brooches, clasps, pot sherds and a broken pot associated with an early medieval burial
Devil's Ditch	Male whose hand had been amputated	Two throwing axes, iron spearhead and two other spearheads	Spur and stirrup
High Dyke		Sword, pommel, various spearheads, two shield bosses and a knife	
Bedwyn Dyke	Skeletons slain in battle		
Bokerley Dyke	Eight burials		

could also be related to cavalry rather than peaceful equestrian activities. The exception is the loom weight from Wat's Dyke found near the bottom of the ditch and is probably just a casual loss rather than an indicator of the original function of the earthwork.[2] The burials are not just dating evidence, but give evidence of purpose of the earthworks and it is striking how many of those burials suggest a violent death.[3] These include many 'deviant' burials, a term that is applied to burials that often lay outside organized cemeteries. These types of grave are usually shallow, the bones often have signs of injury and the bodies are often hunched up in what we would regard as a rather undignified manner. When Morris mapped early Anglo-Saxon burials with evidence of weapons trauma (sites he interpreted as 'massacres'), it is telling that they were concentrated near Wansdyke and the dykes of Cambridgeshire.[4]

There certainly are some Anglo-Saxon burials far from dykes where the bones show unambiguous evidence of weapons injuries, like the six male skeletons dating from the seventh or eighth century found at a Roman villa near Eccles in Kent.[5] Unfortunately, most of the burials associated with earthworks predated modern scientific methods, but there is a clear link between dykes and death. Nearly 800 bodies of people butchered at six different earthworks is quite clearly evidence that the dykes were related to warfare.

There are finds that are suggestive of typical furnished early Anglo-Saxon burials (for example, where a warrior is laid to rest with his weapons) at three possible early medieval earthworks in Cambridgeshire, though significantly none at the nearby earthworks of Miles Ditches or Brent Ditch, which are not early medieval dykes.[6] In 1822, workmen levelling a section of the Devil's Ditch at Newmarket Heath found two throwing axes, an iron spearhead, spur and a stirrup, possibly from a disturbed Anglo-Saxon furnished burial, though the exact relationship of the finds to the dyke is not known. About 4.4 miles (7km) north of Devil's Ditch, archaeologists at Fordham uncovered four skeletons dating from the mid-eighth to the tenth century aged eight to fifteen years of age that had been decapitated.

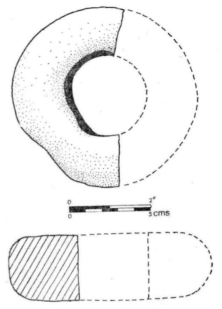

Loom weight found at Wat's Dyke at Mynydd Isa in 1957 (by permission Flintshire Historical Society, original image Varley, W., *Flintshire Historical Journal*, 27, 1975–6, pp.129–37).

In the Museum of Archaeology and Anthropology in Cambridge there is a sixth-century spearhead found in 1918 during levelling of the racecourse next to the Devil's Ditch (catalogue number Z 27370) and another Saxon spearhead was found in 1972 in a rabbit hole (at TL621613) in the inner edge of the ditch. A skeleton dating from about AD1000–1300 of a male in his early twenties, whose right hand had been amputated, was found in the fill of the Devil's Ditch in 1973.

Skeletons and Anglo-Saxon weaponry (sword, pommel, various spearheads, two shield bosses and a knife) from the High Dyke in Cambridgeshire might be a disturbed furnished cemetery burial in the fill of an abandoned ditch, but, in the absence of a scientific excavation of the area, they might be victims of war. As well as these examples found within the structure of individual dykes, there are numerous Anglo-Saxon burials (both inhumations and cremations), especially from the sixth century, found around the dykes in Cambridgeshire. Even in the unlikely situation that all these burials are not people slain in battle at the earthworks, these dykes do seem to have a clear association with warriors and death.

In 1923 and 1931, archaeologists investigating Bran Ditch in Cambridgeshire found the remains of over fifty bodies in the berm, buried not in a pit, but in individual graves.[7] The berm (the flat area between the bank and the ditch found on some earthworks) was unusually wide at this point, though it was impossible to tell if this was because the dyke respected an existing cemetery, or the bank had been moved to accommodate the burials. Only two of the burials were female and the report estimated the age of the rest from twelve to 'old men', as well as a possibly unassociated new-born baby buried near a posthole. To the archaeologists at the time, the burials also contained finds that seemed to date approximately between the fifth to the seventh century in appearance, such as fastenings, pot sherds, brooches, a broken pot and a knife. The knife was found at the hip of a body, suggesting it had been hanging from a belt; the body was twisted, the head thrown back and the hands seemingly clasping the neck. The pot was broken and the pieces placed round the head of a body.

The finds have not survived and the interpretation of the objects, having been done in the 1920s, is possibly suspect. The author showed the pictures of the finds to archaeological experts without telling them the context of the items so as to not prejudice their conclusions; they concluded that the brooches illustrated in the dig report dated from the late Iron Age or possibly early Roman periods. The knife with its angled back looks Anglo-Saxon and the broken pot is probably late Roman, as the original archaeologists suspected. Many of the bodies were lying in a twisted posture; some had no skull or their skull lay at an angle to the body, often with cut marks on the upper vertebra and damage to the jaw, suggesting that they were beheaded. One body had facial wounds, probably caused by a spear. Although they were in separate graves, there were also some loose skulls and

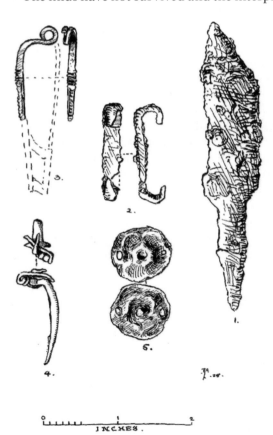

Finds from the burials at Bran Ditch (Lethbridge, T. and Palmer, W., 'Excavations in the Cambridgeshire Dykes: VI: Bran Ditch Second Report', *Proceedings of the Cambridge Antiquarian Society*, 30, pp.78–96, 1927–8).

The pot found with the Bran Ditch burials (Palmer, W., Leaf, C. and Lethbridge, T., 'Further Excavations at the Bran Ditch', *Proceedings of the Cambridge Antiquarian Society*, 32, pp.54–5, 1930–1).

graves containing more than one skull. Most of the bodies showed clear evidence that they had been buried long after death (the lower parts of the body seem to have become separated, possibly when they were moved into the grave and then placed with the rest of the body).

The initial assessment that they were buried piecemeal by a small group of gravediggers who were not sure which head belonged to which body seems plausible. The fact that they were buried with some care suggests the locals held them in affection, so they are less likely to have been criminals or invaders; perhaps they were people who fell defending the area. Recently this view has been challenged and scholars classify them as ritual or judicial executions. Gray thought that the Bran Ditch skeletons were from a Viking massacre and Lethbridge speculated that they were defeated invaders, but Hill, noting how the burials had separate graves, thought them executed criminals from the period AD900–1080.[8] There is some evidence from other dykes that may corroborate Hill's ideas, as archaeologists have uncovered evidence for postholes that could be a sign of a gallows at Rowe Ditch and Combs Ditch, though of course these may post-date the earthwork by centuries.[9] A charter dated 957 (S 647) for Stanton St Bernard possibly also records a gallows on Wansdyke, though the wording is ambiguous.[10] Evidence for capital punishment might reflect the rise of kings, with the growth of a justice system that executes transgressors being an embodiment of regal power, like the as two execution cemeteries found clustered around borrows at Sutton Hoo and at Wolkington Wold in Yorkshire.[11]

Some (myself included) have been more sceptical of the gallows theory as an explanation for deviant burials. Prior to the invention of the long drop, hanging caused death by strangulation, resulting in little or no damage to the neck vertebra; the bodies at Bran Ditch and other sites suggest beheadings. The person with the facial spear injury was unlikely to have been killed in a formal execution. The dating of the finds from Bran Ditch suggests a much earlier date than that proposed by Hill; the only certain Anglo-Saxon find was the knife, an unusual object to be carried by a condemned man to his place of execution, who surely should have been disarmed. The layout of the cemetery is very different from other probable early medieval execution sites. The possible execution burials at Sutton Hoo and Walkington Wold contain far fewer victims than at Bran Ditch and are buried across a wider area in a scattered haphazard fashion on different alignments. At Bran Ditch, the graves are in a long, neat row with little or no space between most of the burials. To explain the number of burials, the small, scattered communities of the Cambridgeshire fens would have had to have a judicial system that carried out the death penalty with ferocious determination.

Unfortunately, it is difficult to differentiate among people executed, massacred, killed in battle, suicides and sacrificed. It is hard to make firm conclusions about deviant burials, even with modern forensic techniques – with some deviant burials, there is a suggestion that the victims' hands were tied before death (especially if the wrists are together and there are no marks of defensive cuts on the hands and arms), but such binding is inferred as no material evidence has survived. With the Bran Ditch burials, it is possible to make a case for the bodies being beheaded criminals buried by a long-abandoned earthwork, but I believe that they were either the victims of a massacre buried piecemeal by the few survivors, or perhaps were publicly killed at a newly built dyke that carried the death penalty for crossing without permission. The odd skulls, the baby and the facial wound point to frenzied brutal killing, rather than the administration of justice.

Outside Cambridgeshire, there is burial evidence and finds of weapons associated with other possible early medieval dykes, though most were not excavated using modern methods. Where Bokerley Dyke crosses the Roman road, eight burials (unrelated to the Roman cemetery previously mentioned) were excavated in the fill of Roman ditches, which may mark the location of an Anglo-Saxon execution cemetery.[12] At a site visible from the dyke and just over 1.9 miles (3km) to the south-west, Pitt Rivers excavated seventeen skeletons (most decapitated) inserted into Wor Barrow, a Neolithic burial mound.[13] In 1838, at Buttington, where Offa's Dyke reaches the Severn near Welshpool, 400 skulls were found, while in 1930 Fox found a 'lance head' on the 'floor' of the ditch of the fort at the western end of Beachley Bank near the mouth of the Wye.[14] The Buttington remains have not been accurately dated, but they could be related to a battle with the Vikings recorded there in 893 in *The Anglo-Saxon Chronicle*, though recent scientific analysis by the National Museum Wales on two of the skulls suggests that they were more recent in origin.[15]

In 1783, locals found pieces of swords, spears, spurs and bridle-bits at the Grey Ditch in Derbyshire (either a furnished warrior burial or evidence of a fight), while in 1892, skeletons described at the time as 'slain in battle' were found at Great Bedwyn near the Bedwyn Dyke.[16] At Poulton Down near Mildenhall a female skeleton with associated sixth- or seventh-century objects was found thrown down a well just 3.7 miles (6km) north of the eastern end of East Wansdyke.[17] A knife carved with an indecipherable Ogham inscription (Ogham being an alphabet normally associated with early medieval Ireland and Scotland) was found about 270m east of the southern end of Fossditch in Norfolk, the most easterly Ogham object found in England and perhaps evidence of Scottish or Irish raiders in East Anglia.[18]

At Heronbridge, the dyke respects (and therefore is broadly contemporary with) a cemetery that contains over 200 bodies of robust males, half of which had head injuries (some even had no skulls); these possibly date from the Battle of Chester c.605–13, which is discussed in more detail later.[19] In 2004, two bodies were removed for paleo-pathological examination, which demonstrated that they had suffered multiple head injuries, probably from a sword; radiocarbon dating suggested that they were from the late sixth or early seventh centuries. The bodies are probably those of Northumbrians (who won the battle), as the neatness of the burials suggests that the victors interred them, while isotope evidence suggests that they came from north-east England or south-east Scotland, which is broadly Bernicia, the heart of the kingdom of Aethelfrith, the victor of the Battle of Chester. This suggests that his army was unusually large, as it could afford to lose 200 men yet still win a battle and have sufficient manpower to bury their dead.

Not all of the dyke burials might be battle victims. If a dyke was a border, then perhaps it would be the perfect place for the disposal of the bodies of outcasts instead of in the community's cemetery. Four burials that seem to have been executions found in the fill of the ditch of the prehistoric South Oxfordshire Grim's Ditch might be evidence that Anglo-Saxons did reuse older dykes to bury criminals sentenced to death.[20] At Aves Ditch, another prehistoric Oxfordshire dyke, archaeologists found a burial lacking most of the skull, which radiocarbon dated to the Anglo-Saxon period (670–870) in the bottom of the ditch.[21] In East Yorkshire, the Anglo-Saxons reused prehistoric dykes to bury their dead as well as barrows; in Wiltshire they also used barrows for high-status burials.[22] A correlation between borders and burials in the early medieval period is specifically mentioned in early medieval Irish law, though this was not of outcasts, but a way of claiming ownership of the adjacent territory.[23]

The burial evidence is rather confused, partly because of the unscientific recording of many early finds. The mass burials tell a much clearer story. The cut marks on the skeletons found at Heronbridge and Bran Ditch argue conclusively against hanging; these are probably victims of massacres or battles. The finds confirm my thesis that dykes and warfare are inextricably linked. The dykes were probably in areas of conflict and acted as a method of controlling the violence as a defence against raiding. Even execution burials could relate to raiding, as the earthworks demarked territory where crossing the border without permission carried the death penalty.

THE DATING OF DYKES

Scientific methods can help us to narrow the timescale of dyke building, though we cannot pin exact dates on individual early medieval dykes without unsupportable speculation. Historians are fairly certain that Offa's Dyke was built during his reign (757–96), despite a recent radiocarbon date suggesting that at least one section is older. From the information in the various dig reports, I have devised a table of the various results given by radiocarbon and Optical Stimulated Luminescence dating of deposits and finds associated with the dykes. For any radiocarbon experts, please note that these results have not all been achieved using the same calibration formulas (though the five Welsh examples were), as there is insufficient evidence from some of the results to attempt a recalibration, so the raw data are given here with that caveat in mind.

The result from East Wansdyke probably represents material dumped into the ditch long after the abandonment of the dyke, while the Harrow-Pinner Grim's Ditch material is probably much older material incorporated into a later structure. The first Swaledale result is of a prehistoric piece of oak incorporated into a later earthwork and the last relates to later silting of the earthwork.[24] Setting aside those odd results, the range of these results suggests that the dykes could date from as far apart as 268 to 1002, but as these represent the extremes of the date ranges this is highly unlikely. Statistically, it is more likely that the dykes date from nearer the middle of the date ranges, which for all of these dykes (bar the last two results) is between 435 and either 715 (if we take Wat's Dyke's radiocarbon date) or 897 (if we use the later Optically Stimulated Luminescence result from Wat's Dyke).

As this book concentrates on the period 400–850, it is perhaps unsurprising that the scientific evidence for these dykes suggests that they were built in the middle of this date range, although I only found evidence of two dykes from the later Anglo-Saxon period, both of which were rather small (Danby Rigg and Combs Bank in Reading). If we set aside the rather late Optically Stimulated Luminescence dates for Wat's Dyke (probably ditch silt that post-dates the earthwork) and the last two results in the table, all of the dykes potentially date from the very late sixth and the first half of the seventh century (590–650). This tentatively suggests that the period 590–650 was possibly the peak period of early medieval dyke construction. This would make Offa's Dyke not only exceptional in scale, but also at the tail end of the dyke building boom.

If dykes had a defensive role, we should expect to find different structures that carried out a similar role and both precede and post-date them. Most enclosed Anglo-Saxon settlements generally date to after or at least near the end of the main period of dyke construction. In western Britain, the fifth- and sixth-century elite often reoccupied Iron Age hill forts and we know in the ninth century the Anglo-Saxons built fortified burhs to defend themselves against Viking raids. Dykes slot neatly into the gap between these two periods of defended settlements, so it seems logical that they carried out similar functions.

Possible Dating Evidence of the Dykes[25]

Name of Dyke	Date Range	Mid-Point of the Range	Material Dated, Original Calculation (where given and calculated differently) and Source
Becca Banks (radiocarbon)	559–674	637	Cow pelvis from ditch fill
Scot's Dyke (Optically Stimulated Luminescence)	420–600	510	Top layer of silt AD510 +/– 90 +/–135
Clawdd Mawr, Llanfyllin (radiocarbon)	630–710	670	Charred organic remains sealed under the bank 1360+/–40BP or calculated 630–710 Two Sigma
Crugyn Bank (radiocarbon)	650–780	715	Charcoal samples sealed under the bank 1310+/–40BP or calculated 650–780 Two Sigma
Giant's Grave, Powys (radiocarbon)	340–530	435	Peat samples found sealed under the bank 1640+/–40BP calculated 340–530 Two Sigma
Short Ditch, Powys (radiocarbon)	410–590	500	Organic samples from the turf-line sealed under the bank 1560+/–40BP or calculated 410–590 Two Sigma
Offa's Dyke (radiocarbon)	430–652	541	Redeposited turf underneath the bank laid down as part of the construction process
Upper Short Ditch (radiocarbon)	540–660	600	Charcoal sealed under the bank 1460+/–40BP or 540–660 Two Sigma
Wat's Dyke (radiocarbon)	268–630	449	The site of hearth sealed under the bank
Wat's Dyke (Optically Stimulated Luminescence)	682–852, 792–1002, 747–927 and 742–952	767, 897, 837 and 847	Ditch silt samples
Fleam Dyke (radiocarbon)	340–640	490	Organic matter, mainly pieces of bone, found in the ditch fill
Devil's Ditch, Garboldisham (Optically Stimulated Luminescence)	660–980 and 650–930	820 and 790	Ditch silt
Harrow-Pinner Grim's Ditch (radiocarbon)	60–340	200	Charcoal within the banks
East Wansdyke (radiocarbon)	890–1160	1025	Charcoal deposits from flint rubble found at the bottom of the ditch

WIDER ARCHAEOLOGICAL EVIDENCE OF WARFARE

As well as the excavations of individual dykes and the artefacts uncovered, other archaeological evidence, such as geophysics, burials, coinage and pollen evidence, gives us further insights into the societies that built these dykes.

One scientific advance that archaeologists have already used to increase our understanding of dykes is geophysics. The earliest recorded uses on British dykes were an attempt to find evidence of a gateway in Wansdyke (the published report gives no exact date, but suggests it occurred between 1966 and 1970) and a resistivity survey in 1976 of Grim's Ditch in Yorkshire.[26] Geophysics can find sections of dykes that farmers in the past have ploughed flat, but care should be taken with this technique. Farmers often utilize dykes as field boundaries and may construct a hedgerow that continues the same alignment past where a dyke originally ended so, unless we excavate, a geophysics reading that suggests a dyke was originally much longer may just be showing a later field boundary. Geophysics therefore has unfortunately mainly given us negative evidence about dykes, in that by failing to find gateways and associated forts we can be certain that such features did not exist.

As well as physical finds, archaeologists can use environmental evidence to ascertain what the principal vegetation was in the past. One of these methods is pollen evidence, a branch of palynology, where the surviving pollen (which is usually only found at waterlogged sites) is analysed in order to ascertain what was the principal vegetation in the past. The science is complex, but the results can be very revealing. Archaeologists take samples from different depths (dated using radiocarbon dating if there are no dateable finds) and then use a microscope to count the different types of pollen. They must be cautious of certain factors, for example the propensity for certain species to produce more pollen per plant, or to be able to spread their pollen wider than other species, so a standardized multiplier is needed. When presenting the evidence, archaeologists can either use absolute numbers of pollen in each layer or percentages (though the percentage method cannot tell us if the total amount of vegetation declines or rises if the overall proportions of different species remains the same). As well as pollen evidence, archaeologists use other evidence, such as macrofossils of large plant remains, the remains of insects, mollusc shells (in particular snails) and evidence of alluvial deposits. Some species of insects and snails thrive in specific environmental conditions and can therefore be very useful indictors of the past environment.

Our inability accurately to date individual early medieval dykes renders largely futile any attempt to use pollen and other environmental evidence from nearby sites to reconstruct the general local environmental conditions at a dyke; we are limited to samples from actual excavations of dykes. There is good pollen evidence from near the Black Ditch on Snelsmore Common and near Bunn's Bank in Norfolk, but as there is no clear dating evidence for these dykes, matching them to specific changes in the adjacent landscape is not possible.[27] Offa's Dyke presumably dates to sometime during his reign (756–97), but the order for the construction of such a long dyke may not relate to circumstances unique to the immediate vicinity of any particular location along the dyke.

Although we do not have environmental evidence from all early medieval dykes, the published studies (like those from the Cambridgeshire Dykes) suggests that most were built across open grassland.[28] Partly this may be because it is hard to dig a ditch through a wood and crossing arable land causes an unacceptable loss of farmland, but open grassland may be typical of the debatable borderlands where raiding took place. Samples from Bran Ditch, for example, suggest that although the land was originally woodland some time before the dyke was built, it was open, possibly grazed, grassland when the builders of the dyke started their work. Macrofossil samples taken from the ditch fill near the northern end of the dyke suggest an area of wetland that presumably 'guarded' the northern flank of the earthwork.

Crampton carried out an analysis of the soils and pollen buried under four dykes, Bedd Eiddil, Ffos Toncenglau, Bwlch yr Afan and Clawdd Mawr Glyncorrwg (Bwlch Garw) in South Wales, and found that all four had been constructed across grassy heathland.[29] Pollen analysis from excavations of East Wansdyke, Becca Banks and Grim's Bank (Padworth) demonstrated that the builders constructed the dyke across open pastureland with no arable and few trees in the vicinity.[30] While there is evidence from West Wansdyke that sections of the dyke cut through areas of former cereal cultivation as well as pastureland, there is no evidence of nearby woodland; the secondary ditch fill does have evidence of shrubs and trees, suggesting that the area was less open after the abandonment of the earthwork.[31]

We can compare the evidence from early medieval dykes with that from prehistoric earthworks to see if their builders also predominantly dug them across pastureland. Dog-leg sections are probably an indicator that a dyke snakes across an arable landscape; it is noticeable how they are found on numerous prehistoric dykes (like the Buckinghamshire–Hertfordshire Grim's Ditch, South Oxfordshire Grim's Ditch, Berkshire Downs Grim's Ditch and Cranborne Chase Grim's Ditch), but rarely on early medieval earthworks. The numerous changes in direction of the Northern Rig (Roman Rig) and pollen evidence from a 1993 excavation suggest that the builders constructed it across an agricultural landscape, respecting existing field boundaries.[32] Pollen evidence from the Grim's Ditch near Leeds (which is probably prehistoric) suggests that the builders of that earthwork dug through grassland, but grew barley nearby.[33] Mollusc evidence and analysis of prehistoric field boundaries suggest that some of the prehistoric dykes on the Berkshire Downs Grim's Ditch do respect arable fields, but others go through a landscape of pastoralism with either free grazing or livestock rearing contained in fields.[34]

Two prehistoric dykes have good evidence that there were trees growing in the vicinity during construction. Pollen analysis of the Scot's Dyke ditch silt samples taken during the 2007 excavation suggest that it was dug through pastureland but with nearby woodland mainly of alder and hazel, while environmental evidence from an excavation of the Devil's Mouth earthwork on Long Mynd indicated ash and hazel trees in the vicinity.[35] Therefore, while early medieval dykes were probably dug across open grassland (either grazed or unutilized), the builders of prehistoric dykes dug them between fields that had patches of woodland in the vicinity.

What can this tell us about our early medieval dykes? It seems that grassland was the chosen landscape through which they were built. The early medieval builders possibly needed good lines of sight to spot raiders, whereas prehistoric dykes seem to be demarking an intensively utilized landscape.

General regional or national trends in environmental evidence give us background evidence of the societies that built the dykes. The published summaries from early medieval Britain all paint a broadly similar picture of no significant increase in tree pollen immediately after the breakdown of Roman rule, implying no wholesale abandonment of agricultural land, although there was some expansion of woodland in marginal areas in northern England, lowland Scotland, the Forest of Bowland, Bodmin Moor and some less fertile lowland areas.[36] This is partly explained by the withdrawal of Roman troops from the frontier zones (like the Hadrian's Wall garrison), which removed a ready market for agricultural produce in areas ill-suited to arable production, so farming was either abandoned or the locals reverted to pastoral activities. There also initially seems to have been a move to pasture and away from cereal production; both pollen evidence and alluvial deposits suggest an intensification of agriculture in the eighth century, especially in areas like the East Midlands and East Anglia, probably linked to the growth in trade and nucleated settlements. This indicates an increasing reliance on cattle in the fifth to seventh centuries. Cattle are mobile and can be herded, so they could become targets for raiders. If dykes were meant to stop raiding, it was probably the threat of the theft of cattle (and a consequential fear of starvation) that stimulated their construction.

As well as the wider pollen evidence, archaeological evidence from sites away from dykes can help us to understand warfare in this period. Unfortunately, the period 400–850 is notorious for the lack of such evidence – while pagan Anglo-Saxon burials have produced numerous finds, the Britons are particularly hard to detect archaeologically. While this could represent a catastrophic decline in population and living standards caused by the end of Roman rule, it is also possible that it is a symptom of the use of less durable materials. Changes from, say, mosaics to ornate rugs and from ceramic to wooden bowls would cause the same apparent decline in material culture. Historians are always cautious of arguing a conclusion from a lack of evidence, but perhaps sometimes a lack of finds from an excavation of a dyke may even be considered evidence in favour of an early medieval date, given the lack of pottery and coins from this period.

Coin evidence is particularly problematic in the early medieval period, as the minting and importation of large amounts of coinage ceased around the same time as the collapse of Roman rule. The growth of metal detecting and the Portable Antiquities Scheme has increased the numbers of coins recorded from the fifth and sixth centuries, but they are usually high-value imported examples valued for their precious metal content (gold and silver coins used as jewellery or talismans), rather than useful tokens for exchange. The almost complete lack of evidence of a monetary system of exchange after the collapse of Roman rule until the eighth century means that we can swiftly discard the theory that dykes were trade barriers. It is unlikely that there was enough internal trade to justify building huge earthworks to control it, especially as only one Mercian coin has been found in Wales.[37]

Anglo-Saxons started to mint high-value gold coins in the early seventh century and in the late seventh century trading settlements emerged, with lower denomination silver coins appearing in sufficient numbers to suggest widespread commerce, though this was mainly restricted to south-east England. Coinage became an expression of royal authority and a medium for royal propaganda; Offa reintroduced the minting of gold coins and was the first king to mass-produce royal coinage, portraying himself as a Roman emperor.[38] Interestingly, neither Offa's nor any other coins picture a dyke, or give the ruler an epithet related to dyke-building (king X 'the dyke builder', for example). Perhaps the rise in trade either led to (or was a symptom of) a decline in internal raiding, though the new trading settlements did attract new foreign raiders: the notorious Vikings.

Dykes and Cultural Borders

While I believe that the main purpose of most early medieval dykes was to stop raiding, they could also mark the limits of distinct cultural groups (especially if such groups were in conflict), or alternatively these earthworks could cause such cultural divisions. If this was the case, we should be able to map the distribution patterns of culturally distinctive artefacts and correlate them with the earthworks. Anglo-Saxon material culture is very distinct from that of the native Britons, though historians argue about how much this is a reflection of a cultural affinity or of ethnicity. British inscribed memorial stones are found overwhelmingly west of either Offa's Dyke or Bokerley Dyke; equally all finds of Anglo-Saxon pagan burials, early brooches and early coins come from east of Offa's Dyke. This suggests there is some correlation on a large scale between the location of those dykes and the distribution of culturally significant artefacts, but does it work on a smaller scale?

Do dykes lie along the fault lines of different Anglo-Saxon subcultures? Historians in the past have followed Bede in dividing the early medieval English into Angles, Saxons and Jutes, but this approach is now largely out of fashion. However, the simple division of Angles in northern England and Saxons in the south might not have just existed in Bede's mind, as we do find some differences. There are definite regional variations in Anglo-Saxon archaeological finds, for example there are more cremations in northern and eastern England and more inhumations in the south, while brooches tend to be saucer-shaped in the south and cruciform in the north.[39] I doubt if it was an ethnic divide, but people in the north and south of early medieval England do seem to have expressed distinct cultural identities through fashion and burial practices. Unfortunately, this division through the Central Midlands and along the Essex–Suffolk border is not marked by any earthworks, though it is possible to argue that the dykes in Cambridgeshire may be a rather inexact match for a small part of the divide. The dykes near the western border of Kent (the Surrey–Kent Dyke and the Faesten Dyke) could mark the western border of the Jutes of Kent, but neither earthwork is properly dated, so the location may be coincidental.

As part of this study, I also examined the idea that Anglo-Saxon dykes were engineered differently to British-built dykes (the latter being those built by the natives, including the inhabitants of Wales and Cornwall). V-shaped ditches, as they are difficult to construct without the sides collapsing, might signify an early British dyke built while Roman military techniques were still common knowledge; later Anglo-Saxon earthworks might be characterized by a more simplistic U-shaped ditch. While it is sometimes difficult to decide who built which dykes (Offa's is obviously Anglo-Saxon, while the Welsh and Cornish dykes are probably British), there was clearly no correlation between ditch shape and the nationality or culture of the builders.

If the dykes do not match the general divisions in material culture in the English zone, then perhaps they do mark subtler regional divides and scholars have tried to match the dykes of East Anglia against the distribution of archaeological material or features. Green *et al.* suggested that the distribution of Anglo-Saxon Illington-Lackford pottery was limited on the west by the Cambridgeshire Dykes, while Scull claimed that the distribution of different styles of early medieval pottery was limited by the various Norfolk dykes, but neither claim bears close scrutiny when the distribution patterns are mapped against the earthworks.[40] Anglo-Saxon funerary customs on both sides of the Black Ditches in Suffolk are too similar to mark a cultural frontier.[41] This inconclusive evidence makes it very difficult to sustain a case for any dyke other than those along the Anglo-Welsh border and possibly those in Dorset marking distinct cultural or even ethnic borders.

Despite much searching, the above is all I can say about dykes as cultural barriers. If they did help to reinforce identities, there is little sign of it in the archaeological record except on the Anglo-Welsh border, which means it was probably an inadvertent consequence of the early medieval dyke-building boom. People usually dug them to keep enemies out, not because the people on the other side were 'different' (with the possible exceptions of those on the Welsh border), although creating or exacerbating cultural/national divides could have been an unintended consequence of dyke building.

Evidence for Warriors and Raiding

While the written sources suggest a society plagued by raiding (more of this later), this could be clerics trying to give a moral message either by pointing out the terrors of secular society or lauding the bellicosity of a king, so it is necessary to examine the archaeological evidence for corroboration. If early medieval war leaders and kings did carry out raids for cattle, we should be able to detect this in the bone finds from elite settlements. At Dinas Powys the bones assemblage initially led Gilchrist to suggest that the source was local dairy production, but more recently it has been reinterpreted as evidence of raiding.[42] As well as the theft of cattle, there is evidence, in particular from the Staffordshire Hoard, that raiders also took high-status metalwork from their defeated enemies. The hoard, dated to 650–700, was found near Lichfield in Mercia; it contained numerous ornate fittings stripped from many swords, knives and shields, as well as jewelled crosses.

What is striking about Anglo-Saxon burials is the number of weapons found with them and these can possibly tell us about early medieval warfare.[43] This phenomenon could relate to status rather than reflect what equipment a person regularly carried – not every person buried with a spear was necessarily a warrior. These buried weapons do look functional, however, and the Anglo-Saxons must have manufactured sufficient arms to allow them often to place one in the ground whenever a loved-one passed away. About 47 per cent of Anglo-Saxon furnished male inhumations contained a weapon; 86 per cent of weapons burials contained a spear, 45 per cent shields, 11 per cent swords, 4 per cent a seax (a type of hunting knife), 4 per cent axes and 1 per cent arrows. Helmets and chain mail are extremely rare. These figures probably reflect the range and proportions of weaponry in Anglo-Saxon society, although bows, being composed entirely of organic material, are possibly underrepresented. The burial evidence suggests that not only are swords rare, but also, like helmets, they are usually found in high-status burials. The balance of an Anglo-Saxon sword is halfway down its heavy blade, implying that it was designed for hacking downwards on the head of an enemy;

Viking and later swords have a balance point nearer to the hilt to allow thrusting and parrying. Most weapon injuries detectable on a skeleton from Anglo-Saxon burials are from the head and shoulders, consistent with the downward sweep of a heavy sword rather than a thrusting motion.[44] It is worth briefly examining the archaeological evidence of weaponry in the Netherlands, northern Germany, Denmark and southern Sweden, the traditional ancestral home of the Anglo-Saxons.[45] In addition to the normal furnished cemeteries, there are mass deposits of weapons in bogs that probably represent the ritual deposition of the equipment of defeated armies. By analysing the numbers of weapons at each deposit, we can see the relative size of armies (with the proviso that we cannot know how many weapons the victors kept for themselves or left on the battlefield). At Esjbøl-North, archaeologists uncovered the remains of 60 swords, 150–175 shields, 203 throwing-spear tips and 191 'lance heads' (tips for heavier spears that were not thrown), suggesting an army of a little over 200. Other sites produced assemblages in similar proportions, suggesting armies between 20 to 300 (finds with more than 300 weapons were almost certainly multiple deposits). These relatively small numbers of soldiers armed predominantly with spears, but led by small elites with swords, are comparable with the evidence from England, though powerful kings like Penda of Mercia could probably mobilize a much larger force when necessary.

So, what can we conclude from the archaeological evidence from early medieval Britain (and the dykes)? The archaeological evidence does suggest that dykes were places where there were violent confrontations (like battles or executions), they were built across open grassland and some were later utilized as places to bury the dead. At the time that they were built, society was reliant upon cattle grazing ruled by people who were portrayed in death as warriors. Warlords with relatively small groups of warriors (none of the possible battle burial sites contain thousands of bodies) raided enemy territory for cattle and other portable treasures.

CHAPTER 3

Analysing the Earthworks

Early medieval warfare left few traces and accounts of the battles are either terse or often written far from the action (in terms of distance and time). The dykes are tangible evidence, but even they are mute and enigmatic features. We can glean information from them, if only we use the right analytical tools. We have no records of the numbers of people involved in building them, but we can measure the dykes and using these figures work how many people would have been involved. As these are the largest pieces of evidence we have, but being just mounds of earth are the hardest to glean information from, I beg the reader's indulgence while I painstakingly reveal how we can unlock the secrets of these features.

HOW MANY PEOPLE BUILT THE DYKES?

Any estimate of the numbers of people needed to build these earthworks will be based on assumptions. Most dykes are intermittent, probably because agriculture, urbanization, industry or natural erosion have destroyed sections; while most writers have assumed that they were originally continuous, it is entirely possible some were not. Likewise, assuming that the section where the bank is highest or the ditch deepest represents the best-preserved section may also be false, if the earthwork, as built, was not uniform in design but varied in scale along its length. A description of a dyke by an antiquarian suggesting that it was originally much larger in scale before the ravages of modern agriculture may be erroneous, if the antiquarian was either exaggerating or had failed to measure the earthwork accurately.

While the bank may be mutilated, we can mitigate some of the guesswork by calculating the amount of earth moved when constructing a dyke by excavating the ditch, even if it is entirely silted up. When a dyke is many miles long and there are only one or two recorded excavations, it is impossible to know if those sections are typical of the whole earthwork. Despite these caveats, by averaging out the measurements given in all the available published studies of these earthworks and measuring as many as possible in the field, I have produced figures that I think are accurate enough to be useful.

To calculate how many people were needed to build the dykes I needed accurate figures and these are given in Appendix I. Once I knew the rough length of the earthwork and either the size of the bank (the width and height) or the depth of the ditch (width and depth), I could calculate the volume of earth moved. I first multiplied the probable length by a cross section of either the ditch or the bank. If an excavation profile was available the ditch was used, as when the silt is removed from a ditch something approximating to the original profile is revealed, but the eroded parts of a bank are lost forever. If archaeologists had not excavated the dyke or they have not published the results, I used either the height of the bank or the depth of the ditch (whichever seemed to best preserve the original profile). As the profiles of earth banks and ditches are irregular semicircles (even a V-shaped ditch is not perfectly triangular), I found by experimentation that the area of the cross section of a ditch or bank is usually 60 per cent of the width multiplied by the depth or height respectively. Therefore, the final figure was produced by multiplying the length of the dyke by the width of the bank/ditch by the depth of the ditch/height of the bank by the multiplier 0.6.

Later spreading of the bank or utilization of the ditch (say as a road or for drainage) can widen them, resulting in abnormally high average width figures, so the largest figures were not always used if this was thought to be the case, as it would result in unrealistically large calculations for the volume. I have only used the dykes that I have good reason to believe are early medieval in this section (the probable rather than the possible examples), to ensure that any erroneously dated earthworks did not skew the figures. I found the dykes ranged from the tiny Bedd Eiddil in south Wales that was a mere 78m^3 to the huge Offa's Dyke at 798,000m^3.

One method of cross-checking my figures is to compare them with those given by other scholars; this is especially useful if other writers have used a different methodology. As three dykes, Offa's, Wat's and the Devil's Ditch in Cambridgeshire, are disproportionably larger than all the rest (these three probably make up two-thirds of the total volume of all the probable early medieval dykes), over- or underestimating the size of these three will skew the results. Fortunately, there are published estimates of the volumes of these dykes against which we can compare. Two studies quote a figure of 500,000m^3 for Wat's Dyke, though neither source says how this was calculated.[1] This figure is very close to the figure given in this book (424,800m^3, which is 85 per cent of the Fitzpatrick-Mathews/Lewis figure) and as I did not discover the methodology behind the Fitzpatrick-Mathews/Lewis figure, we are certainly working independently of each other. A published calculation for Offa's Dyke (750,933.32yd^3 or roughly 574,130m^3) is 72 per cent of the figure, 798,000m^3, from this study.[2] Richard Muir calculated the weight of earth moved to build the Devil's Ditch in Cambridgeshire was 1,360,090,000kg.[3] According to experiments carried out at Overton Down, which Muir himself uses for calculating the man hours needed to build the dyke, 5ft^3 (or 0.142m^3) of earth weigh 5cwt (or 254kg), therefore his figures translate to 760,365m^3, which is just 38 per cent more than the present study's figure of 550,800m^3.[4] Perhaps more significantly, the total of the estimates for the volumes of these three dykes given in Appendix I is 1,773,600m^3, which is just 3 per cent less than the total from these other studies for these dykes (1,834,495m^3). Getting totals with such similar figures (despite the differences in methodology)

Comparison of this Study's Estimates for the Volume of Various Earthworks with those Made by Other Scholars *(note that neither of the two estimates for the same earthwork is less than half or more than double the other)*

Earthwork	This study's estimate for the volume in metres^3	Other estimates	Difference (this study's figure as a percentage of the other estimate)
Offa's Dyke	790,000	574,130 (*see* Tyler, Ch1 note 32)	139%
Wat's Dyke	424,800	500,000 (*see* Fitzpatrick-Matthews, Ch2 note 24; Lewis Ch3 note 1)	85%
Devil's Ditch	550,800	760,365 (*see* Muir, Ch1 note 10)	72%
Antonine Wall (bank and ditch only)	567,000	955,000 (*see* Hanson and Maxwell, Ch3 note 11)	59%

gives me sufficient confidence to make conclusions based on my figures. Before discussing how many people could have built these dykes, it is worth briefly comparing the size of them to other major earth-moving projects from before the Industrial Revolution, so that we can better understand the scale of early medieval dyke building.

Early medieval dykes dwarf the vast majority of prehistoric earthworks, such as Durrington Walls, Maeshowe on the Orkneys, the Great Barrow at Knowlton Rings, the Dorset Cursus and even Silbury Hill, which at 239,000m^3 is the largest prehistoric artificial mound in Europe.[5] Most early medieval dykes are larger than any British hill fort. Camp Tops at Morebattle in the Scottish Borders at just 900m^3 is a typical earthwork, while the unfinished hill fort at Ladle Hill in Hampshire (if completed) would have been a very large example at 11,000m^3, which is still smaller than most dykes. The largest earthen structure built between 850 and the start of the canal age is probably Castle Hill, the huge motte of Thetford Castle built in the twelfth century. It is 100m wide and nearly 20m high, making it approximately 52,000m^3. Nine probable early medieval dykes are larger than Castle Hill.

While prehistoric man and the later medieval period cannot compare, the Romans did outdo early medieval dykes in terms of the volume of earth moved. The only ancient monuments larger than all of the early medieval dykes are the Fenland ditch called Car Dyke and Hadrian's Wall. With the possible exception of the Roman road network, prior to the building of the canal network, Car Dyke and Hadrian's Wall were probably the largest engineering projects in Britain. Car Dyke, which like early medieval dykes is hard to date definitively and whose purpose is unclear, is usually assumed to be Roman; it is 92km long, 12–17m wide and 3.6–4.4m deep, making it about 3,300,000m^3.[6] Hadrian's Wall was 75 miles (120km) long; estimates of the height of the wall vary from 3.5 to 6m and the width between 2.4 and 3m, while the earthen Vallum was around 6–9m wide and 3m deep.[7] With the wall 1,300,000–1,700,000m^3 (a Victorian engineer estimated the size of the wall to be 1,702,115yd^3 or 1,301,360m^3) and the Vallum around 1,300,000m^3, the whole structure is up to 3,000,000m^3.[8] Peter Hill estimated that the ditch in front of the wall (which was probably the source of only a small percentage of the stone used in the wall) was 1,071,846m^3.[9]

The Antonine Wall was 39 miles (63km) long, 3.35m high and 4.5m wide, so I calculate that it was about 569,835m^3.[10] Hanson and Maxwell, however, quote a figure 68 per cent higher for the Antonine Wall, 955,000m^3, claiming this equates to 250,000 man days; they also estimate that with the associated roadways, fortlets, timber breast work and stone base this would be multiplied by up to seven, giving 1,730,000 man days.[11] This suggests that prehistoric and post-850 medieval societies did not have the need, capability or urge to undertake projects on a scale of the larger early medieval dykes, and that only Offa in the early medieval period could match the achievements of the Roman Empire.

It is worth looking next at evidence for the organization of the labour needed to build the dykes before trying to calculate the numbers involved. Higham wondered if the local rulers who ordered the construction of some of the earlier dykes used Roman tax assessments to decide how many labourers each community should supply.[12] Perhaps before the collapse of the monetary economy shortly after the end of Roman rule, a paid workforce could have been hired using the revenue from a Roman-type taxation system. While these scenarios are plausible for those dykes built in the early fifth century, tax assessments, even if they survived, would soon become hopelessly out of date as settlements moved or were abandoned and new ones founded. Slavery was a common source of labour and practised throughout the period, although few individuals probably had sufficient slaves to build a dyke. In the medieval period, people owed obligations to their lord, whether it was a peasant to the local lord of the manor or a minor king to a more powerful monarch. If these obligations were to provide labour service for a set amount of days of the year (for peasants we know from later medieval evidence that this often meant working in the lord's fields), the aristocracy could choose to redirect this by obliging their tenants to help build an earthwork.

Comparison of the Size of Probable Early Medieval Dykes with Other Large Ancient Earthworks *(the latter are in bold italics)*

Name of Earthwork	Volume in Metres³	Length in Metres
Car Dyke	***3,300,000***	***92,000***
Hadrian's Wall (wall and vallum)	***3,000,000***	***120,000***
Offa's Dyke	798,000	95,000
Antonine Wall (ditch and bank)	***569,835–955,000***	***63,000***
Devil's Ditch	550,800	12,000
Wat's Dyke	424,800	59,000
East Wansdyke	244,800	20,400
Silbury Hill	***239,000***	***158***
Fleam Dyke	168,480	5,200
Dorset Cursus	***116,970***	***10,000***
(Mean dimensions of probable early medieval dykes)	109,919	10,331
Bokerley Dyke	95,310	5,295
West Wansdyke	89,100	13,500
Becca Banks	65,520	4,200
Fossditch	60,480	9,000
Thetford Castle motte	***52,000***	***100***
Durrington Walls ditch	***49,604***	***1,173***
Bran Ditch	35,100	5,000
Rowe Ditch	28,125	3,750
The Rein	22,344	1,900
(Median dimensions of probable early medieval dykes)	19,272	3,235
Bury's Bank	16,200	1,500
Crugyn Bank (inc. Two Tumps)	11,750	2,720
Ladle Hill hill fort (if completed)	***11,000***	***750***
Grey Ditch	9,504	1,200
Aelfrith's Ditch	4,350	5,000
Heronbridge	3,654	350
Pear Wood	2,462	400
Great Barrow at Knowlton Rings	***2,318***	***38***
Maeshowe	***2,246***	***35***
Upper Short Ditch	1,575	500
Clawdd Mawr (Llanfyllin)	1,215	450
Short Ditch	1,152	640
Camp Tops hill fort near Morebattle	***900***	***1,000****
Giant's Grave, Powys	780	250
Rudgate Dyke	261	100
Bica's Dyke	216	400

* As this hill fort is bivallate, that is, it has two ramparts, the length figure is twice the circumference of the fort.

From the eighth century, Anglo-Saxon sources specifically cite obligations that include repairing bridges, building fortifications and military service. These obligations and the documents they are recorded in are discussed in detail later. The earliest references are just from Mercia (perhaps this is unsurprising, as that kingdom probably built the largest dykes), but could they reflect older, more widespread, customs that obliged the peasantry to help build or repairs earthworks? Labour to build an earthwork could also have been given voluntarily by local communities, especially if they thought that the dyke would benefit them; this scenario seems most likely with the smaller earthworks. People could voluntarily gather at an agreed time, bringing with them their own tools from their farms or gardens. Presumably, there had to be some form of organization to coordinate the building of the dyke, whether that was a king, a local leader or an ad hoc group of local farmers, but at present we can only really speculate how they gathered a workforce.

The workers required to build an earthwork must have been housed, fed and equipped with tools. For the smaller earthworks, local farms and agricultural implements might have sufficed, but for the larger examples, there must have been some logistical organization. While the workers could have supplemented their diet by hunting or foraging, the numbers needed to build the larger dykes like Offa's probably would have required additional food (perhaps from nearby royal or aristocratic estates, possibly as part of the tribute paid to the leader building the dyke). The line of the dyke needed to be surveyed and marked out; excavations of some of the dykes have provided evidence for marker banks under the main bank, perhaps built by a small group in advance of the main construction party. The larger dykes (Offa's, Wat's, Devil's Ditch, Fleam Dyke and Bran Ditch, for example) all seem to have marker banks, unsurprisingly as they would have needed more planning. This level of organization for the larger earthworks suggests a king was involved rather than a group of local farmers collectively working together. It is estimated that it took thirty men a month to survey Hadrian's Wall; the Mercians could have been less exacting, so could have taken less time to survey Offa's Dyke; though equally they were also likely to have been less experienced than Roman engineers so may have taken slightly longer.

On Offa's Dyke, changes in direction and construction methods suggest that different gangs worked different parts, while evidence from East and West Wansdyke suggests that the builders initially built small quarry pits and spoil heaps before linking them to form continuous earthworks. The water levels encountered during excavation of the earthworks of the Welsh borders mean that the builders must have limited the main construction to the summer months when the ground was drier and this is consistent with studies of the construction of Hadrian's Wall. There is some evidence of the clearance of any unwanted undergrowth or trees using fire; this was probably best done in spring, before the vegetation became so dry that the flames would get out of control. We do know from epigraphic sources that Hadrian's Wall took six years to build (or would have, if war had not interrupted the work) and the Antonine Wall took between two to twelve years due to changes made during the construction work.[13] We may never know if the dykes were built over many years or during a single season, though it seems unlikely Offa's could have been built in a few months (perhaps it was laid out in one year with marker banks, then the main bank and ditch tackled over the subsequent year or two), while the smaller ones could easily have been built in a summer.

What is surprising is that, apart from marker banks, there is little evidence, either written or archaeological, of the bureaucracy, workforce or tools involved in dyke building. There is no evidence of camps for the workers or supply roads built to bring in supplies, which would be essential to mobilize workers from areas outside the immediate vicinity of the earthwork. Presumably, the early medieval people, like their predecessors, used wooden spades and wicker baskets, neither of which usually survives well in the archaeological record, though there is some evidence of both at sites other than dykes.[14] There is evidence that the Anglo-Saxons used iron-tipped shovels to move earth: two eleventh-century Anglo-Saxon calendars in the British Library show people in the March illustrations digging the soil with such shovels.[15] While the shafts may not survive, the iron tip should; I have found no evidence of one associated with an early medieval dyke, which suggests that the labour force is more likely to have been relatively small and/or local, perhaps farmers using their own tools, which they made sure not to break or lose. A much larger workforce would have needed a logistical infrastructure (perhaps even being supplied with mass-produced tools) and it is logically more likely they would have left debris (such as broken equipment) that would be noticeable in the archaeological record.

Scholars have attempted to calculate the number of people needed to build the larger of the early medieval dykes. Patrick Wormald claimed Offa could have built his dyke with just 5,000 men if the construction was spread over his whole reign, while tens of thousands would have been needed if it was built in a single year, but he did not say how he obtained these figures.[16] Stones were found every 1.6m in the marker bank of Wat's Dyke; perhaps if they are taken to represent the section allocated to each labourer, it would presumably have taken 36,875 workers to finish the dyke.[17] Hill used two written sources to make his calculations about how many people Offa employed. First, the *Burghal Hidage* (a tenth-century list of fortified sites), which says that four men were needed for every pole of the perimeter of a fortification; this equates to a man every 4.125ft (1.257m), so 76,000 would have been needed to man Offa's Dyke.[18] Second, he turned to the *Tribal Hidage* (a seventh- or eighth-century administrative document), which implies that Mercian kings could call on 125,000 heads of household. Hill calculated that as the central section was 98 miles long (roughly 157km, which is about 65 per cent longer than the estimate I use) and is divisible into 125,440 units, each 4.125ft long, the Mercians could have used a person from every Mercian household to lay out the dyke one year and finish it the next. Reynolds also used the *Burghal Hidage* to suggest that it took over 15,000 to build the whole of Wansdyke.[19] However, the *Burghal Hidage* tells us how many people are needed to man a town wall, not how many people are required to build it.[20] Far more people are needed to build a fort or a railway than to staff one! Equally, the *Tribal Hidage* gives us a glimpse of how many households the kings of Mercia could tax, not how many they could or did use as labourers.

Some have used work carried out at Overton Down to make estimates of the number of people involved in building the dykes. The work of the Experimental Earthwork Project at Overton Down started in 1960 and the data still form the basis for many modern archaeological assumptions.[21] It involved archaeology students using various pieces of replica period equipment (for example, prehistoric picks) to dig earthworks. The archaeologists estimated that, at best, a person using prehistoric tools can move 5cwt per hour (5ft^3 or 0.142m^3). While it was doubted that this rate could be maintained for long, early medieval peasants were more used to hard labour than archaeology students.

Various estimates have been made of how many people it took to construct various earthworks.[22] Muir tried to estimate the numbers needed to build the Devil's Ditch in Cambridgeshire using the Overton evidence, which he (incorrectly) claimed demonstrated that a man with a pick and a shovel could move 750kg of solid, moist chalk in an hour. He estimated that the soil moved to build Devil's Ditch weighed 1,360,090,000kg, so he calculated it would have taken 500 labourers 400 days (or 1,000 men 200 days) to build the dyke. The Overton dig rates for a man using ancient methods suggest he could dig just 5cwt in an hour, which works out at just 254kg, far less than the figure Muir used. The diggers at Overton only achieved figures comparable to Muir's when using modern steel tools. Fowler likewise used the Overton data to estimate the number of people needed to build East Wansdyke, but gave no calculations; he claimed it would have taken 1,000 men 23 to 30 days to build the dyke. Tyler used the Overton study to calculate that it would have taken 675,839.99 man days to build, so 10,000 people could have built Offa's Dyke in 68 days. Erskine suggested a Roman soldier could shift an utterly unfeasible 20m^3 in a day, which would presumably mean twenty men could easily have built West Wansdyke in a year, though he did not make this final calculation. Lewis claimed that a man can move an entire cubic metre of earth in just twenty minutes (try it in your back garden to see just how hard it would be) and calculated that it would have taken 100 men to build Wat's Dyke in a year.

There also have been some attempts to calculate the number of workers (or rather soldiers pressed into labouring duty) it would have taken to build the Roman frontier walls of Britain and prehistoric earthworks.[23] Seeing if the Romans or prehistoric societies used similar numbers to the later dyke builders can tell us how sophisticated the logistics were of early medieval kingdoms. In 1885, an engineer called Rawlinson estimated that 10,000 labourers could have built Hadrian's Wall in 240 days, using the assumption that a Roman worker could move 8yd^3 (6.1m^3) a day. Hanson and Maxwell claimed that a fit Roman soldier could move 3.8m^3 of earth a day and therefore the ditch and bank of the Antonine Wall would have taken 250,000 man-days to dig. Therefore, it would have taken about 1,500 labourers to build. Peter Hill claimed that a force of 1,800 men could have dug the ditch of Hadrian's Wall in a season and that a force of about 7,200 legionaries plus some auxiliaries built the whole structure over half a year (during the drier months). Richard Atkinson in 1968 said that it would have taken 500 people 10 years to construct Silbury Hill; while Mike Parker Pearson thought that 1,000 could do it in 2 years and 3 years later Geoffrey Wainwright calculated how much labour it would take to construct prehistoric earthworks like Avebury and Durrington Walls. These calculations are summarized here in the table, 'Different Estimates for the Labourers Needed to Build Various Earthworks in a Year'.

While the different estimates made by various scholars for the size of both the early medieval dykes and the Roman frontier works are broadly similar, these estimates of the numbers of people needed to build these structures are quite clearly incompatible. If the ditch of the Antonine Wall only took 1,500 men to dig, it is unlikely that it took 50 times that number to build Offa's Dyke when the two earthworks are of a similar size. With different digging rates forming the basis for these figures, it is unsurprising scholars have produced such varied estimates. It is therefore necessary to investigate further the amount of earth a man can move in

Different Estimates for the Labourers Needed to Build Various Earthworks in a Year *(ancient earthworks are in bold italics)*

Name of Scholar	Date of Study	Dyke	Estimate of Number of Labourers Needed
Rawlinson	*1885*	*Hadrian's Wall*	*10,000*
Atkinson	*1961*	*Avebury*	*325*
Atkinson	*1968*	*Silbury Hill*	*5,000*
Wainwright	*1971*	*Durrington Walls*	*190*
Muir	1981	Devil's Ditch	1,000
Wormald	1982	Offa's Dyke	Tens of thousands
Hanson & Maxwell*	*1983*	*Antonine Wall (ditch only)*	*1,500*
Hill	1985	Offa's Dyke	76,000
Pearson	*1993*	*Silbury Hill*	*1,000*
Fowler	2001	East Wansdyke	1,000
Reynolds	2006	East and West Wansdyke	15,000
Hill	*2006*	*Hadrian's Wall (ditch only)*	*1,800*
Hill	*2006*	*Hadrian's Wall*	*7,200+*
Erskine	2007	West Wansdyke	20?
Lewis	2008	Wat's Dyke	100
Hayes & Malim†	2008	Wat's Dyke	36,875
Tyler	2011	Offa's Dyke	5,000–10,000

* They do not give this final figure; this is my extrapolation from their estimates.
† They do not make this final calculation themselves, but this is based on their assumption that the stones in the marker bank 1.6m apart represent the section allocated to each labourer

a day's work before we have figures that are sufficiently robust to enable us to build theories on them.

Previous studies have relied on a single estimate for the volume of earth somebody can move in an hour or day, but by having as many different estimates as possible, as well as looking at the reasoning behind the calculations, we can make a more informed and balanced estimate. As most dykes (and more importantly the largest of the earthworks) were dug through what we can loosely term soil, we do not have to worry too much about the extra labour needed to quarry the rock (one notable exception is Becca Banks).

As we have seen, experiments at Overton Down suggested that an archaeology student using prehistoric methods (that is, antlers as picks, the shoulder blades of deer as scrapers and wicker baskets to move the material) could move 4.9–6cwt per hour and that 1cwt equated to 1ft^3 or 0.028m^3. The Victorian archaeologist Pitt Rivers managed better results and got his diggers to move 9cwt an hour (roughly 0.25m^3) using antler picks. At Overton Down archaeology students using modern tools found that they could each move up to 17cwt every hour (0.48m^3). Erskine, using data from Roman military handbooks (like *Epitoma Rei Militaris* by Vegetius) and evidence from Roman camps, claimed that a Roman soldier on manoeuvres could daily move 0.75–1.5m^3, but a man unencumbered by military duties could move 10–20m^3 in a day. Bachrach claims that the workers Charlemagne employed in 793 on his failed attempt to dig a canal from the Danube to the Rhine would have had to move 0.3m^3 a day, but gives no source for this figure.[24]

From the nineteenth century, one oft-quoted figure is that a navvy could move 20yd^3 (15.3m^3) a day.[25] However, the Victorian engineer Rawlinson assumed a labourer could only move 8yd^3 a day (6.1m^3) when estimating the labour force needed to build Hadrian's Wall. Dixon, in the excavation report on the Anglo-Saxon settlement at Mucking, claimed that a man could move 0.5m^3 an hour in gravel soil, but gives no supporting evidence, while Lewis asserted that a man can excavate a cubic metre and pile it up in twenty minutes, suggesting that he could move 3m^3 an hour, but also gave no source.[26] A modern archaeologist estimated that, using steel equipment, it is possible to dig a cubic metre of soil in an hour, but once into the subsoil, the rate diminishes dramatically, probably even halves, dropping to about 0.4m^3 an hour in glacial till (Nick Higham, personal communication).

The British Army's standard guide to engineering matters, *The Royal Engineers Pocket Book*, estimates the amount of earth a man can move in an hour to be 0.3m^3.[27] This booklet does add the caveat that this rate is halved in chalk or rock (this would produce a rate less than Pitt Rivers managed using prehistoric techniques); it also notes that the rate decreases if the troops are tired, inexperienced or digging in the dark. Peter Hill looked at records from World War I and estimated that troops could move 90ft³ of earth in a four-hour period when digging a trench under fire, which works out as 0.65m³ per hour.[28] Since 1873, architects and builders have habitually used a reference source called *Spon's Estimating Costs Guide to Minor Works* when costing building work; this includes estimates for excavating different types of ground by hand.[29] Recent editions estimate that a labourer would take 0.6 hours to dig through a square metre of topsoil to a depth of 25cm, which gives a rate of 0.4m³ an hour. The Spon rates for digging a narrow trench are lower, approximately 0.29m³, and for digging through rock it drops to 0.1m³ per hour, but as the ditches of early medieval dykes are much wider and were rarely cut through rock, the rate for digging a pit 1.5m deep at 0.3m³ an hour is probably most relevant.

By putting the information from the various studies in the table 'Different Digging Rates', the data are easier to compare. Because some estimates are hourly and others daily, it is necessary to calculate one figure from the other to make them comparable. As the studies used here have variously estimated the average working day to be six, eight or even ten hours, the figures in square brackets are extrapolations made by this study, which give a range of figures from that of a six-hour day to that of a ten-hour day.

The figures given by Lewis and Eskine seem abnormally high and as they provide no clear reasoning behind their figures, these are best laid aside. It is clear that the rates using prehistoric methods are far lower than those using Roman, eighth-century or modern methods. Roman soldiers and nineteenth-century navvies were possibly better organized, trained and equipped (usually with mass-produced tools) than medieval peasants; modern steel shovels are undoubtedly stronger and more efficient than a medieval wooden spade, but an early medieval labourer would probably have access to far better equipment (like iron-tipped spades and iron axes) than prehistoric antler picks. Therefore, the early medieval rate logically

Different Digging Rates

Study	Type of Equipment	Hour Rate in Metres³	Day Rate
Overton	Prehistoric	0.14–0.17	[0.84–1.7]
Pitt Rivers	Prehistoric	0.25	[1.5–2.5]
Erskine	Roman	0.75–1.5	10–20
Bachrach	793	0.3	[1.8–3]
?Navvy	Nineteenth-century	[1.53–2.55]	15.3
Rawlinson	Nineteenth-century	[0.61–1.02]	6.1
Hill	World War I	0.65	[3.9–6.5]
Dixon	?	0.5	[3–5]
Lewis	?	3	[18–30]
Spon's	Modern	0.3	[1.8–3]
Royal Engineers	Modern	0.3	[1.8–3]
Overton	Modern	0.48	[2.9–4.8]
Higham	Modern	0.4–1	[2.4–10]

should fall somewhere between the prehistoric rates (0.14 to 0.25m^3 an hour) and the figures for those using Roman/nineteenth-century/modern methods (0.3m^3 or more per hour). This means that early medieval labourers could probably move 0.25–0.3m^3 per hour or 1.5–3m^3 a day, a figure surprisingly close to the estimate for Charlemagne's labourers, which is the only estimate originating from the period covered by this book.

By having a dozen different rates, we are on firmer ground than any previous study. With this more trustworthy digging rate, it is possible to estimate with confidence the number of labourers needed to build the probable early medieval dykes. As already mentioned, it is unlikely that the builders of a dyke would work throughout the year. It is difficult to dig the soil in the wetter months and in a pre-industrial society it is probably unlikely that a ruler or community would divert peasants into non-productive projects during the harvest. Therefore, in the table 'Estimate of the Number of Labourers', it is assumed that the working season is the conveniently round figure of 100 days, if the reader thinks that figure is too low and, say, 200 days is a more likely figure, then just halve the figures in the third column.

This table on page 75 applies a different digging rate for dykes with rock-cut ditches, but here this is only applicable to Becca Banks. Spon's and the *Royal Engineers Pocket Book* give hourly digging rates through rock as 0.1 and 0.15m^3 respectively, so this study uses the lower of those two rates, giving a daily rate of 0.6–1m^3.

These figures suggest that for the larger dykes, thousands of labourers were needed, not tens of thousands as in some previous estimates (though they are still major undertakings), but for half of the probable early medieval dykes 100 men or fewer would have sufficed. If the dykes were built over many years, even fewer labourers would have been working at any one time.

Now we know the size of the workforce, we can make conclusions about how they were built. These relatively low figures would explain why it is only on Offa's Dyke that there is clear evidence of different gangs working different sections; on most of the dykes, the workforce would be sufficiently manageable to make piecemeal construction unnecessary. A marker bank of the type found at Fleam Dyke, Devil's Ditch, Offa's Dyke and Wat's Dyke demonstrates the planning and preparation needed when organizing a force numbering over 1,000. It is perhaps a little surprising that the creators of Bran Ditch felt the need to build a marker bank when the labour force was possibly between 117 and 234. For most dykes, such a feature would be unnecessary, as the organizers could easily draw the workforce from local settlements with no need for temporary housing, again explaining the absence of evidence of camps for the workers in the archaeological record. Overall, while these estimates are very similar to those of Muir, Fowler and Tyler, generally they are less than those given by other scholars. If fewer people were involved than previously thought,

Estimates of the Number of Labourers Needed to Build Probable Early Medieval Dykes

Dyke	Volume in Metres^3	Labourers Needed to Build it in a Single Season	Range of Estimates by other Scholars
Offa's Dyke	798,000	2,660–5,320	5,000–76,000
Devil's Ditch	550,800	1,836–3,934	1,000
Wat's Dyke	424,800	1,416–2,832	100–36,875
(East and West Wansdyke together)	333,900	1,113–2,385	15,000
East Wansdyke	244,800	816–1,749	1,000
Fleam Dyke	168,480	562–1,123	
Becca Banks [through rock]	65,520	655–1,092	
Average	**168,480**	**397–785**	
Bokerley Dyke	95,310	318–635	
West Wansdyke	89,100	297–594	20
Fossditch	60,480	202–403	
Bran Ditch	35,100	117–234	
Rowe Ditch	28,125	94–188	
The Rein	22,344	74–148	
Median	**19,272**	**64–128**	
Bury's Bank	16,200	54–108	
Crugyn Bank (inc. Two Tumps)	11,750	39–78	
Grey Ditch	9,504	32–63	
Aelfrith's Ditch	4,350	15–29	
Heronbridge	3,654	12–24	
Pear Wood	2,462	8–16	
Upper Short Ditch	1,575	5–11	
Clawdd Mawr (Llanfyllin)	1,215	4–8	
Short Ditch	1,152	4–8	
Giant's Grave, Powys	780	3–5	
Rudgate Dyke	261	1–2	
Bica's Dyke	216	1–2	
Total	**2,638,066**	**8,794–17,587**	

it is less surprising that dykes are rarely mentioned in the contemporary chronicles.

So, how does this compare with the one ancient civilization where there are records of how many people were needed to build large linear earthworks? Documents from the construction of the Great Wall of China demonstrate that a man could build a rampart 18ft long (roughly 5.5m) in a month; as Offa's Dyke is about 95,000m long, this would suggest 5,278 Chinese labourers could have built Offa's dyke in 100 days.[30] This figure, based on actual experience rather than a historian's guesswork, is reassuringly far closer to this study's figure of 2,660–5,320 than Hill's 76,000 or Wormald's tens of thousands. Although the final stone Great Wall seen on tourist posters is obviously different from the earthen bank built by Offa, many of the earlier structures built by the Chinese are similar.

While our knowledge of the administration of early medieval kingdoms makes it difficult to know how many people the kings of, say, Mercia could mobilize for a civil engineering project, we can compare these estimates from the known figures of armies from other periods. When the Romans invaded Britain, their force probably numbered 40,000; by the end of Roman rule it had declined to just 10,000–20,000.[31] Figures for the size of armies in the Anglo-Saxon and Viking periods are more problematic, as chroniclers often exaggerated the size of enemy forces. It is likely that most Viking armies numbered between just a few hundred and a few thousand men. Estimates of the size of the English army at the Battle of Hastings in 1066 average around 7,000 and in the thirteenth century most armies numbered just a few thousand because they could not support more through foraging.[32] While Edward the First mobilized over 15,000 troops, he used just 968 diggers to divert the River Clwyd when building the castle and town at Rhuddlan and a mere 360 men with scythes to harvest all the crops on Anglesey to prevent them being used by his enemies.[33] He controlled all of England, Aquitaine as well as parts of Wales, Ireland and Scotland and his conquest of Wales was notoriously grandiose, entailing the building of the largest castles in Europe, yet it has been claimed that rulers of Mercia mobilized tens of thousands not to conquer Wales, but to keep the people out.

Figures for the numbers of workers that the Angevins could put to work building fortifications survive from around the year AD 1000 and suggest a ten-hour day was the norm.[34] The core of their territory contained 60,000 people (roughly half that of Mercia), but they could only spare 140 men at any one time to build fortifications and those people had to be supported by 460, over three times as many, to provide the necessary food. According to one scholar, Charlemagne mobilized 60,000 to work on his failed Rhine–Danube canal, though others give a much lower (and more realistic) estimate of just 4,700–6,000.[35] These figures suggest that it is highly unlikely that early medieval kings who only ruled a part of England or Wales could have gathered tens of thousands of labourers. The population of Wales in the late thirteenth century was only about 300,000 and in the early medieval period probably considerably lower; if, as Hill suggested, Offa could have put the 125,000 men in the field, the Mercians would surely have destroyed the Welsh rather than wasted time building a dyke.

The dyke builders of early medieval Britain were not mobilizing people by the tens of thousands as the Romans did when they invaded. Only a few dykes needed thousands of labourers, which is what we would expect from unsophisticated early medieval kingdoms. As half of the probable early medieval dykes could have been built with fewer than 100 workers (and half a dozen of them with fewer than ten), we are probably looking at local communities or perhaps minor warlords building them. The largest may have been ordered by kings, but most of these earthworks were local reactions to enemy raids.

THE STRUCTURE AND LOCATION OF DYKES

After estimating the numbers of diggers needed to build the dykes, we can now examine their structure. The average length for probable early medieval dykes is 10,331m, though because this is skewed by a few very large earthworks we should note that the median length is just 3,235m (that is, the middle amount if the numbers are arranged in size from the smallest to the largest). It gives a more typical figure than an average, which can be skewed by a few abnormally small or large figures. For possible early medieval dykes (those where the evidence for a date is far from certain), the figure is even lower, the average being just 1,990m, but as smaller dykes are less likely to be excavated or securely dated, shorter dykes are more likely to be in the possible rather than the probable category. Dykes from other periods are generally longer than most probable early medieval dykes; the reused/rebuilt prehistoric/Roman dykes average at 3,606m in length, the prehistoric/Roman dykes at 6,172m and the later medieval dykes at 7,960m. The range of lengths for probable early medieval dykes is unusually large at 94–95,000m, while the range for all the others is 100 to just 25,300m.

In terms of volume, the average for probable early medieval dykes is very high (109,919m^3), again because of the larger earthworks, but the median figure is just 19,272m^3. The volume estimates for possible early medieval dykes, 10,748m^3, are even lower. The volume figures for reused/rebuilt prehistoric/Roman dykes (38,722m^3), prehistoric/Roman dykes (33,438m^3) and for later medieval (35,257m^3) are all very similar to each other, but much higher than for most early medieval dykes. In summary, probable early medieval dykes are usually quite small in scale, but a minority, notably Offa's and Wat's, are unusually long and large, so distorting the average. The short ones probably had very specific roles, cutting a routeway for example, while a larger grandiose dyke like Offa's was making a statement about the power of that king.

The probable early medieval dykes generally have a single bank and ditch, both of which are relatively large, whereas prehistoric dykes often have multiple banks and ditches, which are usually much smaller. The ditches of probable early medieval dykes are on average 2.1m deep and 6.2m wide, while the banks average 1.8m high and 8.3m wide; the size of these features seems to vary less than prehistoric dykes. A study of the earthworks of lowland Scotland found that the dimensions of surviving later medieval features are much smaller than early medieval dykes.[36] The

A profile of a typical early medieval dyke (a hypothetical model based on an aggregate of numerous profiles of different earthworks).

average depth of the ditches of agricultural boundaries was 0.412m, of head dykes was 0.23m, of park pales was 0.23m and wood banks 0.27m, with widths and bank sizes equally significantly smaller than probable early medieval dykes. The banks and ditches of probable early medieval dykes generally dwarf those from earthworks of other periods. The most likely explanation is that early medieval dykes were designed to look formidable, to put people off trying to cross them and, if necessary, were imposing enough to be defensible.

The ditches of probable early medieval dykes are more likely to have V-shaped ditches than prehistoric dykes, where the spilt between V- and U-shaped ditches is more even. The angle of the sides of ditches is roughly similar for dykes of all time periods (between 38 and 43 degrees), implying that the angle is more a factor of how steeply a ditch can be dug without it immediately collapsing than changing practices over time. The differences between the two different styles of ditch are significant. A V-shaped ditch is harder to cross, but the sides collapse over time. A U-shaped ditch is more stable and requires less maintenance. It is perhaps significant that none of the probable or possible early medieval dykes with evidence of a counterscarp bank have an unequivocally U-shaped ditch, which suggests the counterscarp is a product of clearing out a V-shaped ditch. The prehistoric ditches were probably boundary markers, so needed to remain as features in the landscape for years or decades, while early medieval dykes are short-term physical barriers.

Many (though by no means the majority) of probable early medieval dykes have features like counterscarp banks, marker banks, berms, revetments and ankle-breakers, but these are rare or unknown on prehistoric or later medieval dykes. Though berms and revetments usually fulfil the same purpose, that is, stopping the bank slipping into the ditch, the Devil's Ditch and West Wansdyke have both (the bank of the former is so tall that it is understandable that the engineers adopted both methods to stop it collapsing). While many of the prehistoric dykes have right-angled corners and branches (the prehistoric dykes of Dorset and Hampshire form a spidery network), these features are rare in early medieval dykes. Even the branch in Bokerley Dyke, the Epaulement, is more likely a turned-in terminus, rendered obsolete when the dyke was extended, than a branch. This is because prehistoric dykes are boundary markers, so often respect field boundaries.

There is no clear evidence for a gateway in any early medieval dyke (unsurprisingly, as they are designed to stop people crossing them), but also even less evidence of palisades. Some have argued that palisade evidence has eroded away, but we do have evidence from prehistoric earthworks like North Oxfordshire Grim's Ditch that clearly demonstrates that original gateways or palisades are detectable by excavation.[37]

The surviving remains of any earthwork may not be indicative of what the original designer envisaged if they were left unfinished, but while it is

ANALYSING THE EARTHWORKS

The relative sizes of the larger early medieval dykes (note that the smaller ones cannot be shown on this scale).

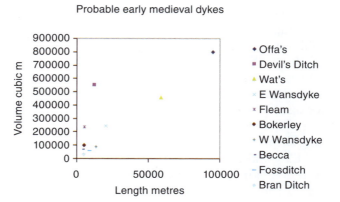

easy to speculate that a dyke was originally meant to be longer, it is difficult to prove. If there was archaeological evidence of a marker bank or ditch extending beyond the built sections it would indicate an unfinished section, but such a feature has not yet been recorded.

Early medieval dykes vary enormously in length and volume. When plotted on a graph the magnitude of some probable early medieval dykes becomes obvious: three dykes, Offa's, Wat's and Devil's Ditch (four if we count the two halves of Wansdyke as one) stand out. However, the graph suggests a graduation in scale rather than there being two distinct groups separated by a clear gap, suggesting that the larger and smaller dykes are part of the same phenomenon. Most early medieval dykes cannot be shown clearly on a graph, as they would be bunched up in its bottom left-hand corner.

The ten largest early medieval dykes (Offa's, Devil's Dyke, Wat's, East Wansdyke, Fleam, West Wansdyke, Bokerley, Becca, Fossditch and Bran Ditch) are not only longer, but

A simplified map showing the topography of Britain and the distribution of early medieval dykes.

are also larger in scale than the smaller dykes. The ditches of the largest ten average at 2.7m deep, whereas the rest of the probable early medieval dykes average just 1.6m; the banks of the ten largest are on average 2.6m high, whereas the rest of the probable early medieval dykes have banks on average of just 1m. The larger ones often seem more sophisticated in design. Half of the top ten largest probable early medieval dykes have signs of a marker bank (Offa's, Devil's Ditch, Fleam Dyke and Bran Ditch), possibly because their length made such a feature essential when laying them out. Though Offa's Dyke probably did not have a revetment or ankle-breaker, these features do seem more common in the larger dykes. While the shorter examples may be more hastily constructed, all sizes generally have the same number of banks and ditches as well as no evidence of palisades, forts or original gateways, suggesting a similarity of construction and purpose.

When the distribution of early medieval dykes is mapped on a national scale against the geology or topography, there are some interesting patterns. There are few dykes in granite areas, either because it is harder to dig a ditch there or because such areas are usually upland with very low population densities. Alluvial areas also contain few dykes, most likely because of the difficulty of constructing an earthwork where there is such a high water table. The chalk hills of lowland England contain many dykes, which is probably unsurprising as such areas are free draining with a relatively soft geology. Dykes are to be found scattered along the length of the Pennines, usually blocking narrow valleys that are still used as routeways across the hills.

Generalizations about the location of early medieval dykes are worth making, though we should remember they are rather subjective impressions. During fieldwork, it was noticeable that views across the landscape from most early medieval dykes are panoramic, often spectacularly so; even with those built across valleys there is usually a nearby hill that gives good views (the views from Lose Hill near Grey Ditch are stunning). Conversely, the dykes are often difficult to locate even with a good map; this is in sharp contrast to prehistoric hill forts, burial mounds and cross-ridge dykes, which are invariably located in prominent locations that make finding them much easier. Two dykes are easy to find: Offa's Dyke snakes across a series of hills, so if one part is hidden in the lee of a hill then another section is in view; and Devil's Ditch in Cambridgeshire is a tall monument in a flat landscape. Later damage to earthworks (for example by ploughing) may have reduced the visibility of many of the dykes, but it was probably a part of the design; even those near prominent natural escarpments are rarely located on the skyline. All but the largest dykes were not designed to overawe attackers; they would be placed in ideal locations for an ambush on hostile raiders by rising up unexpectedly on them.

Views from the dykes were probably even better when they were in use.

Apart from the evidence of a solitary tree removed during the building of Wat's Dyke, pollen evidence suggests that the builders constructed early medieval dykes across open ground.[38] East Wansdyke was built across chalk, yet excavations imply that the builders kept the turf taken during the digging of the ditch to one side and used it to cover the bank. This stabilized the bank, but also meant that it did not stand out as a white line across the green downland.[39] Though the banks of most dykes were simply made by piling the quarried material on the grass next to the ditch, there is evidence that the builders of Offa's Dyke stripped turves from behind the earthwork or stacked turves at the front to stabilize the bank.[40] The main reason for covering the bank with turves was probably structural and it was used by the Romans on their frontier works in northern Britain, but it would also help to camouflage the earthwork. Most dykes were not designed to be seen, but to see from.

Most dykes face downhill, that is, the ditch is downhill of the bank, though there are a few exceptions such as dykes that are on flat or gently undulating ground (such as those in Norfolk). Bapty has noted that sections of Offa's Dyke in Radnorshire and south Shropshire have ditches on the east (that is it 'faces' Mercia not Wales); Stanford suggested this is because it faces such a steep slope as to make a western ditch both unnecessary and hard to dig without the bank falling into it.[41] Fieldwork, however, demonstrates that there is a large section 2.5 miles (4km) south of Knighton on Hawthorn Hill (SO285680) where the dyke is on a relatively shallow slope, yet the ditch seems to be on the eastern side. There are a number of possible explanations, perhaps as simple as some of the gangs building Offa's Dyke not following the plan. Feryok plausibly suggests that the eastern ditch was where the builders had stripped turves from the rear of the dyke and the western ditch has long silted up; I have found no example of an excavation that proved the existence of an eastern ditch.[42]

Most of the dykes seem to cut routeways like the ancient ridgeways that bisect Britain as we would expect from defences against hostile raiders. The Cambridgeshire Dykes bisect a route flanked by marshes, many of the Welsh dykes bisect ridges, some dykes (Fossditch, Bran Ditch and Rowe Ditch, for example) cut Roman roads and some (the Grey Ditch and Rowe Ditch) cut valleys. The termini of many of the dykes are next to wide rivers or streams in steep-sided valleys. Often the dykes are in parallel rows, all facing in the same direction (Offa's/Wat's, the Cambridgeshire Dykes, Bury's Bank/Crookham Common earthworks or Giant's Grave/Crugyn Bank/Upper Short Ditch). The longer dykes that snake across the landscape usually run parallel to an escarpment rather than perpendicular to it (as with prehistoric cross-dykes, for example). Some of these longer dykes have gaps where large rivers link the sections, suggesting the rivers could perform the same functions that the dykes served in deterring attackers. Only about a quarter of the total length of all the early medieval dykes is contiguous as parish boundaries or other administrative boundaries, probably because as stop lines against raids they are set back from borders.

In terms of general distribution, it is noticeable that probable early medieval dykes are not distributed randomly or evenly across Britain, but mainly concentrated on the fringes of Mercia (with the exception of Bokerley Dyke). Perhaps the dykes facing Mercia were reactions to the creation of a strong expansionist central Anglo-Saxon kingdom that carried out predatory attacks or raids against its neighbours, while those facing outwards are evidence of Mercia's power. There is a noticeable lack of dykes within Mercia, so perhaps the subkingdoms of Mercia acted as buffers and the central core of the kingdom did not need defending or defining.

There are other significant groupings among early medieval dykes. Nearly half of the rebuilt prehistoric dykes are in East Anglia and, rather

A simplified map of early medieval dykes plotted on a map of Anglo-Saxon kingdoms (background picture is public domain).

than being in parallel lines facing in the same direction like many early medieval dykes, these often face each other. They seem to subdivide the kingdom of East Anglia and perhaps mark stages in the creation of that polity when it was divided into two mutually antagonistic groups or kingdoms. Unfortunately, there are few written sources from Anglo-Saxon East Anglia to help us to understand these earthworks and historians tend to rely on archaeological evidence to fill the gap between the fall of the Roman Empire and Bede's day, when East Anglia was already a single entity. There is also a series of undated dykes across southern Wales that face north, blocking ridgeways that give access to the lowlands, and a group of dykes in Cornwall that seem to defend peninsulas.

As well as central Mercia, there are other areas where there are no early medieval dykes – Devon, Sussex, Essex, most of western Wales, Cumbria and northern Scotland, for example. This suggests that dyke building was not a universal phenomenon in early medieval Britain and perhaps the inhabitants of some areas had no need to build them. Some of these areas are infertile and the population density was likely to have been low, so perhaps people only built defensive dykes where there was population pressure; however, there are dykes in central Wales, which was probably sparsely populated. Sussex is hardly infertile, especially the coastal plain, but the large number of prehistoric hill forts reoccupied in the early medieval period in the county (like Highdown, Cissbury Rings and Mount Caburn) possibly fulfilled the defensive role taken by dykes elsewhere. If dykes were built to help stabilize and defend newly created kingdoms, perhaps they were not necessary in places like Sussex, Gwynedd, Devon and northern Scotland, where kingdoms with obvious natural frontiers formed very early after the end of Roman rule.

One stimulus for building dykes in the early medieval period was the existence of similar earlier (usually prehistoric) structures in the locality, which acted as an inspiration. Devon has neither prehistoric dykes nor early medieval dykes, while many of the early medieval dykes in Norfolk and Suffolk are rebuilt prehistoric examples. There are numerous prehistoric earthworks in Dorset, including one rebuilt in the early medieval period (Combs Ditch), which may have provided a template for the builders of Bokerley Dyke. In Cornwall, there was a long history of digging earthworks to defend peninsulas, from Iron-Age cliff castles to the ditch defending the early medieval settlement at Tintagel; these examples possibly stimulated the builders of the dykes that defended Cornish peninsulas, such as the Giant's Hedge. There are many prehistoric dykes in Yorkshire and many examples of probable/possible early medieval dykes in the county.

CHAPTER 4

Written Evidence

So far, we have seen how warfare has been underplayed, examined the previous approaches that scholars have taken in the study of early medieval dykes, examined archaeological evidence for warfare and looked at how defensive dykes were built. It is necessary to turn to other evidence before further analysis of early medieval warfare is made. This means turning to written sources, so we must leave archaeology for history, starting with administrative documents, then charters and finally chronicles.

ADMINISTRATIVE DOCUMENTS

I will examine charters later as they are such useful mines of information that they deserve a section of their own, but first I will discuss what other administrative documents can tell us about early medieval society. With the written evidence, we should exercise some caution, as much of it was written long after the events being described, or only later copies survive, which may have been amended by later scribes. Most medieval sources were written by clerics, often in monasteries, and as this book is about warfare, monks are perhaps not the best eyewitnesses.

The *Tribal Hidage* is a document thought to date from the seventh or eighth centuries. The earliest surviving copy is a tenth-century text in Old English, but the later texts are in Latin.[1] It lists communities (kingdoms, tribes and regions) according to the number of hides each was assessed at (broadly speaking, a hide was an area of land large enough to support a family of free and law-worthy status). The lists seem concerned mainly with the Midlands and the South; it does not list Northumbria, so it is either a Mercian administrative document or one drawn up by a Northumbrian overlord listing the areas that owed him tribute.

The largest group is the West Saxons calculated at 100,000 Hides (a figure that seems suspiciously rounded), but there are many smaller units like the *Spalda* of Lincolnshire at 600 Hides and the *East Wixna* at just 300 Hides. As we have seen above, many early medieval dykes seem to fringe Mercia and the *Tribal Hidage* suggests that Mercia is surrounded by smaller communities, which later disappeared from history after becoming absorbed into the central kingdom.

The *Tribal Hidage* can be used when calculating the number of people in each kingdom and the number of possible labourers each king can call upon. The obligation clauses in Anglo-Saxon charters suggest the practice was that one man per hide was obliged to help build fortifications and bridgework, but only one man per five hides was obliged to turn out for army duty.[2] Using this formula and cross-referencing with the *Tribal Hidage*, the kings of, for example, the East Angles could summon 30,000 labourers and 6,000 troops, but as we have seen in the previous section, just 3–6,000 men could have built the Cambridgeshire Dykes. The West Saxons could easily have built Wansdyke with 100,000 families to draw labour from; with 30,000 hides the Mercians could undoubtedly have built Wat's and Offa's dyke. As most dykes needed 100 or fewer labourers, it follows that the smaller communities could manage the logistics of building the lesser dykes.

The *Burghal Hidage* is another Anglo-Saxon administrative document that can possibly help in understanding the logistics of building an early medieval dyke. It survives in seven different texts, the earliest of which dates to the eleventh century, but they all seem to be copies of a West Saxon document from about AD910–20, which lists the number of hides attached to various *burhs*.[3] A *burh* was a fortified settlement or fort; though some have earlier origins, the main impetus for their construction was ninth-century Viking attacks. As previously discussed, this document gives a calculation of how many men were needed for a given length of a fortification, which equates to one every 1.25m. It does takes more people to dig an earthwork than man it, so the document is of little use in calculating the amount of labour needed for construction and if they were never permanently garrisoned, it does not help in indicating how many people manned them. There is good evidence that the majority of Mercian *burhs* date to after the construction of the dykes. As the earthworks were military, the *burhs* probably took over their role, making further dyke-building redundant.

Surviving early medieval law codes can perhaps give us some insights into early medieval warfare. The earliest Anglo-Saxon law code (that of Ethelbert of Kent c.602–3) dates from the middle of the period covered by this study.[4] Such law codes are very different to modern law and we cannot be sure how they were used; they may even have been a written ideal and not actually put into practice. Though the early written law codes are in English, they are inextricably linked with the Latin-based literacy associated with Christianity. Despite being evidence for the rise of kingship, literacy and Christianity, the early law codes stress the control of violence and regulate compensation rather than punish guilt. They suggest that Anglo-Saxon society was one of retribution, in which kings tried to control feuds, vendettas, the theft of mobile property (like cattle and slaves) and raiding.

Law codes may give us a biased view of attitudes to war and violence in this period. While they suggest societies in which feuds, vendettas and vengeance were common, these are far more complex phenomena than a modern reader sitting in a peaceful study perhaps realizes. A raid may provoke a counter-raid that satisfies both parties that the two wrongs cancel each other out, but equally it could lead to a long-running vendetta. Such feuds may have been ended by arbitration between groups acting as equals, or a solution (possibly involving the exile of perceived transgressors or material compensation) imposed by a higher authority (a bishop or king, for example). Some vengeful raids may have been designed not to end a feud by simply righting a wrong in a simplistic 'eye for an eye' manner, but may have been undertaken to highlight a grievance that the group looked to a higher authority such as a king to rectify. While a king might see raids between kingdoms as legitimate violence and an ecclesiastical figure might sanction attacks on unbelievers (especially if it was justified as retaliation for a pagan attack on Christians), we can only guess what smaller communities that left no written records thought of the rights and wrongs of raiding in much of this period. We have some written law codes, but unwritten rules and conventions leave little, if any, evidence.

The late seventh-century laws of the West Saxon Ine define a group of up to seven people crossing into the kingdom with hostile intent as thieves, up to thirty-five as a band and thirty-six or more as an army.[5] The figure for an army seems rather low and, though this may be a deliberate ploy to bring a higher penalty down on small groups of outlaws, it does suggest relatively small groups attacked other kingdoms. As we have seen, fewer than 100 men could have built most of the early medieval dykes, so many raiding armies were probably equally small. Law codes suggest that deep mistrust existed towards strangers (whether traders or travellers), especially those not travelling on roads, assuming that if they did not announce their presence, they were thieves. Vikings often switched seamlessly from raiding to trading and the Byzantine Empire used traders as spies.[6] As these law codes imply that small-scale raids by small groups of armed men were common, it was probably very dangerous for traders to move unannounced into neighbouring kingdoms.

There are numerous references to slaves in Anglo-Saxon law codes.[7] In West Saxon law codes and similar documents, the word for a Briton and the word for a slave become synonymous, perhaps because the West Saxons absorbed large British areas. Slaves could be a by-product of raiding other communities and possibly were a source of labour to build dykes.

Unfortunately, for the study of early medieval warfare, law codes from the rest of Britain only survive from a much later date. The earliest surviving (and the most influential) Welsh law code is that traditionally associated with Hywel Dda (who died around 950). Though it probably draws on older Welsh laws, the earliest surviving copies are thirteenth century in date and are likely to include many later revisions.[8] Like their Anglo-Saxon equivalents, the Welsh law codes mention slaves (probably obtained through raids) and give a great deal of attention to compensation, with heavier penalties for theft than murder. The law codes mention gangs of thieves or marauders, the king's bodyguard raiding other kingdoms and there is a large section on aliens; this also suggests a society where warfare and small-scale cattle raids were common and strangers were distrusted.[9] The Welsh codes mention Offa's Dyke, suggesting that the earthwork, or rather which side of it a person lived, defined whether or not they were Welsh, but this definition could have entered the law codes over three centuries after Offa died.

One of the earliest laws issued in Scotland is the late seventh-century 'Law of the Innocents' issued by Adomnáin of Iona; it specifically sought to protect women and children from the ravages of war.[10] This attempt to curb the worst excesses of early medieval warfare might explain why Christianity became popular in this period – if the churches and monasteries often provided a safe haven, this would alleviate the effects of warfare. Other surviving law codes from Scotland and Strathclyde date from the eleventh century; they have similarities to early Welsh and Anglo-Saxon law codes. A code written in the early eleventh century shortly after the Scottish capture of Strathclyde called *Leges inter Brettos et Scottos* makes reference to fines (what the Anglo-Saxons would term a *wergild*) paid in compensation for murder or injury.[11] *Wergilds* were possibly an attempt to curb violence and particularly vendettas, by turning compensation into a monetary fine; it is likely that the Church (which introduced written law codes) actively promoted monetary fines over violent revenge. To kings who had embraced Christianity, this regulation of unrest which converted bloodshed into financial compensation was warmly welcomed. Like English and Welsh law codes, these suggest that early medieval Scotland was prone to endemic violence; not large armies fighting set-piece battles, but small-scale disorders (feuds, harrying and raiding), in which non-combatants were often harmed.

William the Conqueror's 1086 survey of the landholding of England commonly known as the *Domesday Book* was compiled roughly 300–600 years after the period under discussion in this book, but intriguingly two local Hundreds mentioned in it are named after dykes: Concresdic, named after Combs Ditch, and Flamingdice in Cambridgeshire, named after Fleam Dyke. These two examples may possibly suggest that certain dykes had administrative areas attached to them; perhaps the inhabitants of these Hundreds had responsibilities to build, maintain and man the dykes.

The *Domesday Book* survey provides the earliest national population picture, so may give insights into the distribution of the defensive dykes. Although the survey of the north-west seems incomplete, the data for Lancashire suggest that it was very sparsely settled, which may explain the lack of dykes there. The population of Essex and Sussex, areas also lacking dykes, was higher, but heavily wooded areas on the borders of these shires may have acted as a buffer, making dykes either unnecessary or impossible to construct among the tree roots.

Charters
Early medieval charters mainly record grants of land. Historians find such charters to be useful sources when looking at aspects of early medieval society, such as the landscape or patronage, but can they also help us to understand early medieval warfare? While conflict is rarely mentioned, they do record dykes more often than any other source. If some dykes were defensive, as I maintain, charters can help us to differentiate between dykes that were stop lines set behind borders, or those that were administrative boundaries. The historian Peter Sawyer catalogued them, so when an Anglo-Saxon charter is mentioned the Sawyer number is cited, for example S 176 refers to the charter with Sawyer number 176.[12]

While charters can act as dating evidence for individual earthworks (if a dyke is recorded in a document the earthwork must have existed when the scribe was writing), they can also potentially provide wider evidence about early medieval society. It would, however, be unwise to presume that the authors of later medieval charters, like one dated 1185–91 which mentions Hodic (or How Dyke) in Swaledale, were privy to lost early medieval sources.[13] I primarily focus on Anglo-Saxon charters, as they are more numerous than charters from other kingdoms.

The charters used to date individual dykes are documents that specifically mentioned the earthwork when describing the bounds of an estate. These documents invariably give the earliest recorded name of the dyke and tell us if it either formed an estate boundary or was merely a landmark. The survival of such documents is patchy – no early charters record dykes from Scotland or northern England. Though a tiny number of charters purportedly date from as far back as the early seventh century, most survive only as later (often modified) copies; some were forged or modified and even the authentic charters were not written verbatim as the king actually granted the land, but probably compiled later in a monastery. It is difficult to differentiate among later accurate copies and deliberate forgeries, especially as there is no sharp dividing line between the two, as later copyists often 'improved' the document they transcribed. Some embellishments were designed to give the document more authority, like additions to the list of witnesses or changes in the donor; scribes usually copied the estate boundaries from older documents with care. For the sake of simplicity, I usually presume that the date given on the charter was the date that the original scribe wrote the document (it would be impossible to discuss concisely the known or conjectural textual history of each individual document without making this book unnecessarily long). In the following section, some mention is given where the authenticity of a particular document is in doubt. The earliest charter record of each dyke is summarized in the table 'References to Dykes in Charters'.

References to Dykes in Charters

Name of Dyke	Charter Sawyer Number	Purported Date of Issue	Given Name of Dyke	% of Dyke Contiguous with Estate Boundary or Relationship Between the Dyke and the Estate Boundary
Probable/possible early-medieval dykes:				
Fullinga Dyke	S 69	672–4	Fullingadich	100%
Bedwyn	S 264	778	Vallum	43% (1,200m)
Faesten Kent	S 176	814	Fæstendic	39% (900m)
Wandsyke (East)	S 272	825	Ealdandic	Bisects dyke
Inkpen	S 336	863	Readan dic	Bisects dyke
Wandsyke (East)	S 1513	900	Ealdandic	Bisects dyke
Devil's Ditch Andover (Wonston)	S 360	900	Greatean dic	Bisects dyke
Wansdyke (East)	S 368	903	Wodnes dic	Bisects dyke
Combs Ditch	S 485	942–3	Cunucces dich	Contiguous with dyke for a distance?
Combs Ditch	S 490	942–3	Cunnucesdic	Contiguous with dyke for a distance?
Bokerley Dyke	S 513	944–6	Lang dich	81% (4,220m)
Bica's Dyke	S 564	955	Bican dic	100%
Beachley Bank	S 610	956	Dic	Uncertain
Aelfrith's Ditch & Short Dyke	S 828	956	Ælfredes beorh & dic	100%
Aelfrith's Ditch, Short Dyke & Old Dyke	S 603	956	Ælfðryþe dic, scortan dic and dic	100%
Rowe	S 677	958	Dic	11%
Wansdyke (West)	S 694	961	Wodnes dic	Bisects dyke
Aelfrith's Ditch & Short Dyke	S 829	965	Ælfredes beorh & dic	100%
Aelfrith's Ditch, Short Dyke & Old Dyke	S 758	968	Ælfþryðe dic, sceorton dic & ealdan dic	100%
Festaen Hampshire	S 1558/ S 1559	973–4	Festaen dic	13% (300m)
Fleam	S 794	974	Dic	58% (3,000m)
Bichamditch	S 1108	1053	Bichamdic	100%
Vervil	N/A	?	Crug	100%
Probable prehistoric dykes:				
Great Ridge Grim's Dyke	S 336	860	Ealden dic	
Berkshire Grim's Ditch	S 354	878–99	Grim gelege	
Cranborne Chase Grim's Ditch	S 513	944–6	Strete dich	
Great Ridge Grim's Dyke	S 612	956	Grimes dic	

Some Anglo-Saxon charters do suggest that certain early medieval dykes were not military but functioned as estate boundaries, even if this was not their original purpose. A charter dated 1053 (S 1108), for example, cites Bichamditch in Norfolk ('*Bichamdic*') as one boundary of an estate.

Four charters (S 603, dated 956; S 758 dated 968; S 828 dated 956; and S 829 dated 965) record Aelfrith's Ditch ('*ælfredes beorh*'), and two other dykes, Short Dyke ('*scortandic*') and Old Dyke ('*ealdan dic*'), as the edge of estates at Kingston Bagpuize and Fyfield. A charter of 955 (S 564) mentions Bica's Dyke ('*Bican dic*') and although, like Aelfrith's Ditch, the whole earthwork is contiguous with the estate boundary, it only demarks a small proportion of one side of the estate where it bisected the ridgeway. Fullinga Dyke in Surrey is recorded in a charter dated to 672–4 (S 69, one of the earliest authentic Anglo-Saxon charters) in the bounds of an estate granted by a subking called King Frithuwold as an ancient ditch 'which is Fullinga Dyke': '*antiqua fossa id est Fullingadich*'.[14] The description of the dyke as an ancient ditch suggests that the middle Saxons reutilized an older earthwork. As already mentioned, the depth of the ditches and the heights of the banks of Aelfrith's Ditch, Bica's Dyke and Fullinga Dyke are approximately one-third of the size of other early medieval earthworks; this slightness in scale coupled with the charter evidence confirms that these earthworks were mere estate marker boundaries, not defensive dykes.

In the tenth century, large Anglo-Saxon estates (sometimes known as multiple estates) were broken up in a process called estate fragmentation and the new estates were often noted in charters that recorded the bounds in more detail than previously. Small boundary dykes like Aelfrith's Ditch that mark the edges of estates are part of this process to define estates with greater accuracy than before. The new smaller estates often form the basis for subsequent parishes, making them easy to locate today.

While some of the oldest charters record the larger estates, far more Saxon charters are products of this reorganization process. As can be seen from the table 'References to Dykes in Charters', in most charters only parts of most earthworks are contiguous with the estate boundary. In the case of many Wessex dykes, the estate boundaries cited in charters bisect the earthwork without deviating, for example East Wansdyke slices straight through the middle of the estate defined by the charter dated 957 (S 647) at Stanton St Bernard, suggesting that the dyke was then being treated as a mere landmark. As many early medieval dykes like Offa's often ignore parish boundaries, they probably predate the process of estate fragmentation. Perhaps dykes like East Wansdyke originally ran through rough pasture on the edge of a kingdom, which, centuries later when border raiding had subsided, was parcelled up by the West Saxons, creating new estates that largely ignored the now redundant dyke.

The names of dykes may help us to understand who built them and why, although they are a potential minefield for misinterpretation. Combs Ditch in Dorset appears in two authentic-looking Anglo-Saxon charters as *Cunucces dich* and *Cunnucesdic* (S 485 and S 490), both dated around 942–3. This name possibly derives from a personal Celtic name, 'Cunuc' or 'Conec', but it could also be a form of *cynig*, the Anglo-Saxon word for king, so making the name King's Dyke. Two charters dated 973–4 (S 1558 and S 1559) record the Festaen Dyke in Hampshire as *festaen dic*, while the similarly named Faesten Dyke in Kent is first recorded as *fæstendic* in the boundary clauses of a charter (S 175) dated 814. *Festaen* is Old English for stronghold, bulwark or fortification, suggesting a military purpose rather than a boundary marker, although it has been suggested that the name means overgrown.[15]

The earliest surviving written reference to East Wansdyke is a charter (S 272) dated 825 that strangely merely calls it '*ealdandic*' or 'old dyke', the next charter, though, dated 903, does gives the name of Woden (or rather '*Wodnes dic*') to East Wansdyke (S 368). Reynolds suggests that a charter (S 647, dated 957) records a wrongdoers' gallows ('*wearh roda*') on the East Wansdyke, suggesting that the dyke was a place of execution, although this interpretation is far from certain.[16] West Wansdyke is recorded in a series of tenth-century charters, the earliest of which dates to 961, as '*Wodnes dic*' (S 694, S 711, S 735 and S 777).

The earthwork at the mouth of the Wye, Beachley Bank, is mentioned as a landmark in a charter dated to 956 (S 610). Fox makes much of this charter, claiming that because part of the Beachley peninsula was let to Welsh boatmen (*scipwealan*), this confirms his theory of an agreed frontier with concessions to the Welsh.[17] I wonder if life was so amicable along the Welsh border; this charter post-dates Offa by 160 years and it is possible that so too does the agreement. This earthwork is merely recorded as '*dic*' and was probably not even part of Offa's scheme.

We have good evidence from charters that they cut the routes taken by marauding armies. A Saxon charter giving the bounds of Brimpton (S 500) dated 944 records a *herepath* (or army path) along the ridge that Bury's Bank and the Crookham Common earthworks cut. Note that the estate boundary follows the road and bisects the earthworks without mentioning them. One of the charters that records Combs Ditch (S 485) mentions a nearby *herepath*. The Anglo-Saxon charters granting land around the East Hampshire dykes do not mention the nearby earthworks, though again they record *herepaths*.[18] Charters also record *herpaþes* (*herepaths*) in the vicinity of Wansdyke, S 449 records one about 3.1 miles (5km) north of East Wansdyke near Avebury and others like S 711 and S 735 record such roads near West Wansdyke. While this tenth-century evidence post-dates the construction of the dykes by a few centuries, routeways (especially along obvious ridges) have a great longevity in the landscape, confirming that many dykes cut tracks in areas traditionally used by marching armies.

There are a few relevant charters in Wales. Clawdd Seri is recorded in the Aberconwy Charter of 1200 as a township boundary, but this is relatively late and as Gresham points out, the fact that the dyke already has a name suggests it is a pre-existing feature.[19] A charter in the twelfth-century *Book of Llandaff* (which possibly draws on older sources) records Vervil Dyke as '*cruc*' or '*crug*', which is the Welsh for 'mound'.[20] Interestingly, approximately a quarter of all Llandaff charter boundary clauses mention banks and/or ditches, suggesting that the Welsh were using existing earthworks as landmarks when defining an estate rather than digging new ones to delimit specific areas. Some of the Llandaff charters suggest south Wales was an area that suffered from widespread fighting and slavery was common. One charter dated 740 mentions a possible captured Saxon woman, while another dated c.745 implies an area near Hereford was devastated in border warfare.

As well as providing evidence of the use of dykes, these documents can give us an insight into how labour was organized. As mentioned before, Mercian charters from the eighth century onwards often cite military obligations (or exemptions from them) required from the people on the estate recorded.[21] The obligations include bridge work (either building or maintaining them), fortification work (often called *burh* work) and military duty. There is a debate as to when these obligations became established, as some of the best evidence for them (like the early eleventh-century estate management document called *Rectitudines singularum personarum* or 'The Rights and Ranks of People') is much later in date.[22] Squatriti has suggested that perhaps there were earlier obligations to build dykes that formed the basis for the later practice of *burh* work.[23] Unfortunately, neither the charter obligations, nor *Rectitudines singularum personarum*, mentions dyke repair or building. *Rectitudines singularum personarum* does mention slaves and the lack of references to dyke building in the obligations associated with estates could be due to them undertaking the work. Unfortunately, this rather murky evidence connecting slave labour or *burh* work obligations with dykes is all we have.

Although most early medieval dykes were designed to prevent raids, we must briefly entertain the possibility that dykes also controlled trade. Though Anglo-Saxon charters (S 86 for example) mention tolls, other documents, such as Charlemagne's correspondence with Offa, usually refer to tolls in the context of maritime not overland trade and significantly no charter records any dyke as a place where tolls were collected.[24] Incidentally, Offa's correspondence with Charlemagne is an example of Offa promoting his power on a European stage; possibly his dyke was another example of his self-promotion. The lack of toll booths suggests that dykes were never trade barriers.

When discussing the names given to dykes in early medieval charters it is worth reiterating that many of the earliest charter references date to approximately 2–300 years later than the average radiocarbon dates for early medieval dykes. Indeed, the words *ealdandic* and *antiqua fossa* suggest that scribes thought that the dykes were already old. Some of them were given monikers like *greatean dic*, *festaen dic* and *fæstendic*, suggesting that people realized dykes were no mere hedgerows, although others are not named, merely called a *dic* or *vallum*.

Though the earliest charter referring to Wansdyke is rather suspect, it is noticeable that in it the earthwork is not named after Woden. In fact, many dykes have no names in the earliest charters, especially those that came to be named after Grim, the Devil and Woden. Probably the naming of dykes (in particular after supernatural figures) occurred long after the building of the earthworks when their practical function as defensive structures had ended.

Charters and other similar written sources suggest that dykes had a short-term primary function and many were soon relegated to anonymous landmarks in the countryside. As we have seen, charters can be highly useful in providing a *terminus ante quem* for dykes, but with so many documents only surviving as later copies even this evidence must be approached with caution. As charters only record dykes when describing the extent of an estate and possibly post-date most earthworks by centuries, they are of limited use in understanding why they were built. The charter evidence demonstrates that early medieval people wished to subdivide and demark land, especially in the ninth century onwards when numerous charters survive, but the dykes by this time were often unnamed earlier features reused merely as reference points. The numerous references to *herepaths/herpaþes* (or army paths) seem to suggest that many of the dykes cut routeways to keep out other (hostile) groups. There is no evidence to link dykes to the control of trade and though later obligations (like *bur*h work) may have evolved out of a duty to help build dykes, this cannot be proved.

ANNALS, CHRONICLES AND HISTORIES

Other early medieval sources, like the ninth-century *Historia Brittonum*, the c.1010–16 'The Sermon of the Wolf to the English' by Wulfstan and early medieval biographies of saints all suggest that early medieval society was dominated by kings, warfare, raiding and slavery.[25] I shall examine some of these documents in turn to see what they can tell us about early medieval warfare.

Bede's *The Ecclesiastical History of the English Church and People* is probably one of the finest works of early medieval history, though with Bede we must be cautious that his brilliance as a scholar should not blind us to any biases he has or omissions he makes.[26] Being based on north-east England we can perhaps excuse how the coverage of events in Wessex, Mercia and East Anglia is patchy at best. His book, written in 731, is meant to give an account of the history of England from the time the Romans first landed, but earlier sections are hampered by Bede's sources, or lack of them, so it is probably best just to focus on those parts related to the seventh and early eighth centuries. It is mainly an account of the conversion of the Anglo-Saxons, but there are records of warfare. In around 633, an Anglo-Saxon king, Osric of Deira, besieged a British king in a stronghold; suddenly the British sallied forth, destroyed the English army and then ravaged the whole of Northumbria. In 651, we hear how King Oswin disbanded his army when he realized he was outnumbered rather than have it destroyed and hid, only to be betrayed and murdered by his rival Owsy. These examples suggest that decisive set-piece battles were probably best avoided and even a ravaged kingdom could be rebuilt. Incidentally, Bede mentions Oswy building a monastery at the site of the murder of Oswin to atone for his sins at a place called *Ingetlingum*, which is sometimes identified with Gilling, the village adjacent to Gilling Dyke, though others identify it with Collingham. Even if it is Gilling, Bede's account makes no mention of an earthwork.

The Anglo-Saxon Chronicle is a series of related texts (A, A2, B, C, D, E and F) that probably have their origins in late ninth-century Wessex and though some entries were contemporaneous with events, earlier ones often drew on older sources.[27] The two texts that mainly concern us are A (the entries of which are up to 891 in a single hand, so that section was probably compiled in the late ninth century) and E, a twelfth-century copy from Peterborough.

In general, *The Anglo-Saxon Chronicle* makes much of kings, as well as the kingdoms they forge, and while we would expect a source probably founded by the West Saxon kings to promote the kings of Wessex, other Anglo-Saxon kingdoms also feature. The earliest sections were almost certainly not written contemporaneously with events and are probably based on oral traditions, so are of questionable use. For example, it records in 571 the West Saxons winning a battle at Biedcanford and capturing various settlements in the Chilterns, then in 577 defeating the Britons at Dyrham capturing Gloucester, Bath and Cirencester. Both entries are rather suspicious: in a ninth-century document written at a time when the kings of Wessex were encroaching into the territory of their fellow Anglo-Saxons in Mercia, this document claims that the West Saxons were the first to take these areas from the Britons. Even if these two battles did happen and are not ninth-century propaganda, before a monastic tradition of chronicling events it is unlikely they have been recorded with any accuracy.

I prefer to focus on the entries between 787 (that is, the first mention of the Vikings) and 600 in the A text, which is roughly when the Anglo-Saxons began to be converted to Christianity; unlike the sixth- and fifth-century entries, those are more likely to have been recorded by literate Christian priests at the time of the events. As well as numerous references to the growth of Christianity, this section contains over a dozen references to 'battles', but from the mid-sixth century onwards references to conflicts become more varied – perhaps chroniclers with more detailed source material could add some subtlety. Raids are recorded (661, 676, 686 and 687); kings making war or fighting against other kingdoms rather than a simple battle (722, 741, 743 and 753); a fortification torn down (722); and a king driven out (755). In fact, over a dozen entries mention kings being killed without a battle being recorded. While some of these instances of regicide may be due to war, we can imagine ambushes and assassination caused some of the others. For some of these entries it is difficult to locate the site as place names have changed and even when we can identify the location (for example, the fortifications of Taunton being torn down in 722), there is simply not enough detail to analyse tactics without straying into supposition.

The entry for 755 in *The Anglo-Saxon Chronicle* is different, as here the narrative gives us some more particulars.[28] A king of Wessex, Sigeberht, is driven out by Cynewulf, who is then declared king. Sigeberht is eventually killed by a herdsman, but his brother, Cyneheard, surrounds Cynewulf in a stronghold in Merton and the latter is killed. Unfortunately for Cyneheard, the followers of Cynewulf are outraged by the suggestion that they should follow their dead leader's murderer and through a great display of loyalty kill Cyneheard. The lengthy detail of this entry suggests that killing a leader in this manner was shocking enough to warrant detailed recording, but perhaps killing a king of another kingdom in an ambush may not have broken the early medieval bonds of loyalty. Exactly where in Merton the events took place, though, is anyone's guess

The Anglo-Saxon Chronicle makes only one direct specific reference to dykes (the Cambridgeshire Dykes) and the almost total absence of references to dykes in a document that records the great deeds of kings suggests that most were not built to promote kings or unify kingdoms. The 904 entry in the A text records King Edmund harrying between the River Wissey and the Cambridgeshire Dykes (*dicum*) in retaliation for a raid by Vikings based in East Anglia. The entry seems to use the dykes as a geographic reference point that needed no explaining to the reader, rather than fortifications used in the fighting; as we have seen, the radiocarbon dates for Fleam Dyke suggest the events of 904 almost certainly post-date the dykes by some centuries.

The burials at Heronbridge can be linked with a fair degree of confidence to events recorded not only in *The Anglo-Saxon Chronicle*, but also in Bede and the Welsh Annals, the *Annales Cambriae*.[29] They are probably casualties of the Battle of Chester, which is recorded in *The Anglo-Saxon Chronicle* (605 in the E text, 606 in the A text) and in the Welsh Annals in 613. Here, an earthwork can with confidence be linked through early medieval sources and archaeology to a decisive battle. According to Bede, Aethelfrith of Northumbria massacred 1,200 British monks who had come to pray for a British victory at the battle, though *The Anglo-*

Saxon Chronicle puts the number at just 200. The earthwork is only 1.2 miles (2km) south of Chester, so a distant chronicler would probably record any major event at Heronbridge under the name of the better-known Roman city. Unfortunately, we can still not pinpoint the exact site of the battle and relate the topography to any tactics employed. The bodies could have been moved, so the main fighting could have been elsewhere, for example nearer to Chester, closer to Heronbridge or elsewhere in the immediate countryside. Presumably the Welsh assembled from the west (and survivors possibly fled in that direction after the rout), while the Northumbrians would have come from the east.

Scholars have often tried to link Wansdyke to events in *The Anglo-Saxon Chronicle* despite the lack of any references.[30] If it was a defence against the West Saxons, they do not claim to have overcome the earthwork; if West Saxons built it, they fail to mention the fact and if the West Saxons had nothing to do with it they could easily have claimed it as an act of propaganda. *The Anglo-Saxon Chronicle* mentions the Woden's Barrow near Wansdyke, previously mentioned in the charters as the site of two battles in 592 and 715; the name of the dyke and the barrow are considered in more detail later. This suggests that the barrow, which is just 0.8 miles (1.2km) south of East Wansdyke, was on an obvious invasion route into Wessex or near a contested border area. The lack of a reference to the actual dyke in the chronicles suggests it was a short-term defensive measure.

As well as the Anglo-Saxon sources, there is a series of Welsh annals/chronicles briefly mentioned above, the earliest of which is the Latin *Annales Cambriae* (the earliest surviving text dates to about 1100, but was probably composed around 955 and draws on older sources), while later versions, like *Brut y Tywysogyon* and *Brenhinedd y Saeson*, are in Welsh.[31] Most entries relate to political events (like the English sources these are often violent, such as raids, the devastation of enemy territory, battles and the deaths of kings) and religious ones (deaths of saints, for example). Let us concentrate on the first section up until the first mention of the Vikings (447–796). These entries include fourteen battles, ten using the Latin word *Bellum* and four with the Old Welsh *Gueith* (though why these two different terms are used is a matter of speculation). During the reign of Offa and his sons, three massacres (*Strages*) and three devastations (*Vastatio*) are recorded. There is also a besieging on an island, a hammering (*Percussion*), where a monastery is burnt and a king killed. The burning of a monastery may have been worth recording because it was a rarity; the date, 645, may indicate that the attackers were pagan Mercians. Like *The Anglo-Saxon Chronicle*, these entries describing violence take up about one-third of all the entries, but if we take account of the years where no events are recorded, conflict is mentioned in a relatively small fraction of the entries (roughly 7 per cent of the years in the relevant section of the Welsh Annals and less than 20 per cent of the years of the part of *The Anglo-Saxon Chronicle* mentioned above). This could mean that conflict was not endemic and there were significant periods of peace, or that violence was not always recorded as it was not unusual enough to be worthy of note, or that the scribe simply did not get news of the event.

Although two entries record Offa attacking the Britons (in 778 and 784), the earliest texts make no mention of dykes. Offa's Dyke is mentioned in a later annal (specifically the *Brenhinedd y Saeson* found in the fourteenth-century *Black Book of Basingwerk*, BM. Cotton Cleopatra MS. B v.), but this post-dates the earliest texts by some centuries and is probably a later interpolation.[32] The authenticity of the entry is further undermined by the fact that it describes the north end of Offa's Dyke being near Basingwerk (Ddinas Basing), when we know that Offa's Dyke did not reach that far north.

The *Historia Brittonum* (often ascribed to Nennius, although it is possible he did not write it) is a Welsh source that purports to be a history of Britain and dates to 828–9, so should provide us with good contemporary evidence of early medieval Britain.[33] It certainly describes lots of battles, including twelve that are ascribed to (King) Arthur, but how much is real and how much mythical is very open to debate, as it includes prophecies and miraculous wonders liable to spark scepticism in modern readers. The location of most of the battles is highly debatable, making it impossible for a modern historian to relate topography with battle tactics. Some of the conflicts mentioned in the text are confirmed with entries in other documents, for example the wars of Cadwallon of Gwynedd against Northumbria (recorded in chapters 61 and 64, as well as being referenced in the entries for 629, 630 and 631 in the *Annales Cambriae*). Like many early medieval sources, it is very binary in its description of people – they are of one nation (Picts, British, English and so forth) or another, with no sense that these identities were at all fluid. Whether this is an oversimplification or not, it does suggest that identity was both important and self-evident to early medieval people. Like most of these sources, the descriptions of battles are usually terse and lacking in much detail.

Asser was a Welsh monk who wrote a biography of King Alfred of Wessex, having been appointed Bishop of Sherborne by Alfred in 893.[34] While some scholars (in particular Smyth) have raised doubts about the authorship and veracity of Asser's work in the past, most scholars accept it as genuine. His book tells of Alfred's many battles with Viking raiders and invaders that involve events after the period under review in this book, but also records that Offa constructed a great dyke between Mercia and Wales from sea to sea (though only as a way of establishing who Offa was). This claim that the earthwork ran from sea to sea is probably false, though it could be an echo of an original boastful piece of Mercian propaganda designed to reinforce Offa's imperial pretensions. This suggests that Offa's Dyke was designed to demonstrate the power of the king, as well as being a utilitarian feature. Asser saw the dyke as an Anglo-Welsh divide, not a Mercian–Powys one as Hill proposed, but in Asser's day the Welsh kingdom of Powys no longer existed, having been broken up after the death of Cyngen in 854.

Gildas was a British writer who probably wrote in the early sixth century; his book, *The Ruin of Britain*, is more of a sermon than a straight historical account.[35] The book is divided into 100 chapters, with the final two-thirds consisting of discussions of Biblical prophesies concerning what will happen to the wicked and a long discussion of how standards must be raised in the British Church. The first twenty-six chapters are an introduction that contains an outline of recent historical events, including the struggles of the treacherous British against the Romans, the coming of the Saxons and the ruinous wars between them and the British. Chapters 27 to 36 are a vicious attack on five British kings, describing them as being sunk low in sin and guilty of acts of violence against their kin as well as their enemies. His is a violent world divided between a Church in desperate need of reform and greedy secular kings with a lust for war, sex and decadence. He is probably exaggerating the sins of his times, as his book is a call to religious reform and salvation, but if he had fabricated every part it would have not resonated with his audience enough for them to preserve his work. In Chapter 26 he describes recent events, saying that although wars with external enemies had ended (probably temporarily, though Gildas was not to have known this), there were fights among British kingdoms so that the land was depopulated and in ruins. He names the location of one battle, Badon, but historians have yet to identify the site satisfactorily. Gildas, like Bede and many other early medieval sources already mentioned, makes numerous references to warfare (plunder, raids and battles), the importance of Christianity and to the power of kings.

Although Gildas is the only British source from the early part of the floruit of dyke building and while he does not mention dykes, he intriguingly recounts the building of the frontier works by the Romans in Britain, which might give us some clues as to how early medieval Britons defended their territory. Gildas says that the Britons were advised by the Romans to build walls to scare away enemies and act as a protection. Gildas talks of earthworks being funded publicly and privately, the Romans leaving military manuals, a crowd or mob of labourers building them in the 'usual manner' and how they were meant to keep the enemy at a distance, suggesting that they were sited back from the frontier. They were possibly patrolled by the *speculatores* Gildas mentioned earlier in his text, assuming they are watchmen. The idea of private and public funding seems more Roman than early medieval, but the reference to military handbooks could be the Roman military manual *Epitoma Rei Militaris* by Vegetius, which we know was used later in the medieval period.[36] When Gildas wrote of large gangs of labourers, he probably meant Roman frontier works that required thousands to construct rather than most early medieval dykes, which probably only required about 100 men to build. The reference to the 'usual methods' of construction suggests that building earthworks was such a common occurrence that there was no need to describe the methodology.

POETRY

Surviving Anglo-Saxon and Welsh poetry can provide evidence of early medieval warfare, though most surviving copies of such poems date to after the period under study.

One Anglo-Saxon poem, '*Widsith*', may give us clues as to Offa's motivation in building a dyke and a possible explanation as to why the name of the adjacent dyke is Wat's.[37] The surviving poem is a fragment of an older work that lists various famous Germanic heroes, mainly kings and folk heroes. Lines 35 to 44 mention an earlier continental king of the Angles called Offa who 'marked with his sword' the boundary with the Myrgings (an otherwise unknown German tribe probably from north-east Netherlands) at Fifeldor: '*Ane sweorde merce gemærde wið Myrgingum bi Fifeldore*'. Perhaps the earlier continental Offa inspired the later Offa of Mercia to try to emulate his namesake by marking the western border of Mercia with a dyke, though fixing a boundary with a sword could mean using violence rather than digging an earthwork (there is no evidence of a dyke near Fifeldore).

Intriguingly, the legendary Germanic folklore character Wade, who gave his name to the adjacent Wat's Dyke, is associated with the continental king Offa in the poem '*Widsith*'. This may be coincidental or an echo of a lost longer legend linking these two characters, which inspired the Mercians to build and/or name dykes after them, but with such fragmentary evidence theories are easy to make, but difficult to substantiate.

The great Anglo-Saxon epic *Beowulf* gives an evocative picture of an early medieval warrior, though the only original copy to have survived was penned about AD1000.[38] It records the hero Beowulf fighting against three monsters (two in Denmark and one in southern Sweden) and although it is hard to date exactly, the eight century seems as good a guess as any. Like *Widsith*, it also mentions the continental Offa (lines 1,949 and 1,957), saying he was a king renowned for the defence of his homeland '*eðel sinne*' (line 1,960). There is a sequence when Beowulf lands in Denmark where he encounters a coast-watcher on a wall (line 229); perhaps similar figures patrolled the coasts, borders and dykes of Anglo-Saxon England. In the poem, kings and even princes are recorded as having an entourage of experienced warriors who are loyal to their leader, partly through oaths, but also because they are rewarded with gifts like swords and rings (for example, lines 1,023 and 1,195). Like many other written sources, the poem gives an impression that raiding was commonplace (Hygelac dies on a raid and Hrothgar gives out treasure after a career of raiding) and the fact that Beowulf's crew from a single boat was considered a war party helps to confirm the idea that raiding parties were not large. It mentions Danes on a mission in Frisia being killed in an ambush, suggesting that forays into enemy territory were susceptible to counterattack (lines 1,071 to 1,159).

The Anglo-Saxon poem 'The Fortunes of Men' describes the various trials and tribulations of a man's life.[39] It certainly describes a violent world, for example in line 15 it describes the many ways a man can die: 'one being spear slain, one hacked down in battle'. It spends ten lines of the poem describing how alcohol can lead to anger, fighting and death. The picture painted may be exaggerated for moral or poetic effect, but this was a world where violence was not uncommon.

One battle recorded in some detail that unfortunately does fall outside the period under study here is the Battle of Maldon in 991, but with so few written sources dating from before 800 that give any detail it is worth briefly considering.[40] It records how local Anglo-Saxon levies were raised by a regional leader to help repel a group of raiders from Scandinavia. Before the fighting started there were attempts at negotiations as well as threats and boasts. It tells how the Anglo-Saxons moved to and from the battlefield on horseback, but fought on foot. The arms and armour most commonly mentioned are spears and shields, though arrows, swords and chain mail are also mentioned. It talks of the loyalty of the warriors to their leader and how after he fell some fled, while others chose to die alongside the man to whom they had sworn oaths of loyalty. The battle finished in a rout, but unfortunately the end of the poem does not survive.

Warfare was the major theme of early medieval Welsh poetry, but unlike Anglo-Saxon poetry it does contain some references to dykes, so we can link the words to actual places. Overall, these poems give a picture of a society where kings gained glory through military deeds, usually raiding neighbouring areas for plunder. The works of the sixth-century poet Taliesin makes a reference to the British king Urien of Rheged fighting at a dyke: '*Ossid uch yng Hlawd, neud Urien a blawd*' ('If there be groaning in the dyke, it is Urien who is smiting').[41]

The Welsh border dykes are possibly mentioned (though not named) in a Welsh poem about a British king called Llywarch Hen.[42] It recounts a fight '*ar glawd gorlas*' on Gorlas dyke (possibly a slip for Morlas, a stream that crosses both Offa's Dyke and Wat's near Selattyn) and elsewhere cryptically refers to the dykes enduring, but those that built them being no more. Although the language used in the text does seem to suggest a ninth-century date for the composition, the surviving texts (the thirteenth-century *Black Book of Carmarthen* and the fourteenth-century *Red Book of Hergest*) are much later. Llywarch Hen was a northern British king who, according to early Welsh sources, was driven out by the

English and fled south to Powys (therefore lived near the Mercian dykes), but as he was a sixth-century figure he possibly predates the earthworks in the Welsh borders. At best, this source suggests that Welsh poetry associated the dykes with conflict against the English and exile, though we should note that there is no reference here to Offa. A ninth-century poem called '*Marwnad Cadwallawn*' ('The Elegy of Cadwallon') records a battle between Cadwallon and Edwin of Northumbria at Caer Digoll, which is the Long Mountain near Welshpool close to the line of Offa's Dyke.[43] Such a battle confirms that dykes were built in a contested frontier zone, even though the battle predates Offa by over a century.

The poem '*Y Gododdin*' was written by the early medieval British poet Aneirin about an unsuccessful British raid on Anglo-Saxons based at Catreath, which is possibly Catterick.[44] It tells of an expedition from what is now the Edinburgh area, in which warriors gathered from all over northern Britain to travel nearly 186 miles (300km) south, but when they arrived the Anglo-Saxons destroyed them. As well as having groups of warriors linked by bonds of loyalty raiding enemy territory and describing how the raiders could be overwhelmed by defenders, it also gives an actual description of how a dyke was used in war. It describes in lines 567–69 a warrior who 'trampled on spears in the day of battle in the alder-grown dyke' – '*Sengi waywawr, Yn nydd cadiawr, Yng nghlawdd gwernin*'.

Perhaps the dyke mentioned in the poem was Scot's Dike near Richmond. The earthwork might be 3.1 miles (5km) from Catterick, but it is not implausible that a battle fought at Scot's Dyke could have been given the name of a nearby town when it is 4.4 miles (7km) between Senlac Hill, the site of the 'Battle of Hastings', and the actual town of Hastings. Today there are numerous alder trees at the southern end of Scot's Dike and pollen analysis of the ditch silt samples taken during a 2007 excavation found alder was one of the dominant species.[45] Though the dyke is possibly a little far from Catterick, Catreath could have been located where the Normans later built Richmond, although directly linking archaeology with early medieval poetry is usually best avoided.

'*Y Gododdin*' seems to provide further evidence of the mutual antagonism between the Britons and the English, although some historians have cast doubt on the idea that it was a simple battle consisting of just Anglo-Saxons on one side and the British warriors on the other.[46] One of the British warriors of Gododdin has a father with the very Saxon name of Golistan (probably a mutation of the English name Wolston, line 951), possibly suggesting that the sides were slightly racially mixed. It is worth remembering that names do cross the ethnic divide in the early medieval period: Anglo-Saxon sources record Englishmen with British names like Cadwalla, Chad, Cedric and Cedd. There are clear references to the heroes as Britons (lines 204, 209, 637 and 923) and the enemy as Saeson or Saxons (126 and 532) coming from Lloegr or England (451 and 899), so without arbitrarily discounting large sections of the poem it is clear that Aneirin thought the battle was a British defeat at the hands of the Anglo-Saxons.

'*Y Gododdin*' gives us interesting evidence about early medieval warfare. It is a poem of warriors, death and glory (like those written by Taliesin or those about Llywarch Hen), suggesting that raiding and warfare were common and praiseworthy among the elite. Only 333 warriors embark on the raid, but perhaps we should not take this to be a typical number as it seems a rather artificially symbolic figure. The poem contains some references to axes, swords, shields and chain mail, but the description of the fighting suggests spears were the most common weapon in battle. The poem shows the English standing on a dyke using spears to counter an attack by British cavalry. A dyke is an advantageous structure for getting infantry to stand their ground and would slow or even break up a cavalry charge.

A great corpus of medieval Irish poetry survives and though most of the surviving manuscripts date from the twelfth to the fifteenth centuries, the language of the earliest stories is dateable to the eighth century, while the events referred to date to the seventh century.[47] Although little directly relates to Britain, it does give a flavour of what early medieval society was like, where wealth was reckoned in cattle, with warfare, unsurprisingly, taking the form of cattle raids.

SAINTS' LIVES

Many biographies of saints who lived in this period survive, though most were written long after they died and are of dubious worth as historical evidence, as some episodes are more likely to be there to impart a moral message than to inform us about actual events. Like the works of Gildas, many do not paint secular leaders of the time in a very favourable light: they are both rapacious warlords preying off the humble and robbers stealing cattle, as in the *Life of St Nynia*.[48] One of the earliest Anglo-Saxon examples is the *Life of St Wilfred*, written by Eddius Stephanus in around 720.[49] In Chapter 19, it records years of peace in Northumbria, but this was due to victories abroad. In Chapter 17 a king grants lands that had been gained by driving British clergy out at the points of hostile swords.

One saint who wrote his own story was Patrick, whose Confession gives us a rare insight into the early fifth century.[50] Not only does he record being captured by raiders and made into a slave, but a letter he wrote condemning a British king for making Christians slaves also survives. Patrick's writings show how dependent the early Christians were upon the goodwill of kings in Britain and Ireland to protect the Church and how slaves were occasionally released, although a ransom often had to be paid.

INSCRIPTIONS

Early medieval inscriptions are rarer than those from Roman Britain. At Aberlemno in Scotland there are some sixth- to ninth-century Pictish stones that have carved images of warriors.[51] They show people fighting with spears and shields, but oddly many of them are mounted. It has traditionally been assumed that early medieval people fought on foot rather than horseback (though they may have used horses to travel to battle). Perhaps these stones suggest otherwise, though they are rather simple stylized figures.

If dykes were built to bolster the power of kings rather than being practical stop lines to prevent raids, it is odd that no king bothered to raise a stone monument to their efforts by any of these earthworks. One piece of epigraphic evidence often quoted in association with early medieval earthworks is the Pillar of Eliseg. It was erected during the reign of Concenn of Powys (or Cynan who died in 854) and is dedicated to the memory of his great-grandfather, Eliseg, King of Powys, who presumably ruled at the same time as Offa.[52] It was built on an older mound in Welsh territory about 4.4 miles (7km) west of Offa's Dyke; although it is just north of the River Dee, it overlooks this valley, which is a perfect route for raiders or traders moving between northern Wales and the Midlands. The inscription mentions Eliseg taking land from the power of the English with his sword 'by fire': '*E potestate Anglo/Rum in gladio suo parta in igne*'. This is a frustrating source that merely tells us there was fighting on the border between Powys and the English to the east. Interestingly, an earthwork, Clawdd Llesg, 21 miles (34km) to the south, may once have been named Clawdd Eliseg (Elisedd).

The early medieval Britons (the forefathers of the Welsh and Cornish) set up inscribed stones to commemorate their dead mainly across Wales and Cornwall, but five (variously dated between the late sixth and the ninth centuries) were discovered by Victorians during the rebuilding of a large Saxon church (Lady St Mary) at Wareham in Dorset. These are deep inside what is traditionally seen as Anglo-Saxon territory. Perhaps these stones and the dykes built across Dorset facing towards the north-east like Bokerley Dyke were part of an ultimately doomed attempt to preserve a British identity in Dorset in the face of advancing Anglicization and an expansionist West Saxon kingdom.

LATER AND EARLIER SOURCES

Later Medieval and Early Modern Sources

Later references to early medieval warfare or dykes must be used with caution. We do not know if the scribes used their imaginations to explain mysterious features in the landscape, or if their descriptions of earlier warfare were based on their own times. A biography written at least 300 years after Offa died claims that he built his earthwork during a

Christmas truce in 775, but even if we suspected this information came from an older source it is unlikely to be accurate, as digging earthworks in winter when the ground is either frozen or too wet is highly unlikely.[53]

One oblique reference may help us to understand the motives behind dyke building. A thirteenth-century chronicler, Matthew Paris, describes the wooded part of Hampshire where the east Hampshire dykes are located as the most infamous for robberies and murders in England.[54] Perhaps these wooded hills were always subject to attacks and lawlessness, so these dykes were built to prevent raids in this part of east Hampshire, but it is not certain that these dykes are early medieval or that conditions in the thirteenth century matched those when the dykes were built.

If raiding did dominate early medieval warfare as I suspect, the lack of evidence for forts or barracks at dykes means that they almost certainly had no permanent garrison, so there would need to be a mechanism to summon locals to man them in times of unrest. The *Orkenyinga Saga*, written around 1200, talks about the extensive system of warning beacons set up around the Orkneys to warn of raiders and to signal the locals to prepare to defend their land and we know the West Saxon kings developed a system to warn of Viking attack.[55] Perhaps a similar set of beacons summoned people to see off raiders, as imagined by Tolkien in *The Lord of the Rings*.

Roman and Early Continental Sources

Although they would obviously have no knowledge of early medieval Britain, there are Roman and early medieval continental writers whose works may give us some relevant insights. We have already mentioned the *Epitoma Rei Militaris* by Vegetius, a Roman military handbook, when calculating the number of labourers needed to build defensive dykes, and suggested that similar books may have been one of the military manuals that Gildas claimed the Romans left for the Britons: '*exemplaria instituendorum armorum relinquunt*'.[56]

If the Britons did have this manual (or similar ones), their dykes should display more evidence of Roman sophisticated military techniques. I have already discounted the idea that British and Anglo-Saxon dykes have different ditch profiles, but what about other techniques? Are Anglo-Saxon earthworks more primitive? Archaeologists have only found good evidence for techniques like revetments and ankle-breakers at Wat's Dyke and West Wansdyke, East Wansdyke, Heronbridge and the Giant's Grave in Wales. Trying to decide which dykes are 'British' and which 'Anglo-Saxon' is highly problematic; the Britons could have built Wansdyke and the Giant's Grave, but Wat's and Heronbridge are west-facing earthworks on the Mercian–Welsh frontier.

Erskine and Fowler have both claimed that excavations of West and East Wansdyke demonstrate that they were built in a Roman tradition, possibly using *Epitoma Rei Militaris*.[57] Fowler asserted that there are gaps in East Wansdyke situated at regular intervals (every 800yd or 730m, roughly half a Roman mile) that were perhaps 'gateways', which worked rather like the milecastles on Hadrian's Wall, while the hill forts in West Wansdyke (notably Maes Knoll and Stantonbury) functioned like the forts of Roman frontiers. However, even his map has the 'gateways' at far more irregular intervals, none have been excavated so they may be later cuts by farmers and none of the hill forts have any evidence of early medieval occupation, so they might have been incorporated merely to save on labour. Interestingly, Erskine found no similar gaps in West Wansdyke. Without proof that the 'gateways' are original features spaced at regular intervals, Wansdyke looks no more Roman in style than, say, Wat's Dyke. Without the forts, milecastles and turrets of Roman frontiers, early medieval earthworks do not look particularly Roman and 'British' dykes look very similar to 'Anglo-Saxon' dykes.

THE NAMES OF DYKES

As we have seen, dykes seem to be located at places of conflict, so while the written evidence is rather patchy, perhaps the names of these earthworks can give insights into early medieval warfare. While some names or the stories of their origins may have far greater antiquity than the first manuscript they appear in, later people were more than capable of fabricating explanations of enigmatic features.

Place names are a potential minefield for historians. The name of Combs Ditch has forms that look early medieval (Cunucces dich, Cunnucesdic, Concresdic and then Combs Ditch), but they have drastically different meanings. The name superficially appears to derive from the old English for a valley (*cumb*), which is incongruous as it is on a plateau, but the local Hundred is recorded in the *Domesday Book* as Concresdic, Old English for King's dyke.[58] As we have seen, though, the name is given as Cunucces dich/Cunnucesdic in Anglo-Saxon charters. *Cun* is often found as a British name element and means chief/lord or hound in Cornish (the nearest Brythonic tongue to Dorset), while the -uc is probably derived from the ak/ek suffix used to make a noun into an adjective, thus Cunuc means 'lordly'. In early medieval British languages, 'dog' was considered a creature of status associated with hunting, fighting and loyalty. Unfortunately, we do not know who Cunuc was; there is no sufficiently similar name in the written or epigraphic evidence from south-west Britain, though he was probably a local leader. Alternatively, Cunuc may never have existed and the scribe merely used a rather eclectic spelling of the Anglo-Saxon word for king: cynig. So, we cannot be sure if it was built by a British leader, an Anglo-Saxon, or if the name is a complete red herring that post-dates the building of the dyke.

We know the identity of one person whose name is attached to a dyke – King Offa, so theoretically we should be able to link it to the politics of late eight-century Mercia, but even here we cannot be totally certain. As we have seen, the first written record, Asser's, post-dates Offa by a century. It is impossible to tell if written references that post-date Asser which also call the dyke Offa's, are independent and can be used as corroborative evidence. Most early references to the earthwork, like Symeon of Durham's in the twelfth century, blatantly copy Asser, but the *Life of St Oswald* (written about 1165), which claims that the dyke was built to stop Welsh raids, is only partly based on Asser.[59] The written evidence from Wansdyke possibly suggests that even this thoroughly Anglo-Saxon name was not the original moniker. As we have seen, the earliest surviving written reference to Wansdyke (the charter dated 825 S 272) calls it 'the old dyke' (ealdandic), though it does record the nearby prehistoric burial mound as '*wodnes beorge*', or Woden's Barrow. Fighting at the barrow is recorded in *The Anglo-Saxon Chronicle* in entries dated 592 and 715, neither of which mentions the dyke. As the earliest charters to call the earthwork Wansdyke (or rather *Wodnes dic*) date to the tenth century, perhaps the earthwork acquired the moniker Woden from the nearby barrow around that time.

Interestingly, many earthworks that are probably prehistoric were named after Grim by the Anglo-Saxons. He was their god of war, suggesting that if the Anglo-Saxons did know why a dyke was built, they were presuming it to be a military structure.

SUMMARY OF THE WRITTEN EVIDENCE

The evidence provided by early medieval written sources is problematic and should be handled with care, as there are gaps and the scribes often had agendas very different to our own. Despite attempts to suggest that this period was more peaceful than the sources suggest, there is no doubt that early medieval authors claim their society was often plagued by conflict, especially raiding (for cattle or slaves). It was a time when kings began to hold sway over the populace and Christianity gradually defeated paganism. Even when battles are mentioned, some of them may have been mere skirmishes in our eyes, though we do have good archaeological evidence from Heronbridge that the Battle of Chester involved at least 200 casualties. As dykes are recorded in charters as mere anonymous landmarks when describing estates, it seems the earthworks were earlier in date and had fulfilled a short-term purpose that had been largely forgotten. That role was countering raiding, which the law codes also attempted to control.

CHAPTER 5

Across the World: Raiding and Dykes from Other Periods and Places

This chapter will examine raiding as a part of warfare and how dykes in other time periods and countries were used to counter such forays. First, I shall examine raiding from other societies, before looking at analogies to early medieval dykes, then earthworks from other periods (prehistoric, Roman and later medieval), as well as examples from other countries.

RAIDING ACROSS THE WORLD

As we lack detailed written descriptions of raiding in early medieval sources, let us examine periods of incessant small-scale military forays from other periods and places. By understanding how raiding worked, it may be possible to see how early medieval dykes functioned as a deterrent. Obviously, we have no records from prehistoric societies, but archaeologists have speculated that cattle raids plagued Bronze-Age British society, usually in the autumn when the harvest had been gathered in.[1] Unsurprisingly, there is evidence of raiding from the Viking period from sources like the *Orkneyinga Saga*; interestingly Viking raiders usually went elsewhere when they faced fortifications, suggesting that dykes would have acted as a deterrent.[2] In the later medieval period, there is evidence that rulers avoided decisive pitched battles and that raiding enriched one side while destroying the other side in a conflict. The raids that characterized life on the Anglo-Welsh and Anglo-Scottish borders in the later medieval period are well attested in written records, as well as in physical remains, like the Pele towers.

The incessant raiding in nineteenth-century East Africa was slightly ritualized, though forays in search of women, cattle and slaves could destroy kingdoms.[3] In World War I, the British Army started systematically raiding enemy trenches, which lead to retaliatory raids along the Western Front. The objective of these raids was to demoralize the enemy, gather intelligence and ensure that all the attackers returned safely to their own lines.[4] Halsall's anthropological study of warfare in societies with a similar technology to early medieval Britain in Sudan, South America, New Guinea and the Maoris of New Zealand suggests that there was a great deal of raiding that involved the theft of goods rather than mass invasions to steal land.[5] Even though these raids were often ritualized, in certain locations they could lead to a large number of fatalities. These studies confirm that raiding has often been an integral part of war. It was sometimes ritualized, usually involved the theft of animals or people, raiders often retreated if they encountered resistance and raids could demoralize or devastate the community under attack.

What these studies of other periods and places suggest is that raiding is often carried out by nomadic societies against more settled agrarian communities (for example, Berber raids on the Roman Empire, Mongol raids on China and Tuareg raids on their neighbours to the south). As well as the largest early medieval dykes, a great many earlier hill forts lay along the Anglo-Welsh border. This is possibly because this is the interface between higher land to the west (which supported a more pastoral economy) and the lowlands (mainly arable society) to the east. The dykes of the Anglo-Welsh border and southern Wales were probably designed to prevent attacks by highland raiders on settled communities to the south and east.

DYKES FROM OTHER TIMES, PERIODS AND PLACES

While it is dangerous to assume that dykes from other countries or even British dykes from different periods fulfilled similar purposes, a study of a phenomenon that treats it in isolation is flawed. It is impossible to go into the same level of detail, especially with foreign dykes, as was undertaken on early medieval dykes, so only those directly relevant are discussed.

Earlier and Later British Walls and Dykes
As we obviously have no written records, we are probably even less likely to understand the purposes of prehistoric dykes than those of an early medieval date. Witness Sauer's study of Aves Ditch that contains fifteen pages discussing the issue, with numerous comparisons with other earthworks, but can only tentatively conclude that it was possibly a tribal boundary. Even then, he adds a question mark to the statement.[6] Some earthworks may have been trackways or cattle droveways; others probably demarked land divisions, or were at the edge of wasteland to delimit a group's cultivated territory; some look like they fulfilled a defensive role, while many appear to be territorial boundary markers. It is perhaps significant that while there are few finds from excavations of prehistoric dykes, they have produced *some* contemporary pottery sherds and metal objects; certainly more than early medieval dykes. Pottery finds from early medieval dykes are invariably prehistoric or Roman pottery sherds sealed under the bank, or residual material incorporated into it. As already mentioned, the pollen

evidence does suggest that prehistoric dykes cut through more intensively cultivated areas. If the early medieval dykes were built in thinly inhabited contested borderlands that would explain the lack of contemporary pottery finds.

Like many early medieval dykes, prehistoric cross dykes are short (sometimes 100m or less in length) and tend to bisect ridges, usually with a single bank and a single ditch, making them difficult to distinguish from some early medieval route-blocking dykes. Perhaps the cross-ridge or cross-valley dykes are prehistoric dykes that fulfilled similar purposes to early medieval dykes in preventing cattle raids.

The Roman frontier works of northern Britain were highly visible features in the medieval landscape, so may have been an inspiration to early medieval dyke builders.[7] Gildas and Bede mention them (though they misdate them to the end of Roman rule). These frontier works may have possibly been an inspiration to early medieval dyke builders, though they probably had little idea of how the Roman frontier works functioned. Roman writers described them as dividing the Romans from the barbarians to keep the latter out, but it is likely that they also controlled trade with the tribes to the north. The blocking of minor gateways in the late second century and early fourth probably represents an attempt to funnel trade through the more important crossing points. It is unlikely there was enough trade to make this the Romans' primary stimulus for building the walls and forts, even if this role occupied much of a garrison's time during periods of peace.

There are some obvious differences with the early medieval dykes. Hadrian's Wall and the Antonine Wall have features not found on early medieval dykes: forts; gateways; a wall or palisade; and clear evidence of a resident garrison. Early medieval dykes are rarely contiguous with administrative boundaries like county or parish boundaries, suggesting that they were not located at borders. Similarly, the Romans set their frontier works back from the frontiers, though they also built signal stations and forts garrisoned with scouts in front of them to give advance warning of attack. Roman frontiers were not sharply defined lines on the ground, but zones. The walls, if properly manned, certainly could stop small groups of people crossing into Roman Britain and they do command good views to the north, but they do not seem designed to repel large-scale attacks. The wall was not wide enough to use as a fighting platform, therefore mobile troops would have to destroy any attackers held up at the frontier. The frontier works probably functioned in a manner closer to the Berlin Wall than the Maginot Line. The Romans would gather troops from the forts on or around the walls and engage large-scale invasion forces in open country, where the superior discipline, cavalry and heavy projectile weapons of their more mobile troops would be used to devastating effect. Perhaps some early medieval dykes worked in a comparable way.

While Romans walls may have influenced early medieval dykes, the latter in turn could have influenced later earthworks. As we have already discussed, the end of dykes probably coincided with the rise of the *burh* and the arrival of Viking raiders, whom the *burh* walls were designed to keep out (internal dykes are not much good at stopping seaborne raiders). The Vikings did build some dykes in England, but these were short features designed to defend a tongue of land, like the one on Danby Rigg in the North Yorkshire Moors, or the bank between the Thames and the Kennet recorded by Asser.[8] Prior to the rise of the *burh*, the only earthworks of a comparable design to the dykes in early medieval Britain were the ramparts of hill forts. In the early medieval period in lowland Scotland these were often new constructions, while in lowland Britain they were reoccupied Iron-Age structures. Like the *burhs*, both Iron-Age and early medieval hill forts have palisades and gateways, of which archaeologists have found abundant evidence.[9] This adds credence to the supposition that early medieval dykes did not originally have palisades or gateways, as the numerous excavations of these earthworks would surely have uncovered some evidence of them.

Europe

British dykes are not unique. There are similar prehistoric and medieval earthworks across Europe, with examples in Ukraine, Hungary, Apulia in Italy, Sweden (Götavirke) and Spain (the 2.5-mile/4km long El Muro near Teverga) and Romania.[10] The nearest is a series of long south-facing earthworks in Ireland, which match in scale some in Britain; they run from Bundoran on the west coast to near Armagh, effectively dividing Ulster from the south.[11] The largest are the Dane's Cast, Black Pig's Dyke and the Dorsey, but differentiating among them, especially the first two, is difficult as locals use the two names interchangeably and all three lie on a similar alignment.

Contact between Ireland and northern Britain may have influenced dyke building on either side of the Irish Sea in the early medieval period. Earthworks found across areas traditionally thought of as the Anglo-Saxon homelands (Denmark and northern Germany) may also have provided the inspiration for Anglo-Saxon dyke builders (and raiders). One European earthwork that British archaeologists have drawn parallels with since Pitt Rivers took a (borrowed) spade to it over a century ago is the Danevirke. This south-facing earthwork runs for 18.6 miles (30km) along the base of Jutland, blocking access into Denmark from Germany.[12] It was built in at least seven phases and though the Royal Frankish Annals attribute it to King Godfred in 808, dendrochronology suggests that the earliest phases of building occurred shortly after 737. Interestingly, the Royal Frankish Annals also claim that it ran from sea to sea, a statement that is as inaccurate as Asser's assertion that Offa's Dyke performed the same feat, as the ends of the Danevirke lie on rivers. Even with a twelfth-century rebuild that clad the front in stone, the evidence for a wooden palisade in the earlier phases is obvious, suggesting that if the British dykes had been furnished with one, we would have found evidence of it by now. The Danevirke had a main gateway where the Hærvej, or army road that runs along the spine of Jutland from Germany, crossed the earthwork. The road is also called the Cattle Road, the Oxen Road, the King's Road and the Main Road, suggesting that cattle under the control or protection of the king (possibly as tribute) walked along it in and out of Denmark. Though the references are frustratingly terse, early medieval battles were fought at the earthwork; the Danish army used to muster along the earthwork during times of international uncertainty up to the nineteenth century.

To the north of the Danevirke, there are at least twenty-eight earthworks in Jutland, many of which cut routeways, as well as six tree barriers built across narrow belts of sea.[13] The most elaborate is the Olgerdiget: this was a 7.5-mile (12km) long stockade made up of large poles, though a 1.2-mile section (2km) has a ditch (1.6m deep by 4m wide) with a bank that is dated to 219 by dendrochronology. It was not garrisoned, but possibly patrolled with defenders mobilized in time of war, and seems to mark the dividing line between the Jutes and the Angles. This means that the Anglo-Saxons and Jutes had a history of building dykes before they gained control of England. Interestingly, this study found no records of dykes in Brittany, a place where so many other aspects of British culture were imported in the fifth and sixth centuries. This suggests that the building of a dyke to combat raiding was initiated in early medieval Britain by Germanic incomers (Anglo-Saxons), rather than being a part of native British culture, though of course prehistoric British dykes might also have been an inspiration. Unfortunately, like their British counterparts, few contemporary sources survive describing many of these European earthworks, so it is difficult to ascertain their original purpose. Even when records do survive (both inscriptions and texts), such as those associated with the 87-mile (140km) long dyke that the Bulgars built in Thrace against the Byzantine Empire, which clearly suggest that it had a military purpose, scholars claim it was purely symbolic.[14] Other scholars (myself included) are less convinced that we should ignore such clear primary evidence. Earthworks were replaced by forts that had a clear military function as the main type of Bulgarian defence, which possibly parallels the change from dykes to burhs or forts that King Alfred built in ninth-century England.

Asian Dykes
With the Great Wall of China, there survives documentary evidence which tells why the Chinese built it and how (this study used evidence from China to calculate the labour needed to build linear earthworks). The earliest walls were anonymous, practical structures built when the

Chinese Empire was weak or their diplomacy particularly unsuccessful to counter raiding by nomads to the north.[15] Many of the dykes of southern Wales, like Tor Clawdd and Bedd Eiddil, seem to block access to the coastal plains from the mountains (where people lived a more pastoral and possibly nomadic lifestyle), while Offa's Dyke and Wat's Dyke possibly fulfilled the same purpose of keeping Welsh raiders out of Mercia. Perhaps Offa's Dyke represents a breakdown of diplomacy with the Welsh during his reign; relations had been much closer when the earlier Mercian King Penda was a close ally of the Welsh King Cadwallon. Alternatively, like the later Chinese walls, whose remains we see today on tourist posters and which were often symbolic rather than anti-raiding defences, Offa's Dyke merely reflected Offa's imperial pretensions. These two very different functions, though not mutually exclusive if these structures were multi-functional, do highlight the danger of cherry-picking analogous examples from other countries or periods.

CONCLUSIONS ABOUT OTHER DYKES FROM ACROSS THE WORLD

Linear earthworks in other countries and periods have controlled trade and delimited territory, but often were designed to protect areas from raiders. While it is possible to make analogies with early medieval British dykes, we should be cautious, as people can build similar structures in response to dissimilar circumstances. Such comparisons do suggest that gateways and palisades would leave obvious traces on early medieval dykes in Britain and therefore we can possibly dismiss the suggestion that they were ever created.

CHAPTER 6

Raiding: The Epitome of Early Medieval Warfare

RAIDING AND EARLY MEDIEVAL WARFARE
With all the evidence measured, examined and weighed, it is now time to put raiding into the narrative of early medieval warfare, where we now know it belongs. Many saints' lives, chronicles and histories contain references to 'battles', but this is possibly because decisive set-piece actions were of more significance to chroniclers than small-scale forays. Although there are examples of indecisive battles, engaging in a battle was a highly risky strategy, as one side will be defeated and the leader could even be killed; raiding carried less chance of a catastrophic defeat, so was probably more widespread. There are clear references to raids in early medieval sources like *The Anglo-Saxon Chronicle* and many 'battles' were possibly merely successful raids. As most early medieval armies were relatively small, raiding would be within their capabilities, but mass invasion probably would not. While it is impossible to quantify the amount of raiding, even on a small scale raiding could have a widespread psychological impact (the fear of something can often have as much effect on people as the likelihood of it occurring). The dykes are evidence that some people decided to do something about the periodic raiding.

The Military Nature of Dykes
While dykes may be the only solid evidence of early medieval warfare that we have in the landscape prior to the building of *burhs* in the ninth century, can we really be sure they relate to early medieval raiding? Although some dykes were mere boundary markers (Bwlch yr Afan, Clawdd Seri, Aelfrith's Dyke and Bica's Dyke, for example) most early medieval dykes look like countermeasures against raiding. A few of the longer ones may have been multifunctional, in that they countered raids as well as promoting the power of a king while bonding his kingdom together (Offa's Dyke, Wat's Dyke and possibly the two Wansdykes, for example).

Despite good evidence that dykes countered raids, some studies still dismiss the idea, so let us briefly recap the evidence.[1] One of our few eyewitnesses from this period, Gildas, does say that the Britons constructed walls to scare off enemies and protect people. We have seen that some early medieval Welsh poems associate dykes with fighting. It is noticeable, for example, that when the ditches of prehistoric dykes in Norfolk were recut in the early medieval period (Bichamditch, Launditch and the Devil's Ditch at Garboldisham are possible examples), the inner face of the ditch was near vertical and the outer side flatter. This would accentuate the face of the earthwork and might have drawn people into a killing zone. There is abundant archaeological evidence of both weaponry and bodies that have suffered injuries at the dykes (beheadings at Bokerley Dyke and Bran Ditch, a battle cemetery at Heronbridge, odd weapons from the Devil's Ditch in Cambridgeshire, skeletons of men 'slain in battle' at Bedwyn Dyke and so forth). We cannot dismiss all of these finds as later execution sites or disturbed furnished graves: archaeological evidence clearly suggests that dykes were places associated with violence. If the slots found in the ditches of a least four dykes were ankle-breakers, they suggest that the earthworks were designed to repel and injure those who tried to cross them.

The scale of the banks/ditches is suggestive of military structures, especially as most give good views vital to defenders of a military feature. Most face downhill, which makes them much harder to storm but more difficult to build – on sloping ground the easiest way to construct a simple delimiting mark in the landscape is to throw the soil from the ditch downhill. The dykes often end at features like marshes, ravines, estuaries or rivers, which would hinder any attempt to outflank them; sometimes the ends curve away, so they look longer than they are. We have seen that written sources like law codes, chronicles, charters, poetry and saints' lives all suggest this was an age of raids and warfare – the poem Y Gododdin, for example, describes a raid that was defeated, with part of the fighting happening at a dyke. There may be no battles recorded at Wansdyke, but there are battles recorded in the vicinity, including two at the barrow that possibly gave its name to the dyke. The written evidence, the physical evidence and the lack of credible alternative explanations confirm that many dykes had a military purpose.

These dykes are deliberately sited to intercept raiders. As well as lying across the path of modern roads, as we have seen there is charter evidence that numerous dykes cut routes in the Anglo-Saxon period. Charters tell us that *herepaths*, or army paths (routes commonly used by raiders or invaders), were cut by Wansdyke (S 711 and S 735) and Bury's Bank (S 500). The East Hampshire dykes (especially the Froxfield earthworks) cut access along vegetation-free stony valleys while their flanks are guarded by thickly wooded clay lands. Many of the dykes in Glamorganshire seem to block routes along ridges that give access to the lowlands to the south.

The struggle against violence, in particular small-scale raids often involving cattle rustling, is a clear theme of all early medieval law codes. The collapse of the Roman Empire ended the use of professional armies in much of Europe and the militarization of the civilian population. The spears found in Anglo-Saxon graves may have had a symbolic meaning, but probably also signify a society where the need for personal protection was a daily concern. Farmers may have had good reason to fear the raids of heavily armed warriors. As very small groups of people could have built most early medieval earthworks, perhaps humdrum rural communities or groups of villages constructed dykes to deter or repel raids.

The lack of more explicit direct written evidence for dykes as defences against raiders is perhaps understandable in an age when few sources survive. Early medieval sources tend to laud victories (or heroic defeats), so as dykes were defensive rather than offensive, perhaps early medieval writers would not think farmers protecting their cattle to be worthy of record. If some dykes worked successfully as a deterrent, there may have been no fighting to record or bodies to bury; there are numerous forts and pillboxes across Britain designed to repel invasions that never materialized.

Surely raiders could simply have gone around the dykes? The answer is no, as most would have been incredibly hard to circumvent. The southern end of Giant's Grave, for example, is at a steep gully while there is a bog to the north, and both ends of the Lower Short Ditch are at steep gullies. Many dykes are in groups; circumnavigating one would just mean an invader faced yet another. No raider could simply go around Dane's Dyke or the Cornish dykes, as the sea or estuaries were the termini of these earthworks. The Giant's Hedge, for example, terminates below the lowest fordable point of the estuaries at either end.

The ends of many dykes were probably guarded by woodlands. Although medieval forests were more open than modern woods, as large mammals like deer (more numerous in medieval times) would keep undergrowth clear, navigating through any wood (or marsh) in good order is not easy. To a historian with an Ordnance Survey map it is obvious how to circumnavigate a dyke, but if early medieval invaders approached even a very short dyke where trees, marsh or a rise in the ground obscured the ends, they would not know how to go around it without sending out patrols.

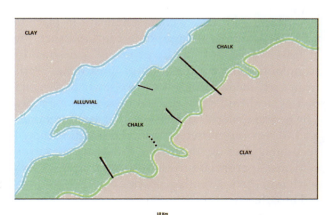

Geological map showing how the Cambridgeshire Dykes (marked in black) block access along a narrow band of chalk.

Even if a raider could go around a dyke, this would cause delay and possibly involve the splitting up of the invading force to reconnoitre a route. When looking for easy pickings, raiders would probably go elsewhere.

The best example of dykes cutting routeways is probably the Cambridgeshire Dykes, which seem to block access to East Anglia along the Icknield Way. They lie across a narrow band of chalk about 3.1 miles (5km) wide, which runs south-west–north-east, and flanked by what were then fens on the north-west side and what is thought to have been ancient woodland on chalky boulder clay to the south-east. An enemy who successfully circumvented one of the earthworks would then be faced with the problem of getting past the next.

Previous studies have often failed to see the significance of these huge earthworks in the story of early medieval warfare. We now need to look at raiding and warfare in detail, fitting these earthworks into the narrative.

EARLY MEDIEVAL RAIDING TECHNIQUES

There is evidence that there were large early medieval armies numbering in their thousands, like the mighty Viking army that invaded England in 866. These large armies led to big set-piece battles like Stamford Bridge and Hastings in 1066, but before 850, smaller-scale conflict was probably the norm. Engaging in battle is a highly risky strategy, as one side will be defeated and in extreme cases the leader might be killed or the kingdom could even collapse; It seems counter-intuitive, but most casualties occur in the aftermath of a battle when one side is in flight; a narrow defeat on the battlefield could lead to wholesale massacre and according to an early eleventh-century sermon, one Viking raider could make ten Anglo-Saxons defenders flee.[2] Small-scale raiding that carried less chance of a catastrophic defeat was probably more widespread and more likely to be within the capability of early medieval leaders.

People were not constantly attacking their neighbours in the early medieval period and there were mechanisms in place to prevent uncontrolled violence. Raiding, though, did occur and such low-intensity conflict (or at least the fear of it) was probably widespread enough to be a major stimulant in the construction of most dykes. Perhaps by using evidence from early medieval Britain and elsewhere we can recreate the mechanics of a typical raid, then discuss how a dyke could counter such a threat. The period under study was one that saw fundamental changes (Britain in AD400 was very different from the situation in AD850), but as we cannot accurately date the dykes, the following scenarios are broadly based on evidence appropriate to the probable peak of dyke building in the late sixth and early seventh centuries.

The collapse of the Roman Empire brought to an end the use of professional armies in much of Europe and the militarization of the civilian population. While farmers could have attacked their neighbours, they were probably usually too busy producing food to do so. Warriors would be more likely to carry out raids, although there was probably no clear division between the two classes for much of this period. Viking sagas suggest that while some made their living purely from raiding, others supplemented ways of feeding their family (farming, trading or a craft) with a bit of seasonal raiding.[3] The leaders of raiding war bands could have been kings, or, especially in the early stages of the period, merely successful warriors; as well as choosing warriors from among their kin, the most successful leaders would attract warriors from other communities. Those who made their living from war would become well armed with shields, swords, helmets and possibly even chain mail. Although rulers did have a band of loyal warriors, *thegns* in Anglo-Saxon times, who were handy with a sword, many people who fought in early medieval battles or raids may have made their living from the soil. Warfare became more professional in the later medieval period, but even well-organized kingdoms like late Anglo-Saxon England would call on local farmers to make up the bulk of their army.[4]

How people prepared for a raid is a matter of speculation, but perhaps poetry can give us some clues. A leader would gather warriors, choose a target and attack swiftly before the victims could organize their defences. Before embarking, oaths of loyalty were probably sworn and the night before we can imagine the warriors boasting about how brave they would be, alcohol possibly helping to exaggerate their ardour. In the early morning, weapons would be checked and sharpened while promises were made about how the booty was to be divided. They would mount horses and set off in the direction of their intended target. There are numerous references in Beowulf to of all these activities, for example when Beowulf prepares to meet Grendel's mother.[5] We do not know if a reconnaissance was made prior to an attack; if a spy was spotted the enemy would be forewarned, so perhaps scouts were not used. The disastrous outcomes of raids like that recorded in *Y Gododdin* suggest that intelligence was not always obtained.

The quickest and easiest way to travel to war would be on horseback. Without detailed maps of neighbouring kingdoms, raiders would probably use Roman roads and ancient ridgeways to penetrate deep into enemy territory without the fear of getting lost or making unnecessary deviations. It is noticeable that along many Roman roads, villages with names of an Anglo-Saxon derivation are located a few miles away rather than on the road; if you drive along the nearest Roman road to where I live there are no villages on the road for about 20 miles (32km). This suggests that raiders did not stray far from these routes, possibly out of fear of ambush or losing their way. It is perhaps significant that the Anglo-Saxon word *rád* not only meant 'to go riding on a horse', but also 'to go raiding' and 'a road'.[6]

As we have seen, in other cultures the ideal raid would be one that met no resistance, or failing that one which swiftly overcame any defenders. Raiders would try to make the enemy break and run (as we have said, most casualties in battle occurred when one side was in flight), but if this was not quickly achieved the attackers might beat a hasty retreat.[7] If raiders targeted farms, the defenders would be local peasants, or *ceorls*, armed possibly with spears and shields as well as the improvised weapons normally used as tools, such as axes, knives or hunting bows. If raiders were confronted by armed enemies, an exchange of missiles would probably occur before handheld weapons were used at closer quarters. If the raiders targeted religious sites, their opposition would have been unarmed priests or monks. They might target the ruler of a neighbouring kingdom, hoping to catch him with only a few members of his entourage to defend him.

While the Anglo-Saxons travelled to war on horses, it is uncertain whether they fought on horseback. They did not have purpose-bred warhorses, nor iron horseshoes that could be nailed to the hooves to protect them on stony ground. They may not have had the stirrup, which is essential when using a horse as a fighting platform.[8] The Anglo-Saxons did pursue a fleeing enemy on horseback, often for many hours after a battle, though during a raid a quick getaway was probably more advantageous than chasing after an enemy. After the raid, the attackers would gather up their stolen goods and head back home along the most direct route (probably a ridgeway or a Roman road), then spend the evening feasting, boasting and drinking in their hall. Raids ignited vendettas that triggered revenge attacks and a cycle of counter raiding; when kings emerged, they tried to curb this partly through the use of written law codes.

A raid could have various objectives: to demoralize an enemy; to reduce their ability to fight back; and to obtain booty. If raiders did try to ambush and kill the leader of a neighbouring kingdom (as happened in Wessex in 755 when Cynewulf was murdered), this might explain the large number of kings recorded as being killed in early medieval sources. The stolen goods could be cattle that raiders could herd back to their own community. The burning down of their victims' farms and food stores would reduce their strength and ability to strike back. The raiders could take slaves (as in the case of Saint Patrick) and high-value goods (such as jewellery); the leader of the raid could use such goods to reward his followers. This largesse would attract warriors to the victor, while the victims might turn on their leaders for failing to protect them. If rape was involved (and Anglo-Saxon sources do suggest it was prevalent in periods of instability), this would further burden the raided area with unwanted young mouths to feed, who might be looked upon with suspicion as their fathers would be enemies.[9] Finds of female brooches made from reused British and Irish metalwork in Viking-age Scandinavia has prompted the suggestion that raiding was also carried out to obtain a bride price, that is, a dowry necessary for a young man to marry.[10] The wealthy and well educated who were less able to fight (such as priests, teachers, lawyers and poets) would flee a community suffering raids, which would further destroy its culture. In numerous kingdoms of early medieval Britain rival factions or branches of royal families fought over control of the realm; perhaps the different groups targeted areas controlled by their rivals to weaken their power.

There are earthworks near Bokerley Dyke in Dorset that confirm that cattle raiding in particular was a real problem in the early medieval period (such raids are a theme of early medieval Irish legends). To the east of Bokerley Dyke (and therefore unprotected by it) are two giant cattle enclosures (soil samples from inside the banks confirm the presence of large amounts of dung).[11] The first, Soldier's Ring, is a 10.5-hectare polygon enclosure surrounded by double banks built near the end of Roman rule, while the other enclosure (39 hectares in size) is 3.1 miles (5km) further east at Rockbourne and overlays Roman fields. These earthworks reflect the widespread move across Britain from arable to pasture in the late and immediate post-Roman period, when the new cattle ranchers needed enclosures to protect their cattle from raiders. Cattle raids probably became such a problem that the locals decided to build the nearby Bokerley Dyke to try to control it.

Weapons Used in Warfare

As well as the finds from continental bogs already mentioned, like those from Esjbøl-North in Denmark, we have evidence from England of what weapons were used. Until their conversion to Christianity in the eighth century, the Anglo-Saxons often buried their dead with objects that symbolized their status; in half of male graves, this meant a weapon. Although I have noted above that some of these weapons may have been symbolic rather than what the dead person used in life, most look capable of causing damage in battle. We cannot know if the proportions of different types of weapons found in graves are typical of what was carried in life. Though bows and arrows are under-represented in the archaeological record, written evidence like the Battle of Maldon poem suggests they were used in battle. We have no reason to assume that the proportions used in Anglo-Saxon England were significantly different from what was found in continental bogs.

Most Anglo-Saxon furnished burials contained a spear (some lighter ones designed for throwing, while others with longer and heavier blades were undoubtedly handheld weapons), nearly half contained shields, 11 per cent swords, and a few knives or axes that may have been tools as well as weapons. Helmets and chain mail are rare. Anglo-Saxon swords were often pattern-welded, that is, bars of iron were twisted together then hammered flat into a blade, giving a surface which, if carefully polished, looks to me like metallic snakeskin. The later Vikings had better steel, so would use a single piece of metal.[12] The reference to the sword breaking during combat when Beowulf fought the dragon may explain why some were buried with multiple weapons, as it would have been advantageous to have a back-up in such circumstances.[13]

While it is possible that people were more likely to bury objects that were easier to replace, it does seem that a spear and shield formed the weapon combination of most people in this period. For the Picts, Scots and the Britons of Wales, Cornwall, Cumbria and Scotland there are far fewer finds to work on and less surviving literature, but it is likely that they used similar equipment. The Aberlemno stone in Scotland does show Pictish warriors using spears and shields, while the British writer Gildas does make reference to swords and spears being used in battle.[14] If they had fought in a very different style using vastly different weapons from the Anglo-Saxons, early medieval authors like Gildas and Bede, who were keen to stress the differences between the nations, would probably have noted it.

Archaeological evidence of weapon injuries that caused skeletal trauma demonstrates the effects of weapons. The seventh-/eighth-century bodies from Eccles in Kent and Heronbridge in Cheshire suggest that warriors hacked down with blows to the head from a heavy sword.[15] The damage found to skulls at these sites confirms the evidence from furnished burials that helmets were a rarity. As has already been discussed, an Anglo-Saxon sword's balance point is halfway down the blade; Viking swords were made from better quality steel, were lighter and had a balance point nearer the hilt. The former was designed for hacking at the upper body, the latter for thrust and parry.[16] Perhaps early Anglo-Saxon warriors expected to attack poorly armed victims, while later Vikings often faced foes also armed with a sword. Early Anglo-Saxon warriors do seem to be partial to using the weight of their weapon to hack down their opponent, targeting the head. Raising a defender up on a dyke makes the attacker's sword far less effective. Spear damage is less easy to detect than heavy blows to the head (especially if bones are not struck), but on display in the gallery in The Collection museum in Lincoln, where the author worked, there is on display a tibia with a spearhead embedded in it that would have caused the victim to bleed to death.

How a Dyke could Counter Raiding

In 1959, Lieutenant-Colonel Alfred Burne published a paper arguing that Offa's Dyke was more likely to be a military structure than an agreed frontier as Fox had suggested.[17] Burne suggested that the reason why there were English settlements west of the dyke was that as an unmanned defensive structure, the Mercians needed sufficient warning to man the earthwork during a Welsh attack, while the other dykes of the Welsh borders were forward and rear lines of an integrated defensive system.

Burne was not an archaeologist, but he was a respected military historian who knew about warfare. If we accept that raiding characterized early medieval warfare, we must examine how a dyke could prevent enemy forays entering the heart of a community.

Dykes could probably function in various ways in a society subject to raiding or the fear of raids. Finding a hostile raiding party in your territory and then intercepting it before it got away would be difficult. Such a raid would need to be ambushed before it could strike, so vulnerable communities blocked routeways with dykes. Dykes could deter attack by being so monumental in size that a potential attacker would deem the force needed to overcome the earthwork would outweigh any benefit from doing so. Dykes could also provide a fighting platform from which defenders could defeat raiders (monumental dykes that failed to deter an attack could obviously also be a place where defenders could make a stand). Communities could dig smaller dykes that were not a visible deterrent, but from which they planned to ambush attackers. Raiders resting before returning home could also dig an earthwork across a neck of land to defend a discrete area (like a peninsula) against counterattack. Similarly, defenders could make a peninsula defensible by use of an earthwork in order to have a refuge during a period when their community was under incessant attack; these last two functions potentially would give rise to very similar earthworks. If we examine these different functions in turn we can see how dykes fitted these four various scenarios.

The largest dykes are the most likely candidates for earthworks designed simply to deter attackers. The Devil's Ditch, for example, is monumental in scale, rising up to 5m above the otherwise flat Cambridgeshire countryside. Kingdoms and communities to the west would undoubtedly have noticed such an earthwork, so while it would not have taken an attacker by surprise, it would certainly have made potential raiders think twice before attacking East Anglia. Equally, the sheer length of Offa's Dyke meant that potential Welsh raiders must have been aware of it and they would have known that a king who could build an earthwork on such a scale was likely to have the resources to punish any attack on his territory. When the Welsh Annals record Offa devastating the British in 784, it was possibly a retaliation against Welsh raiding.[18]

If these dykes failed to deter an attack, they could also have provided a platform to defeat raiders. Anyone who has tried to scale the Devil's Ditch is surely painfully aware of how, if it was manned, it would be hard to overrun. Richard Muir, writing of the Devil's Ditch, made the bizarre claim that: 'invaders, charging in a column, would have overrun the dyke with ease. Despite the formidable appearance of the dyke, our tests showed that a fit young man could run from the outer edge of the ditch over the crest in less than half a minute.'[19] This is nonsense. It is very easy to lose one's step on the bank and roll down to the bottom. As Allcroft put it: 'Wet or dry, its smooth steep slope is as slippery as ice, so you are fain to go up on all fours, if at all.'[20] Even a slight blow from a defender would cause an attacker to tumble. I doubt that Muir's runner was encumbered by shield, sword and spear. Today, the dykes are covered with grass and though we have evidence turf was used to stabilize the banks on some dykes, the ditches at least would have been muddy trenches. In damp weather, the soil would have clung to the attackers' feet as they scrambled through the bottom of the ditch, slowing and tiring them as they tried to gain traction up the slope to where the defender lay in wait.

We can probably also dismiss Muir's claim that the dyke would require too large a force to man, as the marvellous view from the top means that a relatively small force guarding it could easily send men along the bank to block any attempt to outflank them by raiders attacking at more than one point. Such a defensive strategy would not work so well with Offa's Dyke, as its sheer length would surely make it easier for raiders to creep across an unguarded point. Perhaps Offa's Dyke was deliberately set back from the border so that it could not be overrun by surprise (which is why English place names are found to the west) and some scholars have suggested that mounted guards could have patrolled it.[21] Hill suggested that 100 mounted men in three shifts could patrol Offa's Dyke, while beacons could summon defenders from nearby villages when they spotted Welsh raiders.

Mark Bell interestingly suggested that dykes were built by strong groups as a defence against more diffuse groups that they could not control; for example, we know that the stable kingdoms of China built walls against the Mongolian nomads to the north.[22] This theory may explain why many dykes cluster round the powerful and aggressive kingdom of Mercia. Using this argument, perhaps we can suggest that powerful Mercian kings built the dykes of the Welsh borders to face pastoral Welshmen to the west, or perhaps powerful East Anglian rulers may have built the Cambridgeshire Dykes against diffuse groups to the west, which historians often refer to as Middle Angles (groups that were later absorbed into Mercia).

As the majority of dykes were much smaller than Offa's or the Devil's Ditch, they were less likely to deter attack, but communities may have built them as stop lines where raiders could be defeated (dykes like Grey Ditch in Derbyshire, Rowe Ditch in Herefordshire, Pear Wood to the north-west of London, for example). Most dykes are some way back from an actual frontier, so raiders could not easily overrun them, allowing defenders to assemble on the earthwork and plan their strategy before the attackers arrived. Many dykes cut Roman roads, or what charters tellingly refer to as *herepaths* or army paths, the very routes taken by raiders and invaders. The dykes in Glamorganshire, for example, seem to block ridges that give access from the uplands to the coastal plains (in an early medieval context this would mean keeping warriors from Brycheiniog out of Glywysing), often cutting ridges at narrow bottlenecks. Many of the smaller dykes required very few people to build them and some 'rough dykes' (which is the original meaning of the name of Rowe Ditch) were probably temporary measures thrown up at comparatively little notice. The need to build new dykes quickly to counter the threat of raids is possibly why the builders did not bother with a palisade. Raiders who successfully raided an unguarded community may have been surprised by a newly constructed earthwork blocking their progress when they had traversed the same route with ease the previous year.

We know from the complete lack of archaeological evidence of forts, watchtowers or fortified gateways that early medieval dykes were not permanently garrisoned, but, as scholars have suggested when discussing Offa's Dyke, watchmen (like those mentioned in Beowulf or the *speculators* recorded by Gildas) may have patrolled them. These watchmen could then use beacons, flags, horns or messengers to warn the local people of the attack (if the raiders were burning farms as they came, the smoke may have made other warnings unnecessary). We know from later Anglo-Saxon documents that there was a system in each shire whereby the local lords could call on the services of their tenants to fight invaders. This was called the *fyrd* and earlier similar local organizations possibly existed across early medieval Britain.[23] As the local men and the watchmen gathered at the earthwork, messengers could have sought out the local ruler and his warriors.

Previous scholars who have examined the dykes have not discussed the psychological influence of a dyke during a fight. It is likely that the defenders would be a group of (possibly terrified) locals lined up along the earthwork, whereas the attackers would more likely be warriors who derived their wealth and status from raiding. Morale is incredibly important in any battle; the local farmers protecting their land would be susceptible to reacting with panic and the biggest problem with inexperienced troops is that they tend to flee in the face of a determined attack. The attackers would probably travel on horseback to raid and dykes are very effective against cavalry, so would have inhibited the ability of mounted raiders to rout the defenders quickly. As the majority of casualties in battle happen when one side is in an uncontrolled flight, a ditch in front of the dyke which keeps the enemy at a safe distance would be a comfort to the defenders, while the bank would be a safety zone from which the defenders would be reluctant to flee. We know from the Battle of Hastings that manoeuvres like having the cavalry feign a retreat could draw out defenders from a secure position, upsetting defensive formations like a shield wall. Being on a dyke would discourage defenders from leaving their position – who would want to leave the security of an elevated position with good views for a flat field with hostile enemies, possibly mounted, pursuing you?

Perhaps the decapitated burials found at some dykes may have been the remains of defeated defenders who panicked or were overwhelmed by the superior numbers or skills of raiders. The defences of *burhs* later helped comparatively amateur defenders to see off attacks by semi-professional Viking raiders. In modern battles, most conscript soldiers never use their weapon; it is likely that in an early medieval context the defenders would probably hope that the enemy would simply go home. It probably takes four times as many troops to storm a defended position as to hold it, so the raiders would have to outnumber the attackers considerably before they dared to attack.[24]

If the raiders decided to press on with their attack, a dyke would have many advantages for the defenders. The ditch would initially keep the raiders at a distance. Missile weapons (arrows, throwing axes and javelins) would potentially drive off an attacker without the need for the more terrifying prospects of close-quarter fighting. The defenders, if local farmers, would be less likely to own a shield and modern re-enactors state that it is difficult to wield a shield as well as the rather heavy Anglo-Saxon spear, so perhaps they did not form a shield wall on top of the dykes. Projectile weapons are far less effective when thrown or fired uphill, as the loss of momentum makes them easier to dodge and they will do less damage if they hit. If raiders were warriors who made their living from war, they were more likely to be armed with swords and the downward sweep of a heavy early medieval sword would be hard to manage against a defender raised up on a bank.

A dyke could also help to defeat as well as repel an attack. While the raiders, deep in hostile territory, were sustaining casualties assaulting the earthwork, messengers warning of the attack could be bringing more men to the aid of the defenders. If the defenders felt they had sufficient numbers, they could even use the earthwork to destroy the attackers, for example the men on the dyke could send out forays of more mobile and better-trained troops round the flanks of the raiders, then crush them against the dyke. The skulls found at dykes may not have been overwhelmed defenders, but the remains of a destroyed attacking force; perhaps their heads were mounted on stakes to deter other attackers. There are examples from early medieval sources across Europe that suggest displaying the body of an executed transgressor was considered normal.[25] Individual earthworks have particular characteristics that would help to defeat an attacker. Minchinhampton Bulwarks cuts a ridgeway and the ends are located where the land slopes down to a valley; rather than being straight, the ends curve forward to form a reverse 'C' shape, effectively drawing raiders into the centre where the defenders will outflank them. Bokerley Dyke cuts a Roman road, but runs parallel to it for some distance, so that it can be used as a missile platform against attackers approaching from the north.

If the raiders sensibly avoided a frontal assault, even so outflanking the dyke may not have been as easy as modern fieldwork sometimes suggests. With a good map and stout boots on a peaceful sunny day it may be relatively simple to hike round the end, but it would not be so easy during a raid. As most early medieval dykes faced downhill and pollen or other environmental evidence suggest they ran across open country, defenders would have had a good panorama of the ground in front. This would not only give them good warning of attack, but during the fighting it would allow them to react quickly to any outflanking manoeuvre by the attackers. If the raiders tried to go around one dyke and rejoined the road, they may have faced another dyke, as many are found in groups, like those on Crookham Common. As the ends of many dykes are not obvious, a raider either had to send out patrols or guess which way was the best route round the earthwork. If a dyke deflected raiders off the *herepath* they were following so that they had to ford a large river or cross a deep gully, this would provide an ideal opportunity for an ambush. If a raider entered the wood or marsh on the flanks of a dyke, he would be entering an environment where the locals hunted and they could pick off the stragglers. As losses mounted (as raiders were wounded, killed or deserted), the leader of the raid would soon be forced to return to safety. It is likely that many raids were made at night, making it even harder to see the ends of the dyke or to navigate once the raiders had left the road.

The areas where there are no dykes are possibly ones where there was no need to build linear defences against raiders. The lack of dykes in central Mercia might be because the chronicles that record the hostile actions of Mercian kings like Offa and Penda, as well as archaeological evidence such as the Staffordshire Hoard, suggest that the Mercians did more raiding than their neighbours and it is only on their western frontier that they were being raided themselves. The border subkingdoms recorded in the *Tribal Hidage* that surrounded the core of the Mercian kingdom may have absorbed raids from other kingdoms. There are no dykes in north-west Wales, as mountains and tidal rivers that are hard to ford block access into the kingdom of Gwynedd. Big forests lay to the north of both Essex and Sussex (two shires devoid of early medieval dykes) and large tidal rivers or marshes cut their coastlines where defenders could ambush invaders as they attempted to ford these water obstacles. There are no dykes in the Highlands of Scotland, as there are few land routes worth cutting and most raiders would travel by boat.

The dykes built to protect headlands obviously do not block routeways, so perhaps some of these were dug as a defended beachhead by attackers on raids that required at least one overnight stop in hostile territory. We know that the Viking raiders used dykes to protect themselves from counterattack by digging earthworks across a narrow neck of land to make a safe haven, for example Coombe Bank near Reading. Perhaps Park Pale in Yorkshire is a Viking beachhead dug by Vikings attacking the kingdom of Northumbria. It is possible that Anglo-Saxon raiders constructed earthworks to protect themselves when resting during a raiding expedition, either before they settled in Britain or after. On the east coast of England Dane's Dyke is the only earthwork that looks like a possible beachhead constructed by raiders from abroad and the twelfth-century Symeon of Durham claims that a seventh-century Anglo-Saxon king landed there.[26] The source is unfortunately rather late, but the site is extremely well chosen and the earthwork's massive scale makes it unlikely that it was a hurriedly built defence for a group of raiders.

There are problems with the idea that prior to the arrival of the Vikings dykes were built by raiders, but they might have been dug to defend against them. Large cliffs guard the seaward side of Dane's Dyke and very late Roman signal towers along the coast to the north could have provided a warning of raiders, thus allowing the locals to gather their families and animals before retreating behind the dyke.[27] Post-Roman finds and bodies with evidence of a violent death found at these signal stations support the idea that they may have acted with a fortified refuge at Dane's Dyke to protect against raiders in the late and immediate post-Roman period. The earthwork at Heronbridge may have been a refuge or bridgehead for a marauding Northumbrian army, though it looks very well made to be a hurried defensive measure (in particular the careful reuse of Roman material in the revetment). With no gateways or signs of internal structures it does not resemble a fort, but looks like a beachhead defending a fording point. There are no dykes on the west coast of Britain that look like beachheads for Scottish or other Irish raiders; those in Cornwall are surely too long for a hastily erected defence. Therefore, though the Vikings may have used dykes as beachheads, there is little evidence that earlier raiders did, perhaps because their raids were swiftly concluded.

The Cornish dykes do not block routeways, but they do demark headlands, perhaps to defend against raiding, not from the sea but overland. In 815, *The Anglo-Saxon Chronicle* records the West Saxon King Egbert raiding Cornwall from east to west. The shorter dykes (like the one that delimited Stepper Point near Padstow) could have acted as refuges for large numbers of people and cattle. The larger dykes (like the Giant's Hedge that runs between the Fowey and the Looe rivers) could be stop lines set back from a vulnerable border. The area it delimits is too large to just be a refuge, so it was probably designed to defend the core of a Cornish subkingdom, which is why it only covers a small part of the Hundred of West Wivelshire, yet it must have utilized labour from a larger area. The Cornish dykes are set back from the Tamar (and therefore the West Saxons) and beacons, for example St Agnes Beacon (a superb viewpoint enclosed by a dyke called Bolster Bank and visible from as far afield as Camborne), could have warned people to retreat behind the dyke. Similarly, at Tintagel a large ditch, probably early medieval in date, defended the settlement on the cliff-fringed peninsula from landward attack. Raiders could not outflank the Giant's Hedge as it ended below the lowest fordable point on the Fowey and Looe estuaries. Peasant levies will often run in the face of raiders, but a dyke would give them confidence and a fixed point from which to make a stand, while raiders, always looking for easy targets, would leave a manned dyke alone. After the West Saxon raiders went home, the people could rebuild their ravaged farms.

Raiding was probably not always the norm in early medieval Cornwall. The archaeological record suggests a move away from the fortified settlements that characterized the Iron Age in Cornwall, suggesting that there must have been times of stability in the early medieval period. The dykes were temporary measures set back from the border built during times of crisis when the West Saxons threatened. As they rapidly fell out of use, locals soon forgot their names and stories of giants grew up to explain the origins of the Cornish dykes.

By not defending the Anglo-British border as the Britons of Dorset possibly had tried to do at Bokerley Dyke, the West Saxon kings could rampage along the spine of Cornwall, demonstrating their martial might while the Cornish were safe behind their dykes, having avoided being destroyed in a decisive battle. The Anglicization that occurred as Wessex expanded into Devon, Somerset and Dorset never occurred in Cornwall. Uniquely in south-west Britain, the inhabitants of Cornwall claim to possess a Celtic identity. Brythonic place names (especially in the central and western parts) abound in the Cornish entries of the *Domesday Book* and a Brythonic tongue was still the vernacular in western parts into the seventeenth century. The maritime links Cornwall maintained with Brittany up until the Reformation perhaps bolstered a Brythonic culture, but the south coast of Devon is as easy to reach by sea from Brittany, while north Devon and Somerset are only a short voyage from Wales. Control of Cornwall was certainly an attractive prospect to the kings of Wessex, as its mineral wealth had attracted merchants from as far away as the eastern Mediterranean from Phoenician times until the reign of the sixth-century Byzantine Emperor Justinian.[28] The Tamar was never an impassable barrier and the English place names found in eastern Cornwall probably reflect West Saxon colonization of those parts of Cornwall nearest to Devon. The dykes may crucially have provided refuges, allowing Cornish society to weather the aggressive early stages of Anglo-Saxon expansion and so maintain their own identity.

Who Built the Defensive Dykes?
Who built these stop lines is a question for which there is no simple answer. It is likely that people from the delimited estate constructed the smaller dykes that were boundary markers (like Aelfrith's Dyke and Bica's Dyke), probably under the direction of the estate owner, but it is far less certain who ordered the construction of those earthworks that had a military purpose. It is not just that we do not know their names; we do not know what type of people built them or at least ordered them to be constructed. The actual workers could have been local farmers sick of being raided, paid workers following the orders of a king, conscripted labourers, or slaves under the control of a warlord.

It is tempting to link dykes with the rise of kings and certain kingdoms. It is fairly certain Offa ordered the construction of the earthwork that bears his name and equally Aelfrith, Bica, Lawa and Eliseg (if Clawdd Lesg is named after him) may have ordered the building of earthworks to which their names are attached. Without precise techniques for dating dykes, attempts to connect other dykes with individual kings are foolhardy. Geographical location suggests that a Mercian king possibly ordered the building of Wat's Dyke, an East Anglian king those in Cambridgeshire and a king of Wessex possibly ordered Wansdyke, but connecting other dykes with kingdoms, let alone individual kings, is highly speculative.

It is possible that the earthworks can tell us where shadowy lost kingdoms were once located and scholars have linked dykes like the Swaledale Dykes, Tor Dike in Yorkshire and the Giant's Hedge in Cornwall with suspected lost British kingdoms.[29] Unfortunately, these theories usually assume that a later administrative region was once a kingdom, then fit that hypothetical realm to a nearby, possibly unrelated, earthwork. The larger dykes certainly looked planned by an authority with wide-ranging powers (as we have noted, the larger dykes were more likely to have marker banks, ankle-breakers and revetments), but most early medieval dykes are small, simple structures built by 100 men in a single season. The vague descriptive names of many dykes, as well as the supernatural monikers, all suggest that the original builders were soon forgotten; the 'rough dyke' names of some confirm the idea they were hurriedly built. Perhaps kings did not order the construction of the majority of the earthworks and it is likely that small agricultural communities built them to defend themselves against the predatory warlords whose descendants probably became kings. The analysis in this book of the size of labour force needed to build these dykes suggests that most were not the grandiose gestures of a king.

As Paolo Squatriti has rightly pointed out, dykes are exercises in earth moving, that is, they were a typical farmer's solution to a problem, as peasants were always digging the earth, for example for drainage, to get at root crops, to make hedgerows to control cattle, to terrace land for ploughing, to remove tree stumps, to dig out large stones, or to bury the dead.[30] Digging the earth was probably not the natural action of an early medieval war leader. We can only ponder what the role of women was in the growth of dykes. They seem to be excluded from active roles in warfare, except as a victim who was robbed, murdered, raped or abducted into slavery. Perhaps they encouraged men to build the dykes to protect their communities and even worked on them, helping to move the earth themselves. Their male relatives may have even been inspired to build them to protect women in their communities, or alternatively went on raids to capture females. It has been suggested that women kept alive feuds and vendettas with songs and stories; if they were primarily victims it is perhaps unsurprising that they might want to remind others of wrongs suffered by their group in the hope that compensation or at least retribution would be sought.[31]

Evidence for Beacons

When raiding was a problem in the early medieval period people often built beacons to warn of attack. We know the Vikings and their enemies used systems of beacons to warn of the arrival of raiders and the Romans used scouts (*exploratores* and *areani*) to warn of attack.[32] If dykes were not manned (though they may have been patrolled) as archaeology suggests, there must have been a signalling system to alert people to danger so that they could assemble at the dyke. Can we find signs of beacon sites in the period AD400–850? Can we find evidence for a prominent location with good lines of sight at a reasonable number of early medieval dykes?

Hill postulated that beacons were used both to lay out Offa's Dyke and Wat's Dyke as well as to warn of Welsh raiders, but attempts to locate them through excavation have proved fruitless. No charcoal deposits have been found on the top of hills he thought to be signal points.[33] As these dykes are very long, Hill could easily have selected the wrong location to excavate and if a warning beacon was never set alight there would be little evidence of it in the archaeological record. A substantial watch tower, especially if the foundations were sunk into the ground, would leave archaeological evidence, but more flimsy structures could leave no trace. A roving scout using flags or a horn would certainly leave no evidence. If the fires from burning barns gave abundant evidence of a raid in progress, perhaps beacon fires were not needed (obviously, if the raid occurred at night it would be these fires that warned people of attack and flags would be useless). Even so, we should find a prominent hill or similar landmark near every dyke that gives good views towards the area the earthwork faced if they were designed to combat raids and a warning was needed to gather defenders.

Development near some dykes, like Faeseten Dyke in Kent, makes it impossible to tell if there are any good candidates for a nearby signal point, while at Heronbridge and some of the East Anglian dykes the flat landscape means there are unsurprisingly no obvious candidates we can identify. Significantly, at most other dykes there are obvious sites for possible beacon sites or signal points. Despite housing developments (and forestry on Ockham Common) obscuring much of Fullinga Dyke in Surrey, St George's Hill near the north end gives good views, while the hill on which a semaphore tower was built in 1822 at Ockham Common just to the east of the dyke (at TQ089585) is a clear candidate for a signal point. This is assuming that Fullinga Dyke was more than just a border marker, however. Bolster Bank in Cornwall defines a peninsula dominated by a hill tellingly called St Agnes Beacon (at SW710504), which affords superb views across the Bristol Channel and inland. While lines of sight from Tor Dike in Yorkshire down the steep valley to the south are obscured, the high hills that flank the valley on either side would make excellent signal points. An observer on the Swaledale Dykes cannot see anyone approaching from the east until they are quite close, but people on the adjacent hills can. Similarly, the views northwards from Grey Ditch in Derbyshire are rather poor, but Lose Hill (SK153853), 2.5 miles (4km) to the north, commands spectacular panoramic views over a vast area and the hill of Crungoed (SO185711) to the north of Pen y Clawdd dyke in Powys is an excellent candidate for a signal station.

To the north of the dykes in south Wales are the Brecon Beacons, which are so named because of the fires erected on them to warn of English raiders. An observer stationed on the hills near Black Dyke and the Bardon's Mill dykes in Northumberland (like Catton Beacon at NY822592 and Bell Crags at NY772729 where there is actually a fire watch tower today) could have given warning of imminent attack.[34] At Lanreath, near the middle of the Giant's Hedge in Cornwall, a bulge in the course of the dyke encompasses a hill that gives superb prospects to the north. Today, the River Severn forms a rather formidable barrier across a gap in Offa's Dyke between Rhos and Buttington, but before modern flood defences rivers meandered across their floodplains, so it would have been much easier to ford. There are two large hills on the eastern side (Breidden Hill at SJ295144 and Middleton Hill at SJ305133), which give commanding views, so a few watchmen with a beacon fire stationed on the hills could easily warn of any attempt to ford the river by raiders.

For some dykes the evidence is less circumstantial. The views forward from some sections of East and West Wansdyke are hardly panoramic, but the two hill forts incorporated into West Wansdyke (Maes Knoll and Stantonbury), or the Downs just to the north of East Wansdyke (Barbury Hill at SU156761 or Cherhill at SU048694 in particular) overlook large areas.[35] There is evidence of beacon sites across Wessex used to warn of Viking raids (Elizabethans reused many of the sites for Armada beacons), which may have originated in warning systems related to early medieval dykes.[36] To the north of Wansdyke, the late Saxon fort on Silbury Hill or even the *burh* at Avebury could have replaced an older early-warning system for people living near East Wansdyke.[37] They could give advance warning of attackers approaching from the north and then hopefully the locals would have a chance to man the dyke.

The hill of Glastonbury Tor overlooks Ponter's Ball and evidence for early medieval occupation at the site possibly suggests that it was a signal point. Hills obscure the views to the south of the nearby New Ditch, but 1.2 miles (2km) west of that earthwork is the Iron-Age hill fort of Dundon Hill, in the south-east corner of which is a mound called Dundon Beacon that overlays the Iron-Age ramparts.[38] It may be a windmill mound (though that would be better placed on the western side of the hill to face the prevailing winds), or an aborted attempt to build a motte and bailey castle, but the name suggests that the mound was built as a beacon, perhaps working in conjunction with the earthwork. Dundon Beacon overlooks land to the south of the dyke so if watchmen were stationed there and at Glastonbury Tor, it would be almost impossible to cross the area unobserved. Near Bar Dyke and Broomhead Dyke in Yorkshire are two hills surmounted by what are assumed to be Norman fortifications (Bailey Hill at SK312726 and Castle Hill at SK271923), but both could be possible older beacon sites.[39]

As briefly mentioned earlier, along the coast to the north of Dane's Dyke was a line of at least five signal stations, which were probably the last Roman military structures built in Britain. While today many of these sites are no longer inter-visible, they were built on cliff tops subject to erosion, so it is likely that sites that would have connected the chain have long since fallen into the sea. There is evidence of post-Roman occupation at the Filey station and excavations at the Goldsborough signal station found bodies of people who seemed to have died violent deaths dating to just after the end of Roman rule in Britain.[40] Flamborough Head itself would have been an ideal site for a signal station, as later use of the headland clearly shows. Three beacons were erected there in 1588, while in 1674 a lighthouse (the first post-Roman British lighthouse) was built at Flamborough and in 1796 a flag station was built there.[41] While there is no surviving evidence of a Roman or early medieval signal station at Flamborough, quarrying and erosion could have destroyed such evidence. Nevertheless, the Roman signal stations to the north could easily have given early medieval people enough warning of seaborne raiders (Picts or Angles), so that they could gather behind the safety of the earthwork.

This topographical, archaeological and place-name evidence from so many dykes, though not conclusive, certainly suggests people were using hills (sometimes even artificially heightening them) to watch for enemy attacks. We do not know if beacon fires, flags or perhaps mounted messengers (or a combination) were used, but warnings were probably sent to locals. They could then man the earthworks that blocked routeways where they hoped to see off attackers. It is just unfortunate that we do not have the written sources to tell us how many times the earthworks were effective in preventing plunder-greedy warriors raiding their victims.

DYKES AND DEVELOPMENTS IN EARLY MEDIEVAL SOCIETY

Though it would be highly speculative to try to match specific dykes to individual entries in Anglo-Saxon or Welsh chronicles, we can suggest how raiding and counter-raiding measures fitted into processes like the Anglo-Saxon conquest or the rise of kingdoms. Laycock has suggested that dykes are a symptom of the breakdown of Roman rule across Britain and its Balkanization into small British and Anglo-Saxon kingdoms.[42] It could be that it was incessant raiding that caused this fragmentation of the Roman diocese of Britain.

Raiding and the coming together of people to build dykes to combat raids could respectively destroy and build new identities; dykes could have been crucial in the formation of kingdoms and raiding. If a raid led to the ambush and murder of a king, it would lead to a kingdom's destruction. Booty from raids may have helped warlords to become established kings and the concentration of dykes around the border of Mercia could mark a reaction to the growth of that kingdom. Those earthworks around the heartland of Powys may have helped to maintain the power of their kings. The dykes that subdivided East Anglia (like Launditch and Bichamditch) suggest that region was once disunited, though the later written sources give us no hint of that division. The very act of building, maintaining and occasionally fighting at the Cambridgeshire Dykes, probably against Mercia, may have helped to create cohesion amongst those divided communities, which eventually led to the growth of the East Anglian kingdom. The building of the earthworks on the western border of Kent may have helped to reinforce the power of Kentish kings. As already discussed, the act of building and using dykes in Cornwall to counter West Saxon raids probably helped to unite the Cornish and maintain their identity in the face of growing Anglicization. Once kingdoms coalesced and kings gained control of large areas, they would probably try to stop localized raiding (the law codes certainly suggest an attempt to replace reciprocal violence with fines) and the rulers would try to focus energies against external threats. The incessant raids of the immediate post-Roman period may have died down by the ninth century, possibly thanks to the dykes, though they were soon replaced by the incursions of the Vikings. We should note that kingdoms could also form without any need to build dykes, such as the Scottish kingdom of Argyll, as well as the East Saxon and South Saxon kingdoms.

The theory that the fifth to ninth centuries consisted of widespread raiding complements the various theories about the nature of the Anglo-Saxon settlement of England (the *Adventus Saxonum*) and possibly also the Scottish takeover of Pictish territory. Broadly speaking, these movements have variously been characterized as mass invasions, coups by a small group of invading warriors and cultural changes that involved the movement of very few people. Let's look at these theories in turn.

If the Anglo-Saxon invasion involved the replacement of the native population with Germanic incomers, aggressive raiding would help to explain how they could drive out the far more numerous indigenous population. The same logic could be applied to the Scottish takeover of the lands of the Picts. In recent years, such invasionist theories have been less fashionable and the Anglo-Saxon takeover of lowland Britain has often been characterized as a coup by some Germanic warriors. The arrival of a small class of hardened Germanic fighters that had a culture of aggressive and persistent raiding is consistent with the theory that the *Adventus Saxonum* was a takeover by a small elite group of warriors, with very little change in the composition of the majority of the population.

The theory that the Anglo-Saxon invasion was merely a cultural change does not, on its own, explain why the native Britons adopted new Germanic modes of dress, language and religion (nor why the Picts adopted Scottish customs). The theory lacks a driver or catalyst for such changes; people are unlikely to adopt a new language, culture and style of dress on a mere whim. Perhaps raiding was the driving force for these changes. It would certainly explain how a small group of warriors could cause such widespread cultural and linguistic changes. Raiding by small groups of aggressive Germanic incomers could have destroyed the indigenous culture and eliminated the native elite. In the Roman period, across Cornwall and much of Wales native settlements do not seem archaeologically particularly 'Roman'; after AD400, although there is evidence of site continuity, building plans change from round to rectangular, Latin inscriptions appear and there is evidence of Christianity. Perhaps the educated Romanized Christian elite (priests, lawyers and teachers, for example) from the lowlands fleeing raiding Anglo-Saxons arrived in western Britain, as was recorded by Gildas, Bede and the *Life of St Wilfred*. Those left behind in eastern Britain would perhaps want to adopt the cultural identity of the most hostile raiders (their mode of dress and language) in the hope they would be spared from attack.

Not only can these three different models for the respective Anglo-Saxon or Scottish takeovers of England and Scotland (population replacement, an elite warrior takeover and cultural change) complement the idea of widespread raiding, they are not mutually exclusive. While the evidence for violence from Anglo-Saxon cemeteries is rare, this does not preclude victims of raids being less likely to be carefully buried in organized cemeteries, or violence being rare but unpredictable and sporadic. The Anglo-Saxon settlement was probably a complex process, so that at different times and in different areas any of these three theories could best describe the process.

The outbreaks of sporadic raiding may have also helped with the spread of Christianity, which characterized the early medieval period. The Christian Church tried to control violence (for example, St Patrick's letter to Coroticus, Adomnáin laws and *wergilds* in law codes) and while there are records of attacks on monasteries (as in the 645 reference in the *Annales Cambriae*), these were newsworthy to chroniclers possibly because they were shocking and rare. A society constantly plagued by uncontrolled violence is unlikely to grow economically or culturally. The prohibitions around attacking monasteries and churches would make invasions less catastrophic. Christianity, by creating rules around violence and places where killing was considered taboo, provided a brake on the more destructive elements of early medieval society, which made it attractive for kings to adopt and promote this new religion.

THE CHRONOLOGY OF THE RAIDING AND DYKES

Like most human phenomena, the rash of early medieval dyke building and the raids that they were designed to halt probably had a beginning, a peak, a decline and then an end. With so few contemporary documents and so little unambiguous dating evidence from the dykes, we can only make very tentative conclusions about chronology. Sadly, we have more evidence for later reuses of dykes than for their original functions and the end of dyke building is probably easier to date than the origins, due to the lack of written evidence from the beginning of this period. For these reasons, the framework is discussed in reverse chronological order.

The early medieval dykes soon faded from memory from the ninth century onwards. Later people often reuse earthworks in very different ways to how their builders envisioned. Modern walkers use some early medieval dykes as footpaths (Offa's Dyke and the Devil's Ditch). Fieldwork has clearly demonstrated that farmers often use sections of dykes as field boundaries and this has probably gone on for centuries. The medieval scribes who wrote charters often use dykes as landmarks when describing estates. Early medieval people reused dykes as places to bury the dead. Perhaps after their abandonment they occupied a liminal area outside the control of kings and God where the condemned were executed; this would explain why so many are named after the Devil or pagan gods. There is little evidence that they were used (or reused) as meeting places, but equally we cannot be certain they were not.

As has already been speculated, the establishment of more stable kingdoms as well as the raids of the Vikings probably changed warfare forever. New raids came initially from abroad or were a part of wars between large stable kingdoms rather than by local warlords. These changes ended the use of dykes as military structures. When dykes were first built, warlords were raiding neighbouring areas to steal cattle. These warlords gradually set themselves up as kings, who then used raiding to force weaker neighbours to give tribute and/or submit to their overlordship. Gradually these evolved into more stable kingdoms, where rulers extracted surplus production from the land through large agricultural estates rather than raiding.

When the Vikings arrived, raiding resumed, but their raids were unpredictable. The first account of an Anglo-Saxon murdered by a Viking was at Portland in Dorset in 789, hardly the nearest British landfall from Scandinavia. Without obvious land routes to block, people ceased to excavate dykes across routeways. Early medieval rulers did not have the ability to mobilize enough manpower to guard an extended frontier, so they decided to construct points where their troops could hold up or sally forth from if the raiding force looked weaker than anticipated. These strongpoints are the *burhs* of the ninth century. Those dykes that already existed probably then became a nuisance to traders travelling along the routes that the earthworks blocked, so they were punctured where roads passed through the dykes. There does seem to be evidence that the Vikings carried on digging dykes like that at Reading, but they designed theirs to protect raiding parties rather than oppose them.

The radiocarbon and Optically Stimulated Luminescence dates suggest early medieval dyke construction peaked across the very late sixth and the first half of the seventh century. As Offa ruled 757–96, his dyke was probably constructed during the dying days of early medieval dyke building. The massive scale of his dyke and the labour involved could have outweighed any benefit it may have had in deterring Welsh raids. Perhaps this king (whose coinage and whose letters to Charlemagne demonstrate that he wished to be seen as a quasi-imperial ruler) made a massive and grandiose version of a common practical type of earthwork as a demonstration of his power. With better dating techniques, in the future we might discover that the larger earthworks are later in date and reflect the rise of kingdoms, even if this was probably not the original intention of the builders of most earthworks. Dyke building may have helped to create clearly defined kingdoms, but such stability may have signalled the end of the need for the shorter dykes to counter localized raiding.

The origin of early medieval dyke building in particular is more problematic. As this study found no early medieval dykes in the Highlands of Scotland, all the early medieval dykes were probably located in areas that at some point had been part of the Roman province of Britain. Presumably, the imperial authorities would not have allowed locals to build earthworks that blocked the Roman road network, so the dykes must post-date the end of Roman rule in Britain, say 400. If people could not predict the direction from which Viking attacks would come, presumably the same would be true of the early Anglo-Saxon raids from across the North Sea, or other seaborne raids from the north or west (the Irish, Scots or Picts). There is evidence that Iron-Age hill forts like Cadbury in Somerset were reoccupied in the immediate post-Roman period and perhaps these functioned in much the same way as *burhs* later did, as strongpoints against seaborne raiders (Cadbury was rebuilt as a *burh*). However, we should be cautious in assuming that every hill fort was reoccupied for military reasons; their association with the pre-Roman elite could also have been a draw.

Once the raiders from across the seas had established themselves in Britain and local people knew the direction their raids would take along known land routeways, dykes coupled with signal points would then have been the best form of defence. There is a great deal of debate as to when the Anglo-Saxons firmly established themselves in Britain, but from Bede onwards most historians have given a mid-fifth century date and we know from *The Anglo-Saxon Chronicle* that the Viking raids on Britain started in earnest in the ninth century. This gives a date range of roughly 450–850 for dykes to work against overland Anglo-Saxon raiding (though the British could have raided each other prior to this) and this is in fact a close

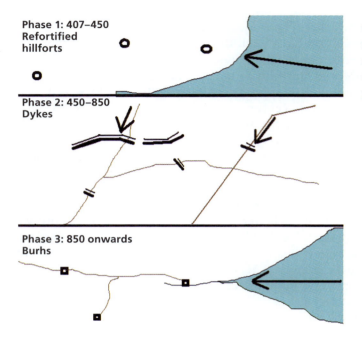

Changing military reactions to raiding in the early medieval period.

match for the archaeological dates of early medieval dykes. Pre-Viking raiding logically peaked in this time bracket. The transition from refurbished hill forts to dykes then to *burhs* can be summarized in the diagram included here. Note that this diagram is partly based on (and indebted to) one made by Stuart Brookes and first publicly shown at a 2007 conference at University College London.[43]

There are at least three possible inspirations for early medieval dyke building. Dykes may have been initially inspired by prehistoric earthworks; there are interestingly no prehistoric or early medieval dykes in Devon, while in Norfolk early medieval people seem to have reused the widespread pre-Roman earthworks. The fact that the Anglo-Saxons gave the name Grim (a god associated with war) to many prehistoric earthworks suggests they thought such dykes had a military purpose. The second possible inspiration (and the one most likely to have inspired the Britons) was the northern frontiers of Roman Britain. Roman signal towers, in particular those on the Yorkshire coast, may have inspired the signalling sites that I have postulated were associated with many early medieval dykes. The third possible source of inspiration for early medieval dyke building (and the structures most likely to have inspired Anglo-Saxon dyke builders) was the numerous dykes found in Jutland just prior to the Anglo-Saxons settling in Britain.

CHAPTER 7

Conclusions

The builders of most of early medieval dykes seem to have primarily designed them to prevent or combat raids. Many are short, hastily built structures with no gateways set back from borders and cutting routeways; 100 labourers could have built most of these earthworks in a summer. While it is likely most either deterred raids or caused raiders to turn elsewhere, there are hints from Welsh poetry and archaeological evidence that a few raiders tried to overcome these defences. Some dykes were probably built by peasants against aggressive raiding. The building and manning of these earthworks probably helped to bind communities together, possibly reinforcing local hierarchies and allowing the growth of small kingdoms in the lee of these earthworks. The raids probably also helped warlords to build up a powerbase and claim lordship over areas.

Towards the end of the dyke-building period, King Offa created an extremely long version of this type of utilitarian military feature along much of the length of the western border of Mercia. While the earlier dykes were simply designed to turn back raids, Offa's Dyke could have been a reflection of his imperialist ambitions, an attempt to manifest his power in the landscape and a way of unifying his people in opposition to the 'foreigners' (the *wealas*) to the west. It probably marked the end of this age of dyke building. Highly mobile Viking raiders could use their ships to attack anywhere along the coast and up major rivers; no longer could the path raiders would take be predicted and blocked, so dykes just became landmarks when laying out new estates.

The raids that these dykes tried to prevent probably had a major effect on early medieval Britain, but we should remember that raiding was sporadic rather than prevalent in all regions and at all periods in early medieval Britain. Farms would be burnt, communities would starve, people would be taken as slaves, women would be raped, artefacts of value stolen and political groupings destroyed. Aggressive and persistent Anglo-Saxon raids were possibly one of the major causes of the Anglicization of lowland Britain. Wealthy members of British society who were less able to defend themselves, like clerics, priests, administrators and teachers, would be obvious targets for raiders, so they would flee westwards or overseas to places like Brittany, as the sixth-century British writer Gildas records. This would undermine British culture and allow the Anglicization of areas with a predominantly British population. There is little evidence of Christianity in the western portion of Roman Britain; however, after the arrival of the Anglo-Saxons, there is good evidence for Christianity (such as stones carved with crosses and bearing Latin inscriptions) in early medieval Wales, Cornwall and Strathclyde. This is possibly because raiding pushed the Romanized Christian literate elite westwards.

Not all dykes were defences built by the Britons purely against the Anglo-Saxons. Raiding was probably endemic at times between and within all groups. The conversion to Christianity and the emergence of stable kingdoms in England from the seventh century onwards was probably widely welcomed, as the clergy condemned raiding and kings tried to curb or control it. Booty from raiding (like the Staffordshire Hoard) may have helped to establish kingdoms, especially Mercia, and collective attempts to stop such raids by building dykes, such as the Cambridgeshire Dykes, may have helped to unify kingdoms like East Anglia. Kings continued to go to war, the Welsh would continue to raid western Mercia and Viking attacks would restart the cycle of raiding, but by the mid-ninth century, localized raiding in England had declined sufficiently to allow the growth of nucleated settlements and trade. Critics may say that the emphasis on raiding made by this study when explaining the purpose of early medieval dykes is a simplistic 'rape and pillage' view of history, but merely claiming that earthworks are 'symbolic' without defining what that means is not an intrinsically more sophisticated theory and does not explain how the earthworks functioned. By ignoring the evidence of low-intensity conflict in the past, we are in danger of creating models that tell us very little about the lives of our ancestors and more about the concerns of modern scholars.

Warfare helped to create and shape early medieval Britain. The dykes that tried to stop the raids are the legacy of that conflict that remain in the modern landscape. Perhaps as we hike across these enigmatic grass-covered structures we can be grateful that we live in more peaceful times.

THE FUTURE OF EARLY MEDIEVAL WAR STUDIES

While this study has gone a long way in codifying the evidence for early medieval warfare, there is a great deal of scope for future scholars to do more. What follows is a list of suggestions to bring further understanding to the study of early medieval warfare. Some of these are ideas this study could not undertake because of time limits or a lack of resources.

Medieval Europe is a large area and a pan-European conference on early medieval warfare and defensive earthworks is needed. It is always interesting to see how others approach similar problems. As well as being divided nationally, scholarship is often split on thematic lines, with military and social historians sometimes seeming to speak different languages. Interdisciplinary approaches could bring new insights into the study of early medieval warfare.

In terms of dykes, science could help us understand so much more about these enigmatic structures. We need radiocarbon or Optically Stimulated Luminescence dates from a much wider sample of early medieval dykes. Though the Environment Agency has mapped large areas of the country using LIDAR, these data are patchy and only recently have they become publicly available (at present only about half of England has been mapped). It can help to find lost sections of dykes and clarify if hypothetical sections really did exist. LIDAR can map the edges of medieval marshland or river plains, putting the dyke into a clearer landscape context. We could see if these earthworks were in thinly settled border areas or in the middle of thickly settled farming land. Geophysics could also help in finding lost sections of dykes, but, as with LIDAR, it cannot differentiate from a later hedgerow built by a farmer that carried on from a dyke on the same alignment. The bones from burials found associated with early medieval dykes, especially those from Cambridgeshire, need re-evaluating using modern scientific techniques to explore the causes and circumstances of death. We need to be certain if these people fell in battle, were massacred, executed, or died of natural causes.

The work on Anglo-Saxon charters and their relationship to dykes carried out by this study is by no means exhaustive. Where charters mention dykes no longer visible in the landscape we should investigate these possible earthworks through archaeological investigation or non-intrusive means (like LIDAR or geophysics).

We live in an age of increasing access to information and even while this book was being written more became available online (journal articles, LIDAR and old maps). The author could use mapping programs to see how dykes fitted into the landscape and simulate the views from them without leaving his chair, though it is far more enjoyable to load the dog in the car and explore the dykes! By using GIS (Geographic Information System) we can analyse the landscape for viewsheds, that is, map what can (and cannot) be seen from a dyke. This increasing access to data will mean that future researchers will be able to find out even more information, more quickly. Predicting how this will affect future scholarship is impossible.

On a practical level, it might be an illuminating exercise for a group of students to try to build a section of dyke using early medieval methods and tools. This would give an insight into the difficulties involved and the amount of labour needed. Then it would be interesting to get some re-enactors to see how easy it is to attack or defend a dyke using replica early medieval weapons.

While I am confident in my ideas, it is likely that future scholars will use the data on the dykes in this book and other new discoveries to find innovative ways of looking at the subject and no doubt draw different conclusions. When writing this book, I was acutely aware of the list of illustrious scholars who have studied early medieval warfare and the dykes built to counter hostile raids: William Stukeley; Sir Richard Colt Hoare; Pitt Rivers, O.G.S. Crawford; Sir Cyril Fox; Sir Mortimer Wheeler; T.C. Lethbridge; Leslie Alcock; Phillip Rahtz; and David Hill. To have stood on the shoulders of such giants was a huge privilege.

APPENDIX I

The Dykes Listed and Measured

This Appendix gives the raw data on which the conclusions about early medieval defences were built. I have divided the dykes by period and listed them giving their main characteristics. For descriptions of the earthworks, *see* Appendix II. If the evidence does not point to a single period when it was initially constructed, then it is classed as a *possible* early medieval dyke, but the reader should note that such dykes could equally be possible prehistoric, possible Roman, possible Viking or possible later medieval dykes.

I have grouped the dykes into the following categories:

- **Probable prehistoric/Roman/early medieval/Viking/later medieval or modern dykes.** Some of these dykes have good documentary or direct archaeological evidence that suggests they are of a certain date. For the rest, there is evidence that brackets their construction to that period, for example, a dyke mentioned in a Saxon charter cannot be later medieval and if it cuts a Roman feature, it is probably post-Roman, so it is defined as a probable early medieval dyke.
- **Possible early medieval dykes.** These are dykes with no good dating evidence, so could be early medieval, but equally they could date from another period.
- **Probable rebuilt prehistoric or Roman dykes.** These have evidence of Roman or prehistoric construction and good evidence (like radiocarbon-dated deposits within the bank) of an early medieval rebuild.
- **Possible rebuilt prehistoric or Roman dykes.** These dykes show signs of rebuilding with some evidence either of a prehistoric/Roman construction or an early medieval rebuild.
- **Probable reused prehistoric or Roman dykes.** These are dykes with evidence suggesting Roman or prehistoric construction and good evidence of use in the early medieval period (for example, there is archaeological evidence that a nearby early medieval dyke would need this pre-existing earthwork to form a complete system), but no sign of rebuilding.
- **Possible reused prehistoric or Roman dykes.** These dykes show no sign of rebuilding, but there is some evidence of early medieval reuse.

I have identified 118 potentially early medieval dykes, which divides up into 24 dykes probably built in the early medieval period, 85 possible examples and 9 earlier dykes that people in the early medieval period may have reused or rebuilt. This is far more than any other study, which allows us to generalize about their size, form, length and location from a far more representative sample. Even if we take into account the fact that this study subdivides some dykes (like Offa's, the Swaledale Dykes and the East Hampshire Dykes), this is a significant increase, even though I eliminated a number of dykes erroneously ascribed to this period by earlier scholars. This is not due to archaeologists finding new earthworks, as apart from the odd discovery, like Cowlod Dyke in 1992, the only significant number of new dykes discovered in modern times were those found in Wales during fieldwork for the Ordnance Survey in the late nineteenth century. Rather, it is because this is the most comprehensive study of these earthworks yet undertaken.

The information I obtained from research and fieldwork is summarized below in a series of tables. Tables are given for each date range group (probable early medieval, possible early medieval, probable prehistoric/Roman and so forth), with columns for the following:

- **Name:** in the order that it appears in the gazetteer (*see* Appendix II).
- **Length metres:** this is an estimate of the probable original length in metres of the earthwork.
- **Boundaries:** the percentage of the dyke contiguous (on the same course) with parish boundaries (if the figure is not 100% or 0%, the length of the contiguous section is given in brackets in metres).
- **Structure:** this is the number of banks/ditches that make up the earthwork, with the lowest feature always given first. For example, CDB means there is a single counterscarp bank (C) downhill of a single ditch (D), which is downhill of a single bank (B). BDB means a single ditch is sandwiched between a pair of banks.
- **Excavated (abbreviated to Excc.d):** if there is a 'YES' in this column archaeologists have excavated the earthwork.
- **Ditch size:** the approximate original depth and width of the main ditch in metres.
- **Bank size:** the approximate original height and width of the main bank in metres.
- **Berm:** whether or not there is evidence of a berm (that is, a level space between the bank and the ditch).
- **Revetment:** whether there are signs of a revetment, though without excavation it is rare to find evidence, especially if the revetment was wooden.
- **Ankle-breaker:** whether there is evidence of an 'ankle-breaker' or 'cleaning slot'.

- **Shape:** whether the ditch is U- or V-shaped and the slope of the ditch sides in degrees.
- **Volume metres^3:** this is a calculation of the volume of earth in cubic metres moved to make the original structure. It is calculated by multiplying the probable length by a cross section of either the ditch or bank, then multiplying that figure by 0.6 (the multiplier discussed earlier applied because banks are not square or triangular in profile, but rather squashed semicircles).

The following rows appear at the bottom of the tables (note that there is a separate table summarizing all the probable/possible rebuilt/reused dykes, as there are too few in each of these categories for any meaningful statistical analysis):

- **Mean:** this gives the mean average of the data in each column.
- **Total:** totals for each column for numeric features like length and width.
- **Range:** the range of values of the data in that column.
- **Median:** this gives the median length and volume; this row only appears in the probable early medieval dykes table because some of the dykes are so much larger than others, thus mean averages are skewed.

Evidence of a marker bank, gateways, palisades, branches and other phenomena only rarely found or the evidence of which cannot be succinctly summarized in a table are discussed after each table rather than having columns with almost no entries.

When looking at the characteristics of early medieval dykes we should remember that the probable (as opposed to possible) early medieval dykes might be unrepresentative, as archaeologists are more likely to investigate larger and more famous dykes for dating evidence. Note that the figure for parish boundaries contiguous with Wat's Dyke is far lower than given in many other studies because this calculation does not count sections where the builders, possibly to save on labour, used a convenient river to fill a gap in the dyke.

There is some sign of rebuilding and reuse for some of the dykes in this category (Bokerley Dyke and both West and East Wansdyke), but there is not sufficient evidence to tell if this was widespread. While Becca Banks was cut through rock, the rest were dug through soil.

There is evidence of a marker bank at Fleam Dyke, Bran Ditch, Devil's Ditch, Offa's Dyke and Wat's Dyke, but no conclusive evidence for palisades or gateways (in fact, many clearly cut roads). The similarities in the construction methods of Offa's Dyke and Wat's Dyke possibly suggest the same group of people built them: they both have a marker bank; a layer of stones at the base of the bank; and a counterscarp in hillier sections to emphasize the ditch. Most dykes face downhill unless they were built in flat areas.

List of Probable Early-Medieval Dykes

Name	Length metres	Boundaries	Structure	Excc.d	Ditch size	Bank size	Berm	Revetment	Ankle-Breaker	Shape	Volume metres[3]
Becca Banks	4,200	0%	DB(?D)	YES	3.25/8	2.4/10	NO	?	NO	U 50°	65,520
The Rein	1,900	100%	DB		2/8	2/9.8					22,344
Rudgate Dyke	100	0%	BDD	YES	1.45/3	?			NO	U 40°	261
Heronbridge	550	0%	BD	YES	3/5.8	1/6	NO	YES	NO	U or V 45–50°	5,742
Grey Ditch	1,200	0%	DB	YES	2.2/6	1.6/7.4	NO	?	NO	V 40°	9,504
Clawdd Mawr (Llanfyllin)	450	18% (80)	DB	YES	1.8/2.5	1.6/3.8					1,215
Crugyn Bank (inc. Two Tumps)	2,720	0%	CDB		0.6/2	1.2/6				V	11,750
Giant's Grave Short Ditch	250	0%	CDB	YES	1.3/4	0.7/4.3	NO	NO	YES	V 30°	780
	640	16%(100)	CDB(D)		1.8/1.5	1/3					1,152
Upper Short Ditch	500	0%	DB	YES	1.5/3.5	0.9/6					1,575
Offa's Dyke	95,000	22% (21,200)	DB (or CDBD)	YES	2/7	2.5/7	NO	NO	NO	V 30°	798,000
Rowe Ditch	3,750	0%	DB	YES	2.5/5	1.5/6	NO	NO?	NO	V	28,125
Wat's Dyke	59,000	4% (2,200)	(C)DB	YES	2/6	2/6.4	NO?	YES?	YES	V 40–50°	424,800
Bran Ditch	5,000	100%	DB	YES	1.95/6	2.1/8.5	YES	YES	NO	U 40°	35,100
Devil's Ditch	12,000	90% (10,800)	DB	YES	4.5/17	5/22	YES	YES	NO	U 60°	550,800
Fleam Dyke	5,200	100%	DB	YES	4.5/12	5/15	NO	?	NO	V 35° then U 60°	168,480
Fossditch	9,000	100%	DB	YES	1.4/8	1/10.5	YES	NO	NO	U 15°–40°	60,480

THE DYKES LISTED AND MEASURED

Name	Length metres	Boundaries	Structure	Excc.d	Ditch size	Bank size	Berm	Revetment	Ankle-Breaker	Shape	Volume metres^3
Pear Wood	400	0%	CDB	YES	1.8/5.7	1.2/8	NO	NO	NO	V 35°–40°	2,462
Aelfrith's Dyke	5,000	100%	(D?)DB	YES	0.5/2.9	0.8/8	YES	NO	NO	U	4,350
Bica's Dyke	400	100%	DB	NO	0.45/2	0.45/2	NO	NO	NO		216
Bury's Bank	1,500	0%	DB	YES	2/9	1.2/9	NO	NO	NO	V 30°	16,200
West Wansdyke	13,500	1.5% (200)	CBD	YES	2.2/5	1.7/12	YES	YES	YES	U and V 45°	89,100
East Wansdyke	20,400 (1,800)	8.9%	CBD	YES	2.5/8	2.5/9.5	NO?	NO	YES?	U and V 40°	244,800
Bokerley Dyke	5,295	81% (4,220)	DB	YES	3/10	3/11	NO	NO	NO	V 40°	95,310
Mean	10,331	27% with parish boundaries (5% with county boundaries)	DB (33% with C)		2.1/6.2	1.8/8.3	NO	NO	NO	V 41°	109,919
Total	247,955	67,100 with parish boundaries (13,295 with county boundaries)			50.2/147.9	42.35/191.2					2,638,066
Range	100–95,000				0.45–4.5/1.5–17	0.45–5/2–22					216–798,000
Median	3,235										19,272

List of Possible Early-Medieval Dykes

Name	Length metres	Boundaries	Structure	Excc.d	Ditch size	Bank size	Berm	Revetment	Ankle-Breaker	Shape ditch	Volume metres³
Bardon Mill	188	0%	DB		?	?					2,000?
Catrail (Picts' Work Ditch)	4,000	0%	D		0.9/6						12,960
Catrail proper	9,500	0%	BDC		0.6/2.7	0.3/2.9					9,234
Wallace's Trench	500	0%	DB		1.25/4.6	1.8/5.5					2,970
Heriot's Dyke (Haerfields)	1000	0%	B		1/2						1200
Heriot's Dyke (Greenlaw)	2,000	0%	CDB		0.85/3	1/4					4,800
Military Way	5,000	0%	DB		1.9/8.3	2/2					12,000
Bank Slack	2,000	0%	(C?)BD		3/6	3/14				V 40°	21,600
Bar Dyke	500	0%	DB		1.8/7	1.5/7					3,780
Broomhead Dyke	1,200	0%	DB		2/3	1/3				V	4,320
Dane's Dyke	4,000	100%	DB	YES	2/10	4.2/20.5	NO	YES	NO	V	48,000
Gilling Wood	500	100%	DB		1.1/6.4	2.3/12				40°	2,112
Park Pale	650	0%	DB		2? /0.5?	1.5/4					2,340
Swaledale western group	960	0%	CDB		1.4/7	2/14	NO	YES			5,645
Swaledale middle group north	580	0%	DB		?/?	1/8	NO				2,784
Swaledale Hodic	580	0%	DB		1.2/9	2/15	NO				3,758
Swaledale Ruedic	680	0%	DB		1.25/7	1.6/10	NO				3,570
Swaledale southern	390	0%	DB		?/?	2/7	YES				3,276
Tor Dike	2,000	100%	DB		3/6	1/3	YES			V 35–55°	21,600
Nico Ditch	6,000	55% (3,300)	D(B?)	YES	2/3.75	(1.3/5?)			NO	U 30–40°	27,000
Calver Dyke	500	100%	DBD		1/2.5	0.5/3					1,500

Name	Length metres	Boundaries	Structure	Excc.d	Ditch size	Bank size	Berm	Revetment	Ankle-Breaker	Shape ditch	Volume metres[3]
Aberbechan	1,200	0%	(?D)BDB		?	2/7.5					21,600
Abernaint	545	25%	BD		2/7	3.5/8					9,156
Bedd Eiddil	94	0%	DB		0.5/2.75	0.4/2.5					78
Bwlch y Cibau (west)	900	0%	DB		?/3.7	1.5/7					5,670
Bwlch y Clawdd	180	0%	B(D?B?)		?/?	1.5/4.3					697
Bwlch yr Afan	192	0%	DBD		1/1	1.25/3					230
Clawdd-trawscae	90	0%	DB		0.6/3	1/3					162
Tyla-Glas	180	0%	DB		0.6/3	1/3					324
Cefn Eglwysilan and Tywn Hywel dykes	1,540	0%	DB		?/?	0.5/4.3					1,987
Cefn Morfydd	400	0%	DB(D?)		0.6/4.3	1/5.8					1,392
Cefn-y-Crug	304	0%	DB		0.6/5.8	0.6/5					635
Clawdd Llesg	170	0%	BD		1/7	1.5/7					1,071
Clawdd Mawr (Dyfed)	1,400	0%	DB		1.2/7.5	1.5/8					10,080
Clawdd Mawr (Foel)	700	0%	BD		?/?	1.75/6					4,410
Clawdd Mawr Glyncorrwg/Bwlch Garw	1,300	0%	DB		?/?	1/(1.5?)					1,170
Clawdd Seri	750	100%	(CDB)D		0.8/7	0.3/2.1					2,520
Cowlod	108	0%	B(D)		?/?	1.2/4.5					350
Ffos Toncenglau	1,200	0%	(D)B		?/4	1.2/4.2					3,629
Fron Hill Dyke	400	(100%?)	(D)B		?/?	1.9/7.3		YES			3,329
Lower Short Ditch	750	100%	DB(D?)		1.3/4	1.5/8					5,400
Pen y Clawdd	260	0%	BD		0.9/6.8	1.9/8.5					2,519
Red Hill	110	100%	BD		1.6/3.3	0.8/4.7					349
Shepherd's Well	140	100%	DB(C)		1.2/4	1/4					403
Tor Clawdd	800	0%	DB	YES	1.2/4.5	0.3/4.5				U	2,592
Ty Newydd	900	0%	DB		0.9/6	2/6	YES	NO	NO	U 20–30°	6,480
Vervil Dyke	188	100%	DB	YES	2.5/9	1.2/8					2,538

List of Possible Early-Medieval Dykes (continued)

Name	Length metres	Boundaries	Structure	Excc.d	Ditch size	Bank size	Berm	Revetment	Ankle-Breaker	Shape ditch	Volume metres³
Wantyn Dyke (northern)	3,000	0%	DB		0.5/4	0.7/7				8,820	
Beachley Bank	1,400	0%	DB	YES	1.5/4	2/10	NO	NO	NO	V 30–50°	5,040
Offa's Dyke in Herefordshire	8,250	19% (1,600)	DB		2/4	2/15					39,600
Offa's Dyke in the Wye – English Bicknor	1,200	0%	(CD)B	YES	1.5/5	2.1/11	YES	YES			5,400
Offa's Dyke in the Wye – St Briavel's	14,000	0%	CDBD	YES	0.6/4	1/10	YES	NO			20,160
Minchinhampton Bulwarks	2,300	0%	DB	YES	2.3/7	1.2/4.9	YES	YES	NO	V 45°	22,218
High Dyke	2,000	0%	DB	NO	0.6/15	1/18					10,800
Bunns' Bank	3,000	100%	DB	NO	?/?	0.7/6					7,560
Horning	800	0%	DBDB	NO	?/13	2/12					11,520
Panworth	500	0%	DB	NO	0.5/4	1/6					1,800
Black Ditch Snelsmore	1,000	0%	DB	NO	1.75 /4.5	1.75 /4.5					4,725
Crookham Common earthworks	1,550	0%	DB and BDB	NO /1.8?	0.3 /1.8?	0.6					1,004
Grim's Bank Padworth	4,600	0%	DB	YES	1.5/7.5	1.3/6	YES	?NO	NO	V 20–30°	31,050
Bedwyn Dyke	2,800	0%	DB	NO	2/9	2/6.3					30,240
Mount Prosperous dyke	250	100%	B?	NO	?/?	?/?					?
Inkpen Dyke	500	0%	?	NO	?/?	?/?					?
Bolster Bank	3,300	0%	DB	NO	1.4/6	3/6					35,640
Dodman	600	0%	CDB	NO	4.5?/?	2/6					4,320
Giant's Grave	350	0%	DB	NO	?/7	2/5					2,100
Giant's Hedge	11,000	0%	DB	YES	0.8/5.5	1.5/3.3	NO	YES	NO	?	29,040

THE DYKES LISTED AND MEASURED

Name	Length metres	Boundaries	Structure	Excc.d	Ditch size	Bank size	Berm	Revetment	Ankle-Breaker	Shape ditch	Volume metres³
Stepper Point	300	0%	DB	NO	?/?	?/?					?
New Ditch	800	0%	DB	NO	1.5/7	2.3/9					5,040
Ponter's Ball	1,050	19% (200)	DB	YES	2.4/8	3.5/27	NO		NO	U 40°	12,096
Battery Banks	2,240	0%	DB		1.5/8	1/7.5				U	16,128
Devil's Ditch Doles Wood	2,100	0%	DB		0.7/6	0.5/3					5,292
Devil's Ditch Pepper Hills Firs	2,000	0%	CDB		1.7/12	1.2/8					11,520
Devil's Ditch Wonston	3,050?				?/?	?/?					?
East Tisted-Colemore	4,000	2% (80)	(C)DB		3/13.5	3/13.5					97,200
Froxfield short dyke A	274	0%	DB		2.4/12	2.4/12					4,735
Froxfield short dyke B	100	0%	DB		2.4/12	2.4/12					1,728
Froxfield short dyke C	100	0%	DB		2.4/12	2.4/12					1,728
Froxfield short dyke D	100	0%	DB		2.4/12	2.4/12					1,728
Froxfield Long Dyke	5,350	5% (290)	DB		2.5/9	2/9					72,225
Hayling Wood (including branch)	2,900	0%	B or BDBD		?	2.2/5					19,140
Festaen Dic (Hartley Witney)	2,200	13% (300)	DB		1/7	1/7	YES				9,240
Faesten Dyke (Kent)	2,400	39% (950)	DB	YES	1.8/6	1.5/7	NO	NO	NO	V 40°	15,552
Fullinga Dyke	20,000	100%	DB		0.8/4	0.5/4					38,400
Surrey–Kent Dyke	320	100%	DB		1.5/9	3/16					2,592
Mean	1,990	24%	DB (13% with C)		1.5/6.3	1.6/7.4	NO (53%)	YES (55%)	NO	V (62%) 38°	10,748
Total	169,213	39,928			95.5/ 425.45	123.45/ 582.4					870,601
Range	94–20000				0.3– 4.5/ 0.5–15	0.3– 4.2/ 1.5–27					78– 72,225

List of Probable Rebuilt Prehistoric or Roman Dykes

Name	Length metres	Boundaries	Structure	Excc.d	Ditch size	Bank size	Berm	Revetment	Ankle-Breaker	Shape ditch	Volume metres^3
Devil's Ditch Garboldisham	2,800	100%	DB?	YES	1/6	1/1.8			NO	U 60°–40°	10,080
Combs Ditch	4,500	56% (2,500)	DB	YES	1.8/7	1.4/7.3	NO	?	NO	U 40°	34,020
Mean	3,650	73%	DB		1.4/6.5	1.2/4.6			NO	U 40°	22,050
Total	7,300	5,300			2.8/13	2.4/9.1					44,100
Range	2,800–4,500				1–1.8 6–7	1–1.4/ 1.8–7.3					10,080–34,020

Note that the volume figures for these and the possible rebuilt dykes unfortunately includes the amount of earth moved to build the original prehistoric/Roman dyke as without highly detailed excavation results it is impossible to estimate just the early medieval refurbishment figure.

Probable Reused Prehistoric or Roman Dykes

Name	Length metres	Boundaries	Structure	Excc.d	Ditch size	Bank size	Berm	Revetment	Ankle-Breaker	Shape ditch	Volume metres^3
Harrow-Pinner Grim's Dyke	7,000	29% (2000)	DB	YES	1.7/5.7	2.4/15		NO		V	40,698
Mean	7,000	29%	DB		1.7/5.7	2.4/15		NO		V	40,698
Total	7,000	2,000			1.7/5.7	2.4/15					40,698

List of Possible Rebuilt Prehistoric or Roman Dykes

Name	Length metres	Boundaries	Structure	Excc.d	Ditch size	Bank size	Berm	Revetment	Ankle-Breaker	Shape ditch	Volume metres³
Bichamditch	5,000	100%	DB	YES	2.7/6	2.5/7	YES	NO	NO	40–90°	48,600
Launditch	5,000	60% (3,000)	DB	YES	1.8/5	1.5/8.5				U 30–40	27,000
Black Ditches Suffolk	7,000	25% (1,750)	DB(D?)	YES	2/8.5	2/6.5	NO?		NO	U 30°	71,400
Mean	5,667	57%	DB		2.2/6.5	2/7.3			NO	U 43°	49,000
Total	17,000	9,750			6.5/19.5	6/22					14,7000
Range	5,000–7,000				1.8–2.7 /5–8.5	1.5–2.5/ 6.5–8.5					27,000–71,400

The Black Ditches in Suffolk have an irregular ditch profile, probably caused by recutting.

The Calver Dyke and Blwch yr Afan volumes are double the ditch figure, as there are two ditches; with the Aberbechan Dyke, it is double the bank figure. There is evidence that Clawdd Mawr (Dyfed), Shepherd's Well, Ponter's Ball and Faesten Dyke in Kent were refurbished. The ditches of Broomhead Dyke, Beachley Bank, Clawdd Mawr Foel, Clawdd Mawr Llanfyllin and Minchinhampton Bulwarks were dug through rock, the rest through soil. There is evidence of a marker bank at Vervil, which also has stones lining the front of the bank, which may have acted as a guideline for the builders. Note how those dykes often thought to be part of Offa's Dyke (including Beachley Bank) are much smaller than Offa's Dyke proper, suggesting that they are separate earthworks.

There is little conclusive evidence for gateways at any of these dykes. While most of the dykes face downhill, Abernaint, Catrail proper, Clawdd Mawr (Foel), Red Hill Cross Dyke and Hayling Wood all distinctly face uphill. Bwlch y Clawdd faces uphill, though this may be due to the steepness of the slope forcing the builders to quarry from the uphill side. Cowlod and Cefn-y-Crug do not have a distinctive uphill or downhill aspect, as they are in saddles of land between two slopes. Clawdd Llesg faces slightly uphill, but has flanks 'guarded' by streams and it has a hill behind it.

List of Possible Reused Prehistoric or Roman Dykes

Name	Length metres	Boundaries	Structure	Excc.d	Ditch size	Bank size	Berm	Revetment	Ankle-Breaker	Shape ditch	Volume metres[3]
Black Dyke	4,000	37.5% (1,500)	BD		1.8/4.3	1.4/4					18,576
Scot's Dyke	12,000	25% (3,000)	CDB	YES	1.5/5.5 /11.75	1.65	NO	NO	NO	U 40°	59,400
Bwlch y Cibau (north)	450	0%	DBDBD		?	?					?
Mean	5,483	27%	?		1.65 /4.9	1.5/7.9	NO	NO	NO	U 40°	38,988
Total	16,450	4,500			3.3/9.8	3.05/ 15.75					77,976
Range	450– 12,000				1.5–1.8 /4.3– 5.5	14– 1.65/ 1.4– 11.75					18,576– 59,400

The only evidence for a gateway for the dykes in this section is on Scot's Dyke, but we should note that the gateway, like the earthwork, was probably constructed in the prehistoric period.

Summary of all Probable/Possible Reused/Rebuilt Dykes

Name	Length metres	Boundaries	Structure	Ditch size	Bank size	Berm	Revetment	Ankle-Breaker	Shape ditch	Volume metres[3]
Mean	3,606	63%	DB	1.8/6	7.7	NO	NO	NO	U 43°	38,722
Total	32,450	20,550		14.05/48	14.2/61.85					309,774
Range	450–12,000			0.7–2.7/ 2–8.5	0.3–4.8/ 1.8– 12.65					10,080– 71,400

List of Probable Prehistoric or Roman Dykes

Name	Length metres	Boundaries	Structure	Excc.d	Ditch size	Bank size	Berm	Revetment	Ankle-Breaker	Shape ditch	Volume metres³
Grim's Ditch (Leeds)	8,800	23% (2,000)	DB	YES	2.2/4.5	2.1/12.65	YES YES	NO NO	NO NO	V 35– V 35–50°	52,272
South Dyke	2,700	0%	DB	YES	1.5/7	1.5/11.5	NO	NO	NO	U 40–50°	17,010
Roman Rig	25,200	24% (6,000)	DB(D?)	YES	1.7/2	2/4.5	?			V 45°	51,408
Whitford Dyke	10,000	4% (400)	DBD	YES	1.6/4.2	0.3/5.4		NO	NO	U	80,640
Devil's Mouth	140	0%	DBD	YES	0.7/5	1.5/6				U	756
King Lud's	1,500	100%	DBD, BDB or BDBDB		1.9/8	1/4.5				U and V	27,360
Foulding Dykes	1,300+	0%	?		?	?					?
Miles Ditches	3,000	0%	DBDBD?	YES	1.2/3.5	?			NO	V 30°	22,680
Bucks–Herts Grim's Ditch	8,591	24% (2,100)	BD	YES	1.2/5.75	1.2/6	NO	NO	NO	V 30–50°	35,567
Aves Ditch	5,000	60% (3,000)	DB	YES	1/3.5	1.8/4	NO	NO		V 40°	10,500
Berks Downs Grim's Ditch	15,000	29% (4,400)	BD?	YES	1.25/5.75	1.1/5.5	NO	NO	NO	V 45–50°	64,688
Hug's Ditch	3,000	100%	DB		?	?					?
Reading–Oxford Road	300	0%	B			4.8/10					8,640
South Oxfordshire Grim's Ditch	6,000	17% (1,000)	DB	YES	2.75/5.7	0.7/5	YES	YES	NO	U 50°	56,430
Cranborne Chase Grim's Ditch	20,000	25% (4,900)	DBD		1/6	0.5/2					72,000
Tisted Cross Valley Dyke (N)	170	0%	DBDB		1/5	1/3					1,020
Tisted Cross Valley Dyke (S)	200	0%	DB		1/5	1/3					600
Riddlesdown Dyke	200	0%	DBDB		?	?					?
Mean	6,172	25%	DB		1.4/5.1	1.5/5.9	NO	NO	NO	V 42.5°	33,438

(continued overleaf)

List of Probable Prehistoric or Roman Dykes (continued)

Name	Length metres	Boundaries	Structure	Excc.d	Ditch size	Bank size	Berm	Revetment	Ankle-Breaker	Shape ditch	Volume metres³
Total	111,101	28,300			20/ 70.9	20.5/ 83.05					501,571
Range	140– 25,200				0.7– 2.75/ 2–8	0.3– 4.8/ 3– 12.65					600– 80,640

Note that the percentage of the length of prehistoric dykes that are on the same alignment as parish boundaries is similar to the early medieval dykes, confirming that the latter were not built as border markers.

List of Probable Later Medieval Dykes

Name	Length metres	Boundaries	Structure	Excc.d	Ditch size	Bank size	Berm	Revetment	Ankle-Breaker	Shape ditch	Volume metres³
King's Wicket	200	0%	DB		?	1/3					360
Deil's Dyke	25,300	0.8% (200)	B		1.5/4.1	2/1.7					86,020
Senghenydd Dyke	12,000	29% (3,500)	DB		1.5/4.1	1.2/4.9					44,280
Double Banks	2,000	100%	DBD		1.8/2.4	?/6					10,368
Reading – Coombe Bank	300	100%	DB		?/?	?/?					?
Mean	7,960	15%	DB		1.7/3.25	1.4/3.9					35,257
Total	39,800	6,000			3.3/6.5	4.2/15.6					141,028
Range	200– 25,300				1.5–1.8/ 12.4–4.1	1–2/ 1.7–6					360– 86,020

When calculating the volume of Deil's Dyke the 60% multiplier was not used as it was a wall of stacked turves rather than an earthen bank, so had a rectangular rather than a curved profile. The volume figure for the Double Banks is double the ditch figure as it has two similar sized ditches. Even though the parochial system postdates some of these dykes, sections of earthworks are contiguous with parish boundaries either because the latter are not as fixed in the landscape as often thought or the dyke followed a pre-existing boundary.

APPENDIX II

The Dykes Described

When analysing the written evidence, it is clear that most of the locations of early medieval conflicts are lost to us. Even where the chroniclers give us the name of a town or river that we can identify, there is rarely the detail to narrow down the location. Looking at the modern landscape with such vague information and thinking we can ascertain the tactics used in the early medieval period is a fool's errand. That said, the defensive dykes do still exist and anyone wishing to walk in the footsteps of early medieval raiders (or people wishing to confront these attackers) can use this section to find the earthworks.

This Appendix lists the possible early medieval dykes of Britain. Although an effort has been made to limit it to earthworks from the period AD400–850, it not only includes every example for which there is positive evidence that it may be from that date range, but also some that scholars have assumed date from that period. This list has a variety of sources, including national and county lists of scheduled monuments as well as various published gazetteers of earthworks. Note that this study assumes that the face of the dyke is the side with the ditch (a dyke with only a bank or a ditch, or a bank with a ditch on both sides obviously does not face in any direction).

This study does not list the dykes alphabetically, as some do not have names and many share the same moniker (often with the 'Devil' or 'Grim' in the name), but they are instead broadly divided into geographic groupings mainly based on historic counties (pre-1974) or groups of associated earthworks. At the beginning of each section there is a paragraph explaining the reasoning behind the grouping (there is some logic to it even if it eludes the reader!).

Although some are inaccessible, being on private land (usually farmland), many run across open-access areas (moorland or downland), or have footpaths that follow them. If you are planning to visit one, I would recommend using an Ordnance Survey map (which is why the grid references of the dykes are included) and of course always respect the Countryside Code.

NORTHERN BRITAIN

This region covers all of Britain north of Hadrian's Wall, including the

156 THE DYKES DESCRIBED

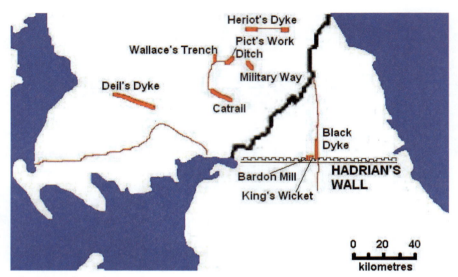

The dykes of Northern Britain.

whole of Scotland, though most are near the Border. Earthworks in this area have survived better than those in more urbanized areas.

Bardon Mill Dyke and King's Wicket

These two west-facing dykes, the 188m long Bardon Mill Dyke (NY797696 to NY797694) and the 200m long western bank of King's Wicket (NY797695 to NY798693), run across open moorland between Bromlee Lough and Hadrian's Wall. Being parallel, they look like they were constructed at the same date, but while medieval ridge and furrow respect the former dyke it is found under the later, suggesting King' Wicket is a late or post-medieval stock enclosure not an early medieval dyke.

Looking north from Hadrian's Wall, with the Bardon Mill Dyke on the left and the King's Wicket on the right.

Black Dyke
This west-facing dyke runs north (with a convex curve to the west) from Whitelee Cleugh on Hadrian's Wall just east of Housesteads Fort for about 2.5 miles (4km) from across some bleak but stunning countryside to Sewingshield Crags (NY780737 to NY799700), with probably 1.2 miles (2km) unmade where the builders utilized natural features. Antiquarians used to think it extended much further at either end, but this is probably not the case. As Hadrian's Wall probably destroyed the southern end, the dyke is most likely prehistoric. However, the builders of the nearby Bardon Mill Dyke possibly chose the site for their earthwork as the Black Dyke and a north–south section of Hadrian's Wall would form a parallel defensible rear line, therefore it is probably a prehistoric dyke reused in the early medieval period.

Catrail (Including Wallace's Trench)
Scholars once thought the Catrail was a continuous earthwork, but it is now considered to be three distinct structures. The northern section (also called the Picts' Work Ditch) is a ditch that runs south-west from Linglie Hill near Galashiels (NT475305) to Mossilee near Selkirk (NT479358). As it is not continuous, it was probably only 2.5 miles (4km) long. The southern section of the Catrail faces south-west and runs from near Hoscote Burn (NT378123) to Roberts Linn (NT538026), a distance of some 12 miles (19km), though this is not continuous and probably only covers approximately half the distance. The third earthwork is the east-facing Wallace's Trench, which runs north–south on Minch Moor (NT386327 to NT386323) for about 500m.

Deil's Dyke
Nineteenth-century scholars mistakenly thought that this dyke ran from the south-west coast of Scotland eastwards to surround Galloway before turning south to the Solway Firth. There is an actual surviving 16-mile (25.7km) long bank called The Celtic or Deil's Dyke in the upper Nith valley (NS617114 to NS839051). As thirteenth- to fifteenth-century pottery was found in the core of the bank in 1981, this earthwork was probably the medieval forest boundary of the foresta de Senecastre (Sanquhar), established by Walter Steward in 1214.

Heriot's Dyke
Scholars once thought that this dyke ran from near Lauder east to the Blackadder Water. Most now consider it to be two separate structures: one a sinuous 0.6-mile (1km) long wall (NT575500 to NT584500) at Haerfields; and a second a straight 1.2-mile (2km) long south-facing dyke (NT704485 to NT721484) across Greenlaw Moor. The first record of the name (spelt 'Herriot') was in 1834; the name could be from Old English: here-geat or 'army gate'.

THE DYKES DESCRIBED

Military Way

This much mutilated earthwork, which faces south-west, runs for about 3.1 miles (5km) (NT512320 to NT549285) between Selkirk and Bowden, though Crawford suggested it extended a further 0.6 miles (1km) northwards (to NT506327) on Faldonside Loch. Although traditionally thought to be a Roman road, this is unlikely, as small lochs like Lady Moss cut it.

YORKSHIRE, CUMBRIA AND LANCASHIRE

The major problem with this region is deciding which dykes to include or exclude, as there are many intersting dykes in the region that are undoubtedly prehistoric or later medieval.

The dykes of northern England (including dykes in Yorkshire and Derbyshire).

ABERFORD DYKES AND GRIM'S DITCH

To the east of Leeds is a series of earthworks: in the valley of the River Cock are the Aberford Dykes (Becca Banks, also called The Ridge, South Dyke and The Rein); and about 3 miles (5km) to the west between Leeds and Garforth is the Grim's Ditch.

Becca Banks (also called The Ridge) is a south-facing earthwork that runs for 2.6 miles (4.2km) from Barwick to east of Aberford (SE403382 to SE445382) on the north bank of Cock Beck. The South Dyke is a north-facing earthwork that runs along the south side of Cock Beck for

THE DYKES DESCRIBED

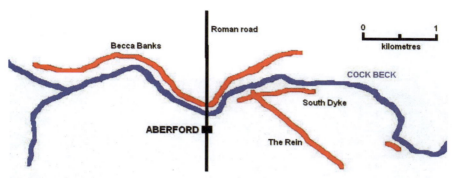

Aberford Dykes.

0.7 miles (1.1km) (SE437375 to SE447376). There is similar earthwork 132m long on the same alignment (SE459367 to SE460367) nearly 0.9 miles (1.5km) to the east, suggesting that it was originally 1.7 miles (2.7km) long. The Rein is a south-facing earthwork that runs for 1.2 miles (1.9km) (SE438376 to SE452365).

Grim's Ditch, an east-facing earthwork that runs south for 5.5 miles (8.8km) from Whinmoor (SE358380), almost to the banks of the River Aire (SE374295) south-west of Swillington, is difficult to see as it has been heavily damaged by agriculture. Becca Banks overlays an Iron-Age enclosure and possibly cuts a Roman road. In the bottom of the ditch fill second-century Roman sherds were found, halfway up was a cow pelvis that returned a radiocarbon date of AD559–674 and near the top of the ditch fill were some possible late Saxon sherds and thirteenth-century pottery. Radiocarbon dates from the ditch fill of Grim's Ditch suggests a prehistoric date.

Bank Slack

Bank Slack is a rather overgrown south-facing dyke that runs for about 1.2 miles (2km) (SE205546 to SE220548), following a sinuous route on the edge of a valley.

Bar Dyke

Bar Dyke is an earthwork facing north-west, which runs for about 500m (SK245944 to SK247948) across rough grazing land in the Peak District.

Looking north along Bar Dyke.

THE DYKES DESCRIBED

Looking south towards Broomhead Dyke (arrowed).

Broomhead Dyke
Broomhead Dyke is a north-facing dyke that runs for at least 1,200m (SK229961 to SK241965) along a ridge overlooking the ravine of Ewden Beck on the moors south-west of Stockbridge.

Dane's Dyke.

Dane's Dyke
Dane's Dyke is a west-facing earthwork that runs from coast to coast for 2.5 miles (4km) (TA213732 to TA216692), cutting off the scenic Flamborough Head from the mainland.

Gilling Wood Dyke
This is a 500m long west-facing dyke (NZ151047 to NZ153051) about 2.5 miles (4km) north of Richmond through the western edge of Gilling Wood (a perfect spot for walking an inquisitive dog).

Gilling Wood Dyke.

Nico Ditch
The earthwork once ran for at least 3.7 miles (6km) eastwards from Platt Fields (SJ849944), then curving north to end at Denton Golf Course (SJ905961), but has largely been obliterated by modern Manchester. There has been a series of archaeological investigations, though none found any dating evidence.

Looking east along Nico Ditch in Platt Fields.

Looking west along Park Pale.

Park Pale

Park Pale is (or rather was, as it has been almost completely ploughed flat) a straight north-facing earthwork that runs for about 650m (SE404754 to SE411755), cutting off a tongue of land between the River Swale and Cod Beck.

Roman Rig/Ridge

This is an east-facing (and heavily destroyed) dyke that runs on the ridge above the River Don from Sheffield north-east to Mexborough. South of the M1 there is only one dyke, the Single Rig, which runs from the

The north-east end of the Southern Rig.

centre of Sheffield (SK356880) about 3.5 miles (5.7km) north-east to near junction 34 of the M1 (possibly SK391916). To the north, there are two roughly parallel dykes. The north-western one, the Northern Rig, runs about 6.5 miles (10.5km) long north-north-east to Mexborough (SK422984 to SE465000).

The easterly branch, the Southern Rig, is about 5.6 miles (9km) long and runs north-north-east for just over 0.6 miles (1km), before turning east to finish just west of Kilnhurst (SK457975). An unpublished excavation in 1973 produced radiocarbon dates of c.AD280 and c.2090BC from the dyke, suggesting that the earthwork is probably prehistoric or Roman.

Rudgate Dyke
Excavations in the 1960s on a north-south Roman road called Rudgate (at SE459422) revealed that someone had utilized the road to build a 100m long east-facing dyke. As the earthwork destroyed the Roman road surface, it is probably early medieval.

Scot's Dyke
This east-facing dyke runs for about 7.5 miles (12km) (NZ197107 to NZ182008) from near the late Iron-Age Stanwick Camp south to the River Swale just east of Richmond. Samples of the silt at the bottom of the ditch tested during 2007 by Optically Stimulated Luminescence and archaeomagnetic dating produced a late Iron-Age date, suggesting a prehistoric date. The possible reference from Y Gododdin mentioned earlier suggests that it was possibly reused in the early medieval period.

The southern end of Scot's Dyke.

THE DYKES DESCRIBED

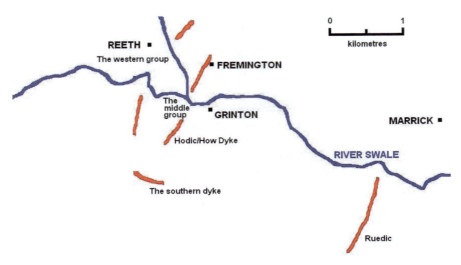

Swaledale Dykes.

Swaledale Dykes
These generally east-facing dykes block access up Swaledale. As they all are markedly larger than the prehistoric, medieval and modern field boundaries, they could just as easily be early medieval as prehistoric.

The Western Group The western group consists of two east-facing dykes, one north of Reeth about 290m long (SE043998 to SE040996) and one south of Reeth 670m long (SE037987 to SE036980).

Looking north along the southern earthwork of the western group of the Swaledale Dykes.

THE DYKES DESCRIBED

Hodic, looking south.

The Middle Group These two east-facing dykes include a 580m long dyke north of the river (SE046993 to SE044988) and the 580m long Hodic or How Dyke south of the river (SE043984 to SE040979).

The Eastern Dyke – Ruedic The eastern dyke near Marrick just consists of an east-facing dyke south of the Swale called Ruedic, about 680m long (SE069975 to SE066969).

The Southern Dyke This dyke is unusual in that it is on the uplands and is south-facing. It runs for about 390m (from SE037975 to SE039973).

Tor Dyke
This south-facing dyke runs across moorland at the head of a scenic valley for about 1.2 miles (2km) (SD976756 to SD991754) at the head of Coverdale.

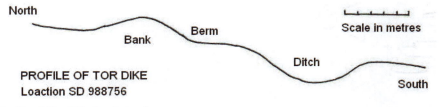

Profile of Tor Dike by the author.

Looking west along Tor Dike.

DERBYSHIRE

There are two possible dykes in Derbyshire.

Calver Dyke

This almost completely destroyed north–south dyke (SK225739 to SK226734) was probably originally nearly 500m long and is also known as Calver Cross Ridge Dyke and Longstone Edge Cross Ridge Dyke.

Grey Ditch

This north-facing dyke cuts a valley near Bradwell. It is in three sections: the western is about 200m long (SK167818 to SK169818); the central is about 900m long (SK171818 to SK179813); and the eastern section about 100m long (SK181812 to SK183812). In 1783, pieces of swords, spears, spurs and bridle bits were found 'on both sides and very near it', while archaeologists found an old plough soil sealed under the bank, which contained thirteen Romano-British pottery sherds, suggesting that it is early medieval.

Looking east along Grey Ditch.

THE DYKES DESCRIBED

WALES

This section does not contain the larger border earthworks like Offa's Dyke, just the shorter dykes from near the Anglo-Welsh border. The possible and probable early medieval dykes in Wales have a distinct distribution: most are in Powys and Glamorganshire. This may be a product of geography (with dykes being of little use in the mountainous west), or politics (especially if dyke building was a product of Anglo-Welsh conflict).

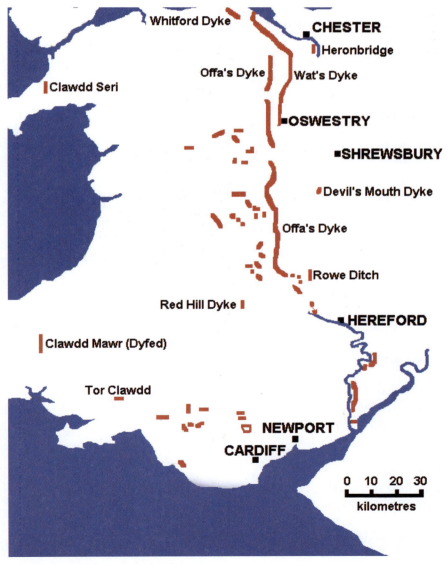

The dykes of Wales and the borders.

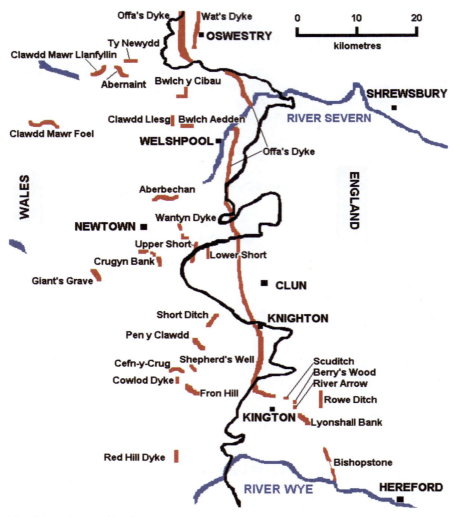

The dykes of central Wales.

Aberbechan Dyke
This south-facing earthwork near Llanllwchaiarnin, Powys runs sinuously eastwards uphill from a stream for approximately 1,200m through the land of a friendly farmer (SO127944 to SO135947).

Abernaint Dyke
This 545m long dyke, facing north-east (SJ122220 to SJ126217), is near Llanfyllin in Powys.

Bedd Eiddil Dyke
Bedd Eiddil Dyke is a 94m long north-facing earthwork cutting a ridgeway (SS969996 to SS972996) on the east side of the Afon Rhondda Fach valley.

THE DYKES DESCRIBED

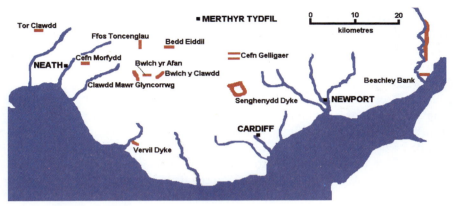

The dykes of south Wales.

Bwlch Aeddan Dyke
This north-facing scarp, which is 366m long (SJ169105 to SJ173106) and near Guislfield in Powys, is almost certainly a natural feature, not a dyke.

Bwlch y Cibau Dyke
Bwlch y Cibau Dyke is near Meifod in Powys (SJ178164 to SJ186171); the central part has multiple ditches and these are probably part of an earlier hill fort or enclosure incorporated into the earthwork.

Bwlch y Clawdd
Bwlch y Clawdd Dyke runs for 180m (SS940945 south-west to SS939944), cutting a narrow ridge just 1.2 miles (2km) east of Bwlch yr Afan.

Looking west along Aberbechan Dyke.

Bwlch yr Afan Dyke
This earthwork runs west to east for 192m, cutting a ridge (SS919950 to SS921951); a study of the soils under the bank suggested it is medieval.

Cefn Eglwysilan and Tywn Hywel Dykes
These three parallel north-facing cross-ridge dykes, running west from the west side of Senghenydd Dyke, are difficult to see nowadays. The most northerly, Tywn Hywel Cross Ridge Dyke, runs for about 440m (ST099999 to ST102912), while the middle dyke, which is unnamed, is about 200m long (ST100908 to ST103909). A small stream divides the southern earthwork and the portion to the west is called Cefn Eglwysilan Cross Dyke West, while that to the east of the stream is Cefn Eglwysilan Cross Dyke East. They are on the same alignment and, if originally continuous, would have been 900m long (ST098901 to ST104906).

Cefn Gelligaer (Clawddtrawscae and Tyla-Glas)
These two north-facing earthworks cut a ridge about 1.2 miles (2km) west of Bargoed. The northern dyke, Tyla-Glas Dyke, is about 180m long (SO110012 to SO111013), while the southern dyke, Clawddtrawscae Dyke (SO116002 to SO117003) is 90m long.

Cefn Morfydd Dyke
This is a north-facing 400m long dyke (SS790980 to SS787982) on a saddle of land between two small valleys.

Cefn-y-Crug Dyke
Cefyn-y-Crug Dyke is a south-facing dyke that runs across a saddle of higher ground near Penybont in Powys (SO160641 to SO163643) for about 304m.

Clawdd Llesg
Clawdd Llesg is an east-facing 170m long dyke (SJ157112 to SJ157114) that cuts a ridge near Meifod in Powys. Surveyors first noted the dyke in 1879 and named it after the nearby settlement. However, the name contains the word for dyke (clawdd) and possibly the name of Eliseg (or Elisedd), the eighth-century king of Powys.

Clawdd Mawr (Dyfed)
Clawdd Mawr is an east-facing earthwork overlooking the Afon Cloddi in Dyfed (SN376336 to SN377328) about 0.87 miles (1.4km) long, which could have formed the eastern boundary of the early medieval kingdom of Dyfed.

Clawdd Mawr (Foel)
This is a south-facing 700m long sinuous dyke (SH974111 to SH980110) near Foel in Powys.

Clawdd Mawr Glyncorrwg/Bwlch Garw Dyke

Clawdd Mawr is an east-facing earthwork that runs roughly for 192m (SS894948 to SS895947), cutting a saddle of higher ground with the terminals located at the edge of steep slopes. Crampton excavated a Bwlch Garw Dyke, which from the location given is presumably the same earthwork and his soil samples suggested that it is early medieval.

Clawdd Mawr (Llanfyllin)

This earthwork facing north-west runs across a ridge near Llanfyllin in Powys for approximately 450m (from SJ064216 south-west to SJ061213) with both ends adjoining streams in deep gullies. A 'rapier' was found on the site in the 1880s, but no details were recorded.

Clawdd Seri

This north–south dyke cuts a ridge in the higher ground east of Llanaelhaearn in Gwynedd. About 750m of the earthwork are marked on Ordnance Survey maps (SH416466 to SH416461), but it was possibly longer. The dyke is recorded as a township boundary in a charter for Aberconwy Abbey dated 1200.

Cowlod Dyke

This possibly east-facing earthwork, about 108m long (SO165634 to SO165635), is located near Penybont in Powys.

Crugyn Bank/Two Tumps Bank/Double Deyches

These three dykes, which face south-west and are collectively known as

Looking south along Crugyn Bank (picture by Helena Grigg).

the Double Deyches/Dyches, run across open rough grazing land just south of Dolfor in Powys. Crugyn Bank is the westerly earthwork, while the two easterly dykes are termed Two Tumps Dyke after nearby tumuli. Crugyn Bank (meaning 'small heap') runs for about 500m (SO101858 to SO106856), while the Two Tumps runs in two sections, the first 600m long (SO115852 to SO119848) and the second 200m long (SO120844 to SO120842).

All three dykes face south-west and cut the Kerry Ridgeway. They are of a similar size, so if they were originally one continuous earthwork (as recent field surveys and aerial photography suggest), it would have been about 2,720m long (SO101858 to SO120842).

Ffos Toncenglau (Ffos Ton Cenglau)
This east-facing earthwork 2.5 miles (4km) south of Hirwaun in Glamorganshire runs for about 0.8 miles (1.2km) (SN917030 to SN920022), cutting a narrow point in a ridge with both ends flanked by steep slopes.

Fron Hill Dyke (Ditch Bank)
This earthwork, which faces south-west, runs north-west to south-east across farmland for 400m (SO195601 to SO198598), cutting a valley south-west of New Radnor in Powys.

Giant's Grave
This southwest-facing dyke runs for 250m (SO043864 to SO044861) across a ridge of high ground just east of Llandinam in Powys.

Looking north-west along Fron Hill Dyke.

Looking south along the central section of the Heronbridge earthwork.

Heronbridge Earthwork
This is a 550m long west-facing dyke sandwiched between Watling Street and the River Dee. It forms a C-shape with the (fordable) river to the east (SJ412639 to SJ411638, then south to SJ411346, then curves eastwards to finish at SJ412635).

Excavations found that the bank overlay part of a cemetery, probably casualties from the Battle of Chester (AD605/613). We do not know where the actual fighting took place, though it was presumably somewhere nearby. We can imagine the Northumbrians marching up from the east; they may have dug the earthwork or taken shelter behind a pre-existing dyke. The Welsh were presumably assembled from the west.

Lower Short Ditch
This 750m long west-facing earthwork (SO223885 to SO222877) is located south of Sarn in Powys.

Pen y Clawdd Dyke
This earthwork, which faces south-west, is near Llangunllo in Powys and runs for 260m (SO187708 to SO187706) from the edge of a steep hill (Crungoed) south-south-east to a steep-sided valley.

Red Hill Cross Dyke
This 110m long (SO150498 to SO150499) east-facing earthwork runs across a saddle of high ground near Paincastle in Powys.

Senghenydd Dyke

This is a four-sided dyke roughly totalling 7.5 miles (12km) in length that surrounds and faces inwards towards a settlement of the same name. The north-west corner is at ST101915; it runs east to ST126921, then turns south to ST137900, where it peters out. It reappears at ST124884, where it runs west to ST120880, then turns north to the starting point. It is probably a deer park boundary built shortly after the annexation of Senghenydd Is Caeach by the lord of Glamorgan in 1267 and not an early medieval defensive structure.

Shepherd's Well

This earthwork, facing south-west, is near Llanfihangel Rhydithon in Powys. It is up to 140m long (SO188649 to SO188651); it cuts a ridge and is flanked by steep ravines.

Short Ditch

This dyke, facing north-west, is near Beguildy and Llanlluest in Powys. It runs on a straight alignment across a plateau for about 640m (SO191750 to SO187746), the terminals of which are located at deep-sided streams (dingles) that guard the flanks.

Tor Clawdd Dyke

About 3.1 miles (5km) north of Clydach in Glamorganshire there is a north-facing 845m long dyke (SN667062 to SN673063) curled in a northward bulging curve about the northern summit of Tor Clawdd. Coal diggings have mutilated it.

Ty Newydd Dyke

This is a 254m long north-facing earthwork (SJ131232 to SJ133232) near Llanrhaeadr-ym-Mochnant in Powys. It is also referred to as Dyke Q and Clawdd Refel. Aerial photography and surveys suggest that it was once 900m long (SJ130233 to SJ137235).

Upper Short Ditch

This 500m long earthwork (SO195872 to SO191867) west-facing dyke cuts the Kerry Ridgeway and the Anglo-Welsh border.

Vervil Dyke

This 188m long (SS888775 to SS889773) dyke, which faces south-west, cuts a narrow isthmus between the rivers Ewenny and Ogmore, with river cliffs or marsh protecting the flanks.

Wantyn Dyke

This earthwork near Kerry in Powys consists of two sections. The main body of the earthwork, the north section, looks more like an overgrown hedgerow and faces south-west. It runs (SO184921 to SO197895) in a straight alignment for 1.9 miles (3km).

The southern section (also called Upper Wantyn Dyke) on a hillside less than 0.6 miles (1km) further south is L-shaped, running for 435m south-west–north-east (from SO200888), before changing direction (at SO203890) and running south-east for about 900m (to SO209884). The two are morphologically very different and the southern section is probably a later unrelated field system.

OFFA'S DYKE, WAT'S DYKE AND ROWE DITCH

This section encompasses three main dykes (Offa's Dyke, Wat's Dyke and Rowe Ditch) and some associated earthworks that run roughly parallel to the English–Welsh border. Sir Cyril thought Offa's Dyke ran from Prestatyn on the north coast of Wales to the River Severn and the modern long-distance footpath roughly follows this route. Later studies have cast doubt on the idea that it was a single earthwork, though all scholars assume the central section is definitely Offa's.

Beachley Bank
This south-facing dyke, which runs for 0.87 miles (1.4km) in two straight sections from the Wye to the Severn (ST540943 to ST552928), is mentioned in a charter dated to 956 (S 610). At the western end is a semi-circular enclosure, possibly a fort; a 1930 excavation found a 'lance head' of an indeterminable date on the 'floor' of the ditch.

Offa's Dyke – Central Section
This section covers the central portion of Offa's Dyke, which runs almost due south from Treuddyn (SJ268577) to Rushock Hill (SO300595) for

Looking south along Offa's Dyke.

about 64 miles (103km). There are two gaps in the earthwork: one 1,350m long from around SJ292420 to SJ283410, where the River Dee fills the gap; and another of 4.4–5 miles (7–8km) (SJ281155 or SJ278158 to SJ248086) covered by the River Severn, making the built earthwork about 59 miles (95km) long. Near Ffrith, the earthwork cuts a Roman settlement and numerous excavations have proved it is post-Roman.

Offa's Dyke in Herefordshire
Fox admitted that south of Rushock Hill there is little evidence of Offa's Dyke in Herefordshire (though south of Bishopstone the River Wye may have acted as a substitute) and efforts by local archaeologists to find a continuous earthwork across Herefordshire have proved fruitless.

Kennel Wood According to Fox, a 170m long part of Offa's Dyke (SO300596 to SO301596) lay east of Kennel Wood, but excavations along this line found only geological features or unimpressive field boundaries.

Scuditch This earthwork lies to the east of Scuditch Wood and runs 250m east–west (SO306600 to SO308600) on the same alignment as the southern end of the central portion of Offa's Dyke.

Berry's Wood This earthwork runs for about 150m (SO323587 to SO323586) south to a knoll in Berry's Wood.

River Arrow This is a section of earthwork running north–south (SO324581 to SO324580) from the south bank of the River Arrow for about 100m.

Lyonshall Bank This earthwork facing south-west lies on the west side of the village of the same name. It may have run for 1.9 miles (3km) (SO326562 to SO348543).

Bishopstone Running from just west of Yazor (SO394474) for 3.1 miles (5km) south-south-east to the River Wye between Byford and Bridge Sollers (SO408427) are hedgerows that may mark the route of a lost earthwork.

Offa's Dyke in the Wye Valley
Along the east bank of the River Wye there are some earthworks, but they are smaller than the central portion of Offa's Dyke and often difficult to distinguish from quarries, lynchets, hollow ways, field boundaries and Iron-Age forts.

There are two main sections commonly called Offa's Dyke on the east bank of the River Wye in Gloucestershire – the northerly English Bicknor section and the St Briavel's section. Surviving sections of the northern

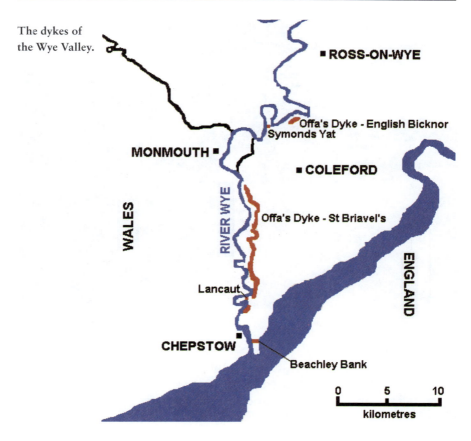

The dykes of the Wye Valley.

earthwork (from SO592173 southwest to SO584168) are 800m long. The southern earthwork starts just south of Redbrook (SO539091), finishing in the parish of Tidenham (ST536951) 8.7 miles (14km) to the south. The course is about 10 miles (16km) long because it follows the river, but there is a gap (ST549976 to ST538953) of about 1.2 miles (2km).

Rowe Ditch
This west-facing earthwork cuts the valley of the River Arrow and should not be confused with the Row Ditch, a later medieval earthwork that defends Hereford. An excavation in 1985 at Vallet Covert (SO379612) found that the northern terminus and the southern end were near Pitfield Farm (SO382575), 2.3 miles (3.75km) to the south. Excavations found that the earthwork cut Roman remains.

Wat's Dyke
Wat's Dyke is a west-facing dyke that runs southwards for 38.5 miles (62km) from Basingwerk (SJ195775) on the Dee to Lower Morton (SJ305238), just south of Oswestry. There is a 1.9-mile (3km) gap where the dyke builders utilized the River Dee and the River Ceiriog.

Looking north along Wat's Dyke.

Whitford Dyke
This earthwork runs north-west–south-east for about 6 miles (10km) (SJ083799 to SJ153746). It used to be thought that it was part of Offa's Dyke, but it is probably prehistoric as it incorporates prehistoric features like the cairn on Cop Hill and Ysceifiog Circle.

THE MIDLANDS

There are few possible early medieval dykes in the Midlands, except those that run parallel to the Welsh border mentioned above.

Devil's Mouth Dyke
This heavily eroded 140m long dyke runs north-east–south-west (SO440943 to SO440942) cutting a ridge on a plateau in Shropshire known as Long Mynd or 'long mountain'. Radiocarbon dates suggest that the dyke is probably from the middle Bronze Age.

King Lud's and the Foulding Dykes (The Three Dykes)
These dykes, collectively called The Three Dykes, run west–east and are almost impossible to locate on the ground and we are reliant on antiquarian's maps and aerial photographs. The northerly Foulding Dyke can still be seen from the air and is about 1.3km long (SK866274 to SK879274). The proximity of prehistoric features in the area, the slightness of the surviving remains and similarities with similar nearby prehistoric monuments suggests that they are probably pre-Roman.

THE DYKES DESCRIBED

Looking south along Minchinhampton Bulwarks.

Minchinhampton Bulwarks
South of Stroud is an east-facing 2,300m long dyke (SO857003 to SO874010), which runs roughly north-east–south-west in a series of straight alignments that form a C-shaped plan. The area is popular with dog walkers and ideal on a summer's day for a picnic or a bit of kite flying.

CAMBRIDGESHIRE

Between Newmarket and Baldock are six dykes that bisect a narrow band of chalk, along which runs the Icknield Way flanked by the Fens on the north-west and mixed glacial tills to the east, which were probably heavily forested. Excavations of these earthworks have proved that most are early medieval.

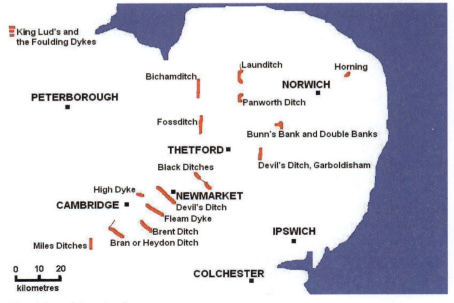

The dykes of East Anglia.

Bran Ditch, looking south.

Bran or Heydon Ditch

This dyke, which faces south-west, runs from the edge of the Fens south–south-east (TL404449 to TL430405) in almost a straight line through farmland for 3.1 miles (5km). Excavations uncovered fifty early medieval burials dug into the berm, either the site of an execution or (in my opinion) the location of a massacre.

Brent Ditch

Brent Ditch runs on a sinuous course near Pampisford (it can be traced from TL505485 to TL521465, though it was probably originally much longer). It consists of a flat-bottomed ditch with steep sloping sides, so most think that it was originally a prehistoric road, not, as is often popularly supposed, a dyke.

Devil's Ditch

Devil's Ditch is one of the most impressive earthworks in Britain and consists of a large 7.5-mile (12km) long (TL566662 to TL653583) almost straight south-facing earthwork. It is possible to walk the length of the earthwork and it affords good views over Newmarket Racecourse. Roman finds discovered under the bank and an Anglo-Saxon spearhead from within the bank confirm it as an early medieval dyke.

THE DYKES DESCRIBED

Devil's Ditch, looking west.

Fleam Dyke

The dyke runs on a slightly curved south-easterly course for about 3.2 miles (5.2km) (TL536557 to TL572523) from low ground near Great Wilbraham to higher ground near Balsham. There is a pleasant walk that runs the length of the earthwork, but do not try to access it from the A14 in the middle. Fleam is probably from the Old English for a fugitive; archaeological excavations have found Roman finds sealed under the bank.

Fleam Dyke, looking east from near the A14.

High Dyke

This south-facing dyke runs from the River Cam east-south-east to Quy Water for about 1.2 miles (2km) (TL481604 to TL509595), cutting off a peninsula of land. Where the Newmarket Road crosses the dyke, two isolated Anglo-Saxon shield bosses and a group of skeletons with associated Anglo-Saxon grave goods (a sword, a sword pommel, various spearheads, a knife and some brooches) have been found.

Miles Ditches

This earthwork runs south for about 1.9 miles (3km) from low-lying ground south-west of Bassingbourn to the edge of an escarpment at Therfield Heath (TL328430 to TL333400). It is difficult to locate without aerial photography, which is due to this earthwork being prehistoric.

Worstead Street

Worstead Street, also called Wort's Causeway, runs south-eastwards from Cambridgeshire towards Colchester. Excavations have clearly demonstrated that it is not a dyke, but a Roman road.

NORFOLK

There are six dykes in Norfolk traditionally ascribed to the early medieval period. Recently, archaeologists have reclassified some as prehistoric, but there is evidence that people rebuilt older earthworks in the early medieval period. Most of the dykes are in two north–south lines on either side of the A1065; perhaps they reflect a lost political divide.

Bichamditch, looking south-east.

Bichamditch

The east-facing Bichamditch (also called Devil's Dyke or Devil's Ditch) runs for at least 3 miles (5km) (TF751116 to TF740064) south from near Narborough to a tributary of the River Wissey. For much of its course the dyke is only visible on aerial photographs, but it is a substantial feature on both sides of where a Roman road (the modern A1122) passes through it. When I walked down this road, I noticed a slight deviation at this point and a few metres to the south there is a shallow cut in the bank. Perhaps it is a prehistoric dyke that later Roman road engineers breached, then in the medieval period people blocked the route, which is why the earthwork is bigger near the road and travellers had to deviate slightly to the south to avoid the obstruction, hence the cut. The volume of road traffic then prompted somebody to reconnect the road, but this was done inexactly, hence the slight deviation.

Bunn's Bank and Double Banks

Bunn's Bank is a fragmentary south-facing earthwork south-east of Attleborough and is about 1.9 miles (3km) in length (TM047929 to TM079947). While it is probably early medieval, it was later used as the northern boundary of a twelfth-century deer park.

Devil's Ditch, Garboldisham

This west-facing earthwork is at least 1.7 miles (2.8km) long (TL989842 to TL987814); field boundaries and parish boundaries on a similar alignment suggest that it reached a further 400m south (to TL987807) to the Little Ouse. There is confusion as to whether the dyke faces west or east, or if it originally consisted of double banks with a ditch in-between. Excavation evidence suggests that the earthwork is probably prehistoric, but recut in the late eighth or early ninth century.

Devil's Ditch, looking north (picture by Helena Grigg).

Fossditch, looking south.

Fossditch

This east-facing dyke is about 5.6 miles (9km) long (TL773958 to TL755869) and runs in eleven straight alignments (also called Fendyke, the Weeting Devil's Dyke and Devil's Dyke) from near the River Wissey south to the Little Ouse. Excavations clearly demonstrated that the southern section cuts through a Roman settlement.

Horning

This dyke, which faces north-west, runs for about 800m south-west across farmland from the floodplain of the River Ant (TG359171) to slopes overlooking the River Bure (TG354166), cutting off a peninsula. The Ant used to flow into the River Thurne, which means that the peninsula was once twice the size it is now. To the east, now cut off by the River Ant, are the remains of St Benet's Abbey and it is possible that the monks either dug it or refurbished/reused an older earthwork to delimit the boundary of their monastery.

The southern end of the dyke at Horning.

THE DYKES DESCRIBED

Launditch
This west-facing dyke is about 3.1 miles (5km) long (TF936191 to TF924146), although originally it may have been longer. It is possibly a prehistoric dyke, part of which was rebuilt in the medieval period to sever a road.

Panworth Ditch
This west-facing dyke runs roughly north–south for about 500m (TF893054 to TF894051; both ends tend to curve away slightly eastwards), although crop marks on aerial photographs suggest that it was originally longer. The dyke lies at right angles to a possible Roman road. Fieldwork for this book suggested that the bank is later than the road.

Looking east across a possible gateway in Panworth Ditch.

SUFFOLK

There is only one possible early medieval dyke in Suffolk.

Black Ditches
The Black Ditches consist of two separate west-facing earthworks on the same alignment, with a gap in-between. The northern section extends across Cavenham Heath for about 1,800m (TL766727 to TL768709). The southern section is 1.2 miles (2km) to the south on Risby Poor's Heath and runs for 1.18 miles (1.9km) (TL772694 to TL777677). If the two sections were originally continuous, it would be up to 4.4 miles (7km) long. Prehistoric finds suggest that it was originally prehistoric, but the profile of the ditches imply that it was possibly rebuilt in the early medieval period.

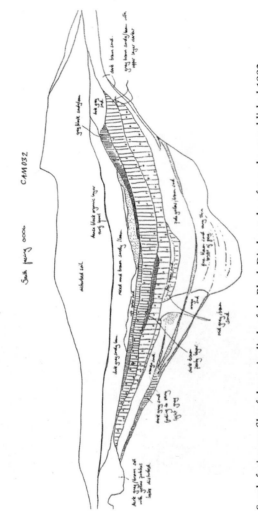

South-facing profile of the main ditch of the Black Ditches taken from the unpublished 1992 excavation; note that the original diagram has no scale (CAM 032, copyright Suffolk County Council Archaeology Service, used with permission).

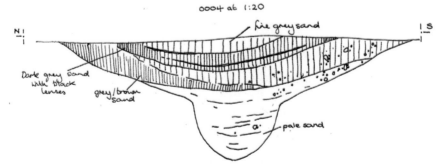

Profile of the smaller parallel ditch of the Black Ditches taken from the unpublished 1992 excavation; note that the original diagram has no scale (CAM 032, copyright Suffolk County Council Archaeology Service, used with permission).

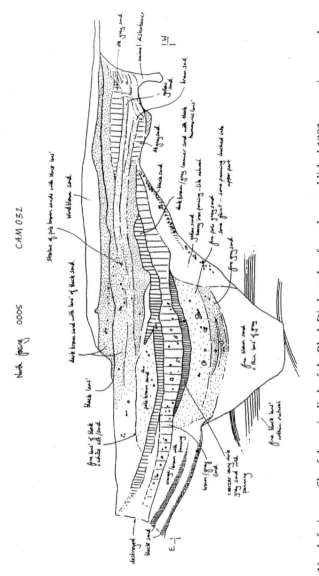

North-facing profile of the main ditch of the Black Ditches taken from the unpublished 1992 excavation; note that the original diagram has no scale (CAM 032, copyright Suffolk County Council Archaeology Service, used with permission).

THE HOME COUNTIES

There are dykes in what was Middlesex running south-west–north-east, facing downhill towards London. Some think they were the boundary of a post-Roman territory based on Verulamium (St Albans), although as there is almost no evidence of activity in the London area for two centuries after 425, it is hard to imagine what purpose they served. There is also a series of dykes along the downs of Buckinghamshire and Hertfordshire called Grim's Ditch.

THE DYKES DESCRIBED

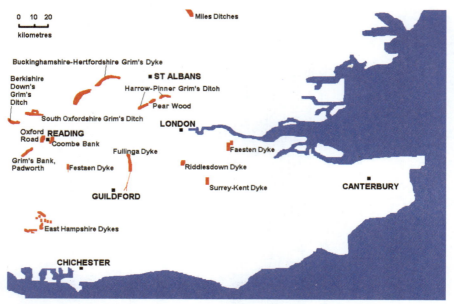

The dykes of south-east England.

Buckinghamshire–Hertfordshire Grim's Ditch

This earthwork, which faces south-east, runs from near West Wycombe north-east to near Dunstable (SU 833979 to TL 008203) along the north escarpment of the Chilterns. Despite some early suggestions of an early medieval date, the earthwork is probably prehistoric.

Pear Wood

This south-facing earthwork between Stanmore and Elstree is about 400m long (TQ170935 to TQ173936). Excavations found fourth-century Roman and early medieval dating evidence from the bottom of the bank and in the ditch fill.

Harrow-Pinner Grim's Dyke

The main surviving part of this south-facing earthwork runs from near Cuckoo Hill (TQ111896) eastwards to Harrow Weald Common (TQ143929) for nearly 3.1 miles (5km). Traditionally considered Saxon, excavation evidence includes Iron-Age pottery sherds found in the bank and a radiocarbon date of around AD50.

BERKSHIRE AND OXFORDSHIRE

There are numerous small dykes in these two adjoining counties, which are considered together as the only two dykes that now lie in Oxfordshire, Aelfrith's Dyke and Bica's, were in Berkshire until 1974 and so are often recorded in Berkshire archaeological journals and guides.

THE DYKES DESCRIBED 189

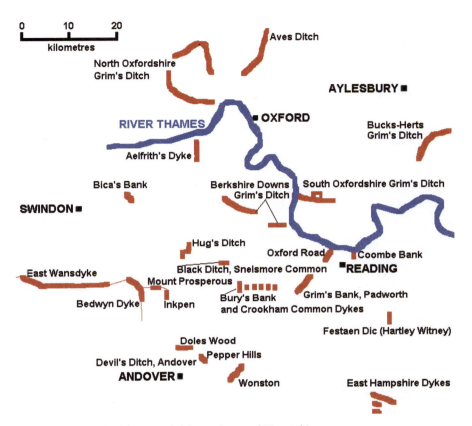

The dykes of Oxfordshire, Berkshire and part of Hampshire.

Aelfrith's Dyke
Though the county Historic Environment Records entry only records a 0.6-mile (1km) long section (SU411989 to SU411978), this west-facing dyke and associated earthworks (Old Dyke or Old Balk to the north and Short Dyke to the south) probably ran from the River Thames southwards for 3.1 miles (5km) (SP413009 to SU409954) to the River Ock.

Aves Ditch
This west-facing dyke was originally at least 3.1 miles (5km) long (SP519248 to SP497211), though it may once have continued further north. Excavations have produced clear late Iron-Age dating evidence.

Berkshire Downs Grim's Ditch
Running along the northern edge of the Berkshire Downs is a series of dykes called Grim's Ditch. The most obvious sections are a 6-mile (10km) section along the north escarpment of the White Hills (SU418842 to SU495839) and a 3.1-mile (5km) section, which runs near Aldworth (SU546785 to SU598796). Finds suggests that they are prehistoric.

Bica's Dyke
This east-facing dyke south-west of Compton Beauchamp is nearly 400m long (SU276866 to SU280862).

Black Ditch, Snelsmore Common
There are two parallel north-facing dykes on Snelsmore Common. The larger dyke is 700m long (the western end being SU458712), the smaller 300m long (starting from SU461712). Both converge before crossing the road (at SU4647101) and peter out just east of it.

Bury's Bank and Crookham Common Dykes
On Greenham Common there used to be a west-facing earthwork called Bury's Bank, while on nearby Crookham Common to the east there also existed five parallel (probably west-facing) earthworks; all were destroyed by the extension to the airfield runway in the early 1950s.

Bury's Bank was 0.9 miles (1.5km) long (SU490653 to SU490638), the Crookham Common earthworks, working from west to east, were: 500m long (SU519648 to SU519643); 500m long (SU527649 to SU525643); 200m long (SU529645 to SU529643); 200m long (SU532644 to SU533642); and 150m long (SU534645 to SU534643). Two rather large pieces of late Roman pottery discovered in the bottom of the ditch suggest that they were newly broken pieces that fell in.

Grim's Bank, Padworth
This dyke, facing north-west, is about 1.9 miles (3km) north-west of the Roman town of Silchester. It runs south-west in a series of straight alignments for about 2.9 miles (4.6km) (SU609636 to SU634666).

Hug's Ditch
This is a west-facing earthwork that runs in a dog-legged fashion north to south. Only crop marks and hedgerows mark the course of the earthwork, but it was at least 1.9 miles (3km) long (SU386746 to SU379734), though originally it was probably much longer. It is of similar length, size and alignment to a series of prehistoric dykes on the Berkshire Downs and as the associations with early medieval figures are dubious, it is probably prehistoric.

Reading ('Oxford Road' and Coombe Bank)
In Reading, there are two banks both about 300m long that lie on the southern side of the River Thames at 90 degrees to the river. The easterly bank is called Coombe Bank (SU698747 to SU698750), but the westerly dyke (SU681747 to SU678744, but with a sharp dog-leg turn) is unnamed, so for convenience is referred to as 'Oxford Road' Dyke. The western earthwork is probably prehistoric, while the easterly dyke, Coombe Bank, may relate to the fighting between Alfred of Wessex and a group of Vikings in 871–2.

THE DYKES DESCRIBED

South Oxfordshire Grim's Ditch

This south-facing earthwork (sometimes called the Mongewell Grim's Ditch) runs for about 3.7 miles (6km) (SU608882 to SU683687) from the River Thames eastwards to Nuffield. Iron-Age finds from various excavations suggests that it is probably prehistoric.

WANSDYKE

Wansdyke runs from near Bristol eastwards across Somerset and through the middle of Wiltshire to end near the western border of Berkshire, but it is possible that it was once longer than the visible remains we see today. Scholars have generally assumed that the name derives from the pagan Germanic god Woden, though the earliest reference (a charter, S 272, dated 825) does not name the earthwork. As it may not be a single earthwork, it is split here into five parts.

First, the possible section from the Bristol Channel to Maes Knoll hill fort (called here the Western Extension); secondly, West Wansdyke (from Maes Knoll to the head of Horsecombe Brook, just south of Bath); thirdly, the Bathampton section (from Horsecombe Brook to Bathford); fourthly, the central section (from Bathford to Morgan's Hill); and finally East Wansdyke. East of Savernake Forest it is unlikely there ever was a single continuous earthwork, but the final section includes various earthworks

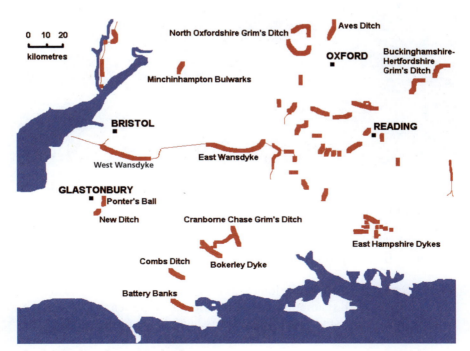

The dykes of south-west England.

often associated with Wansdyke: the Bedwyn, Mount Prosperous and Inkpen Dykes.

Western Extension Some scholars have claimed that the western end of Wansdyke lay near Portbury on the Bristol Channel, but fieldwork, excavations and surveys have failed to find any sign of the earthwork here.

West Wansdyke West Wansdyke runs from Maes Knoll eastwards to Horsecombe Brook (ST598662 to ST747619), with a 1.6-mile (2.5km) section between Publow Brook and the River Chew (ST622652 to ST648647) where rivers fill a gap, making the built earthwork 8.4 miles (13.5km) in length. The builders incorporated two older Iron-Age hill forts: Maes Knoll and Stantonbury. Excavations have uncovered residual prehistoric and Roman finds in the bank, confirming that it is probably early medieval.

Looking east along West Wansdyke from Maes Knoll.

Bathampton Section Some scholars have suggested that there is a section of Wansdyke running across Bathampton to Bathford, but they have probably been confused by a large Iron-Age enclosure and a field system on Bathampton Down.

Central Section A 13.7-mile long (22km) section of the Roman road from Bath to Mildenhall (Cunetio) runs on a similar alignment to Wansdyke, so some have suggested that the road was heightened in the post-Roman period. Most now think that only the easternmost 400m stretch was ever turned into dyke.

East Wansdyke This striking earthwork runs for about 12.4 miles (20km) eastwards from Morgan's Hill to the edge of Savernake Forest (SU023671 to SU195664), making for a bracing hike across some of the finest downland in Britain.

Bedwyn, Mount Prosperous and Inkpen Dykes Bedwyn Dyke, facing north-east, is a 1.7-mile long (2.8km) dyke (SU280658 to SU289637), running south from the Iron-Age fort of Chisbury. Mount Prosperous is a 250m long west–east bank (SU338644 to SU341645), while further east near Inkpen there is a 500m long north–south earthwork (SU351640 to SU352636). Some scholars have proposed that these earthworks were once linked to East Wansdyke, but there is no evidence to back up this claim.

CORNWALL

The convoluted coastline of Cornwall means that anyone building dykes that define an area of land is likely to build them from inlet to inlet leaving monuments that unfortunately can resemble Iron Age cliff castles. As this study does not include defended settlements, Tintagel has been

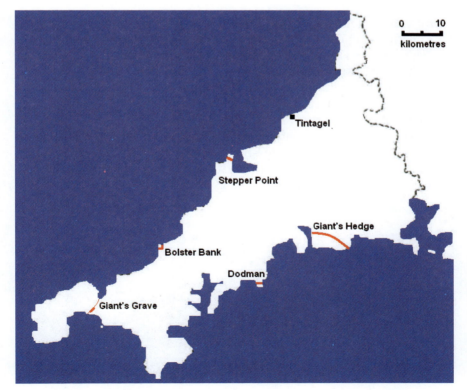

The dykes of Cornwall.

excluded, but that site confirms early medieval Cornishmen were digging earthworks to defend headlands.

Bolster Bank
This south-facing earthwork runs for 2 miles (3.3km) (SW697495 to SW721508), cutting off a peninsula, which includes the prominent hill St Agnes Beacon.

Looking north towards St Agnes Beacon, with Bolster Bank in the foreground.

Dodman
This north-facing earthwork runs for 600m (SW999397 to SX003400), cutting off a steep headland. Most scholars assume that it is an Iron-Age fort, although it seems unusually large and lacks the multiple banks or complex fortified gateways of such structures.

Giant's Grave
This dyke, which faces south-east, is about 350m long (SW508323 to SW505320), but there are suggestions that it was once 3.7 miles (6km) long and followed the line of the A30 north-east to the River Hayle, cutting the narrow neck of land.

The Giant's Grave, looking west.

THE DYKES DESCRIBED

Giant's Hedge
This dyke runs intermittently along an 6.8-mile (11km) long course from the Lerryn River, a tributary of the River Fowey (SX136567) east to the West Looe River (approximately SX254528), facing inland and cutting off a territory up to 8×3.7 miles (13×6km).

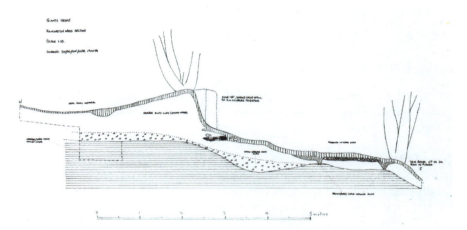

ABOVE: Section of the Giant's Hedge at Kilminorth Wood from 1984; watching brief drawn by Steve Hartgroves of the Historic Environment Service Cornwall County Council (used with permission).

Looking east along the Giant's Hedge (at SX185574).

Stepper Point

This dyke, which faces south-west, originally ran for about 300m (SW909778 to SW911776), separating Stepper Point from the mainland, although there is little to see today. A 2007 Time Team excavation (aired 8 March 2008) of a settlement just outside the enclosed area, Lellizzick, uncovered high-status fifth-/sixth-century Byzantine pottery and there used to be a chapel dedicated to the Byzantine St Sampson on the headland.

SOMERSET

There are two possible early medieval dykes in Somerset, New Ditch and Ponter's Ball. They are just 2.5 miles (4km) apart on a similar alignment, so may be related.

New Ditch

This earthwork runs for about 800m (ST503331 to ST502330) on a north-east–south-west alignment, seemingly blocking a route along the ridge of the Polden Hills. The northern section is in private woods and therefore inaccessible, but the southern section is in the pleasant Combe Hill Wood, which is open to the public.

New Ditch from the west.

Ponter's Ball
This east-facing dyke is approximately 1,050m long (from ST535382 to ST530373) and cuts what used to be the only dry route to Glastonbury.

Ponter's Ball, looking north.

DORSET

As the dykes of Dorset face north-east towards the heartland of Wessex, they have usually been interpreted as British defences against the seventh-century West Saxon advance.

Battery Banks
This is a north-facing dyke that runs along a ridge of land west of Wareham. It exists today in five sections, which add up to about 2,240m. West to east, they consist of: a 1,370m section (SY878880 to SY891874); a 200m section (SY876879 to SY877879); a 210m section (SY866883 to SY868883); a 185m section (SY858886 to SY859885); and a 275m stretch (SY844894 to SY847893).

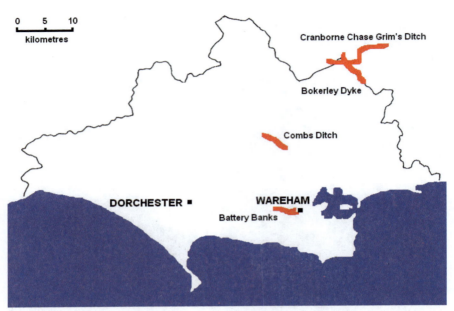

The dykes of Dorset.

Bokerley Dyke

This earthwork faces north-east and runs for about 5,220m (SU023200 to SU063169); there is also a 75m long branch (at SU037196) called the Epaulement. Excavations have clearly demonstrated that the earthwork was built and rebuilt in a series of stages. These started in the very late Roman period and continued into the immediate post-Roman.

Combs Ditch

This earthwork, facing north-east, runs across the top of Charlton Down (ST851022 to ST877000) for at least 2.8 miles (4.5km). Excavations suggest that it is prehistoric but later rebuilt, probably in the post-Roman period.

HAMPSHIRE

In this section there is an isolated dyke (Festaen Dic near Hartley Witney), plus two groups of dykes (the Devil's Ditch group near Andover and the East Hampshire group).

Devil's Ditch, Andover

There are three Devil's Ditches near Andover that may be related: one in Doles Wood; the second centred on a small wood called Pepper Hill Firs; and the third in the parish of Wonston about 8 miles (13km) to the east.

Doles Wood This south-facing dyke follows a sinuous path about 700m long (SU363512 to SU371513), but a 1,400m long crop mark continues eastwards on a similar alignment.

Pepper Hills Firs This west-facing earthwork runs for approximately 1.2 miles (2km) in a curve like a reversed C. The southern end is fairly obvious (SU399472), but the northern terminus is less so; it seems to follow a hedgerow to just north of the nearby Roman road.

Wonston The Wonston section exists today as a completely flattened crop mark 1,750m long (SU494429 to SU498413). If it cut the western estate boundary of an Anglo-Saxon estate as a charter dated 900AD (S 360) suggests, it would need to run at least another 1,300m to the north-east (to SU483442).

East Hampshire Dykes
In east Hampshire, there is a series of dykes to the west of Petersfield,

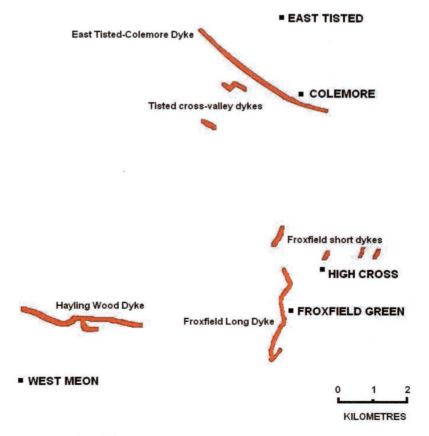

The East Hampshire dykes.

often collectively referred to as the Froxfield Entrenchments or the East Hampshire Dykes. They have individually been given various names, but here they are termed the East Tisted-Colemore Dyke, the Tisted Cross-Valley Dykes, the Froxfield Short Dykes, the Froxfield Long Dyke and the Hayling Wood Dyke. As they face in different directions, it is unlikely that they are contemporaneous. The Tisted Cross-Valley Dykes are much shallower than the rest and the northern one has produced an abraded piece of Iron-Age pottery in its bank, so they are probably prehistoric, but the others are possibly early medieval.

East Tisted-Colemore Dyke The East Tisted-Colemore Dyke faces north-east and stretches for 2.5 miles (4km) (SU683324 to SU711305) across the parishes of East Tisted and Colemore.

Tisted Cross-Valley Dykes The northerly Tisted Cross-Valley Dyke is a south-facing 170m long dog-legged earthwork (SU691311 to SU693310), about 230m to the south-west of the East Tisted-Colemore Dyke, though this dyke faces in the opposite direction. There is a second south-facing 200m long cross-valley dyke just over 0.6 miles (1km) to the south-west (SU686302 to SU687301).

Froxfield Short Dykes The Froxfield Short Dykes consist of four west-facing dykes, the westernmost of which is 1.4 miles (2.3km) west from the most easterly. The westernmost is 274m long (SU702274 to SU700271). The others are all about 100m long (SU711269 to SU711268, SU719270 to SU719269 and SU723269 to SU723267).

Froxfield Long Dyke This is a 3-mile (4.8km) long west-facing earthwork that runs sinuously north–south (SU702265 to SU700244) to the west of the village of High Green. At the southern end there is another dyke nearly 550m long, running almost parallel but veering slightly towards the east (finishing at SU703247), so the pair form a V. It is impossible to tell if this feature is a contemporary feature to strengthen the southern end, or if the two dykes are of different dates.

Hayling Wood Dyke This south-facing earthwork runs for 1.4 miles (2.3km) (SU642256 to SU666253) and is about 4 miles (6.5km) south of the East Tisted-Colemore Dyke. Although for most of the course it runs almost in straight west–east alignment, in the centre of the dyke in Hayling Wood there is a dog-legged section (a right-angled northward turn, followed by a right-angled eastward turn) and then a short 600m section of dyke branches off to the south, which then turns sharply eastward (ending SU658251). On a map these twists in the dyke seem to delimit on three sides of two adjoining rectangles of land.

Festaen Dic (Hartley Witney)

This west-facing earthwork is to the east of Hartley Wintney. Only a 60m stretch survives (SU796585 to SU797584), though it was probably originally 1.3 miles (2.2km) long (SU797590 to SU798569).

SURREY AND KENT

These two counties are grouped together as two of the three dykes are along the western border of Kent.

Faesten Dyke

This is a doglegged 2,400m long west-facing dyke (TQ507729 to TQ502709), though it is possible that it once extended further south. It is difficult to see why the dyke has a dogleg plan, unless it was built in more than one phase, or respected an older feature. The earliest record is in a charter dated AD814 (S 175).

Faesten Dyke, looking east.

Fullinga Dyke

Fullinga Dyke is a west-facing dyke that ran from the River Thames at Weybridge, possibly as far south as the North Downs. The best-preserved sections of the dyke are on St George's Hill and on Ockham Common (a lovely area for a walk to the old semaphore tower). The name Fullingadic seems to relate to the Fullingas, a folk group of Anglo-Saxons who lived in north-west Surrey and gave their name to Fulham.

Looking north along Fullinga Dyke on Ockham Common.

Riddlesdown Dyke

This possibly 200m long (TQ322605 to TQ324607) earthwork, which faces south-east and is near Purley, bisects a ridge of downland. Although it is pleasant to walk along this oasis of downland in the middle of suburbia, the dyke is probably prehistoric.

Surrey–Kent Dyke

This west-facing dyke runs for 320m (TQ432536 to TQ433533) from a prominent hill south across a valley, through which passes across the A25, and up the hill on the other side. Where the A25 cuts the dyke, there is a lump of tarmac about 60cm above the road surface sticking out of the north bank, suggesting that at some point in the past the road had a definite hump. This implies that the bank predated the road.

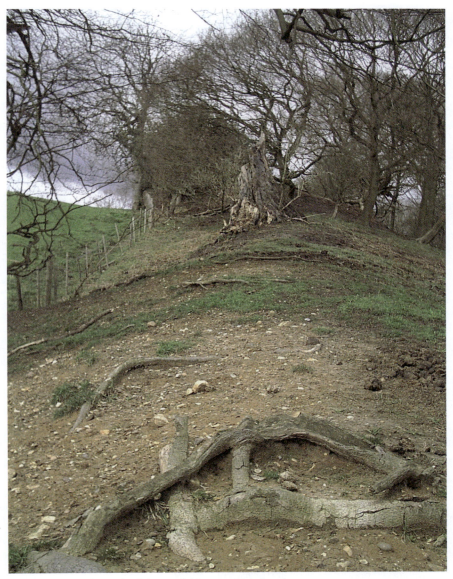
Looking north along the dyke on the Surrey–Kent border.

Endnotes

Chapter 1: Introduction and Methodology
1. Stocker, D., 'The Shadow of the General's Armchair', *The Archaeological Journal*, 149, pp.415–20, 1992.
2. Sawyer, P., *The Age of Vikings* (London: E. Arnold, 1962).
3. James, S., 'Writing the Legions: The Development and Future of Roman Military Studies in Britain', *The Archaeological Journal*, 159, pp.1–58, 2003.
4. Keynes, S. and Lapidge, M. (eds), *Alfred the Great: Asser's Life of King Alfred and Other Contemporary Sources* (London: Penguin, 1983).
5. Wood, M., *In Search of the Dark Ages* (London: BBC, 1981).
6. Osborn, G., *Exploring Ancient Dorset* (Bridport: Dorset Publishing Company, 1976).
7. Fox, C., 'Dykes', *Antiquity*, 3, 10, pp.135–54, 1929.
8. Two examples of authors dismissing the idea of any significant movement of people across the North Sea are Pryor, F., *Britain AD: A Quest for Arthur, England and the Anglo-Saxons* (London: HarperCollins, 2004); and Yeates, S., *Myth and History* (Oxford: Oxbow, 2012).
9. Halsall, G., *Worlds of Arthur* (Oxford: Oxford University Press, 2013), p.113.
10. Muir, R., *Riddles in the British Landscape* (London: Thames & Hudson, 1981), p.159.
11. Hawkes, S. (ed.), *Weapons and Warfare in Anglo-Saxon England* (Oxford: Oxford University Committee for Archaeology Monograph, 1989).
12. Halsall, G. (ed.), *Violence and Society in the Early Medieval West* (Woodbridge: Boydell Press, 1998).
13. Underwood, R., *Anglo-Saxon Weapons and Warfare* (Stroud: Tempus, 1999).
14. Baker, J., Brookes, S. and Reynolds, A. (eds), *Landscapes of Defence in Early Medieval Europe* (Turnhout: Brepols, 2013).
15. Guest, E., *Early English Settlements in South Britain* (London: Archaeological Institute, 1849), p.192.
16. Pitt Rivers, A., *Excavations in Bokerley and Wansdyke, Dorset and Wiltshire 1888–1891: Volume 3* (London: Harrison and Sons, 1892), pp.291–3.
17. Godsal, P., *Woden's, Grim's and Offa's Dykes* (London: Harrison & Sons, 1913).
18. Fox, C., 'Wat's Dyke: A Field Survey', *Archaeologia Cambrensis*, 89, Part 2, pp.205–78, 1934; and Fox, C., *Offa's Dyke: A Field Survey of the Western Frontier-Works of Mercia in the Seventh and Eighth Centuries AD* (Oxford: Oxford University Press, 1955).
19. Fox, C., O'Neil, B. and Grimes, W., 'Linear Earthworks: Methods of Field Study', *Antiquaries Journal*, XXVI, pp.175–9, 1946.
20. Fox, C. and Fox, A., 'Wansdyke Reconsidered', *The Archaeological Journal*, 115, pp.1–48, 1958.
21. Crawford, O., *Archaeology in the Field* (London: Phoenix House, 1953).
22. Major, A. and Burrow, E., *The Mystery of Wansdyke* (London: Burrow and Co., 1926).

23 Crawford, O., 'The Work of Giants', *Antiquity*, 10, 38, pp.162–74, 1936.
24 Erdtman, G., 'Studies in the Micropalaeontology of Post-glacial Deposits in Northern Scotland and the Scotch Isles', *Journal of the Linnean Society*, 46, pp.449–504, 1924; Clifford, E., 'The Earthworks at Rodborough, Amberley, and Minchinhampton, Gloucestershire', *The Transactions of the Bristol and Gloucestershire Archaeological Society*, 59, pp.287–307, 1937; and Crampton, C., 'An Interpretation of the Pollen and Soils in Cross-ridge Dykes in Glamorgan', *Bulletin of the Board of Celtic Studies*, 21, 4, pp.376–90, 1966.
25 Green, S., 'Wansdyke, Excavations 1966 to 1970', *Wiltshire Archaeological and Natural History Magazine*, 66, pp.129–46, 1971.
26 Malim, T., Penn, K., Robinson, B., Wait, G. and Welsh, K., 'New Evidence on the Cambridgeshire Dykes and Worsted Roman Road', *Proceedings of the Cambridge Antiquarian Society*, 85, pp.27–122, 1996.
27 Noble, F. and Gelling, M., *Offa's Dyke Reviewed* (Oxford: British Archaeological Reports, 1983).
28 Hill, D. and Worthington, M., *Offa's Dyke: History and Guide* (Stroud: Tempus, 2003).
29 Muir (1981), *op. cit.* in note 10, pp.149–63.
30 Curta, F. (ed.), *Borders, Barriers, and Ethnogenesis, Studies in the Early Middle Ages* (Turnhout: Brepols, 2005); and Curta, F., 'Linear Frontiers in the 9th Century: Bulgaria and Wessex', *Quaestiones Medii Aevi Novae*, pp.15–32, 2011.
31 Boldrini, N., 'Creating Space: A Re-examination of the Roman Ridge', *Transactions of the Hunter Archaeological Society*, 20, pp.24–30, 1999a; and Boldrini, N., 'When Is a Border Not a Border? The Roman Ridge Re-evaluated', in Cumberpatch, C., McNeil, J. and Whiteley, S. (eds), *Archaeology in South Yorkshire 1996–1998*, pp.100–4 (Rotherham: South Yorkshire Archaeology Service, 1999b).
32 Tyler, D., *Kingship and Conversion: Constructing Pre-Viking Mercia* (Manchester: University of Manchester, PhD History, 2002); and Tyler, D., 'Offa's Dyke: A Historiographical Appraisal', *Journal of Medieval History*, 37, pp.145–61, 2011.
33 Reynolds, A. and Langlands, A., 'Social Identities on the Macro Scale: A Maximum View of Wansdyke', in Davies, W., Halsall, G. and Reynolds, A. (eds), *People and Space in the Middle Ages, 300–1300*, pp.13–44 (Turnhout: Brepols, 2006); and Draper, S., *Landscape, Settlement and Society in Roman and Early Medieval Wiltshire* (Oxford: Archaeopress, 2006).
34 Laycock, S., 'Britannia: the Threat Within', *British Archaeology*, 87, pp.10–15, 2006; and Laycock, S., 'Britannia: A Failed State?', *Current Archaeology*, 219, pp.18–25, 2008.
35 Malim, T., 'The Origins and Design of Linear Earthworks in the Welsh Marches', in Nash. G. (ed.), *Landscape Enquiries*, pp.13–32 (Bristol: Clifton Antiquarian Club, 2007); Hayes, L. and Malim, T., 'The Date and Nature of Wat's Dyke: A Reassessment in the Light of Recent Investigations at Gobowen, Shropshire', *Anglo-Saxon Studies in Archaeology and History*, 15, pp.147–79, 2008; and Malim, T., 'Grim's Ditch, Wansdyke and the Ancient Highways of England: Linear Monuments of Political Control', in George, A., Hawley, D., Nash, G., Swann J. and Waite, L. (eds), *Early Medieval Enquiries: The Proceedings of the Clifton Antiquarian Club Volume 9*, pp.148–79 (Bristol: Clifton Antiquarian Club, 2010).
36 Squatriti, P., 'Digging Ditches in Early Medieval Europe', *Past and Present*, 176, pp.11–65, 2002; Squatriti, P., 'Offa's Dyke Between Nature and Culture', *Environmental History*, 9, 1, pp.37–56, 2004; and Squatriti, P., 'Moving Earth and Making Difference: Dikes and

Frontiers in Early Medieval Bulgaria', in *Borders, Barriers, and Ethnogenesis*, Curta., F. (ed.), pp.59–90 (Turnhout: Brepols, 2005).

37 Rashev, R., 'Remarks on the Archaeological Evidence of Forts and Fortified Settlements in Tenth-Century Bulgaria', in *Borders, Barriers, and Ethnogenesis*, Curta., F. (ed.), pp.51–8 (Turnhout: Brepols, 2005).

38 Hill and Worthington (2003), *op. cit.* in note 28; Hayes and Malim (2008), *op. cit.* in note 35; Malim (2010), *op. cit.* in note 35, p.178; Storr, J., 'Bran, Brent, Fleam and Devil', *British Archaeology*, July/August, pp.46–9, 2013; and Storr, J. (2016) *King Arthur's Wars: The Anglo-Saxon Conquest of England* (Solihul: Hellion, 2016).

39 Bell, M., *The Archaeology of Dykes* (Stroud: Amberley, 2012).

40 Ordnance Survey, *Map of Britain in the Dark Ages – North Sheet* (Southampton: Ordnance Survey, 1938); Ordnance Survey, *Map of Britain in the Dark Ages – South Sheet* (Southampton: Ordnance Survey, 1939); *Ministry of Works, Ancient Monuments in England & Wales List Prepared by the Ministry of Works Corrected to 31st December 1952* (London: Her Majesty's Stationery Office, 1953); and Crawford (1953), *op. cit.* in note 21, pp.240–51.

41 Chalmers, G., *Caledonia Volume 5* (Paisley: Alexander Gardner, 1889), p.237 and Graham, A., 'The Deil's Dyke in Galloway', *Proceedings of the Society of Antiquaries of Scotland*, 83, pp.174–85, 1951).

42 Watson, C., 'The Minchinhampton Custumal and its Place in the Story of the Manor', *Transactions of the Bristol and Gloucestershire Archaeological Society*, 54, pp.203–384, 1932; Darvill, T., *Prehistoric Gloucestershire* (Gloucester: Gloucestershire County Library, 1987) pp.167–9; and Darvill, T., 'Landscapes – Myth or Reality', in Jones, M. and Rotherham, I. (eds), *Landscapes – Perception, Recognition and Management: Reconciling the Impossible?*, pp.11–15 (Sheffield: Wildtrack Publishing, 1998).

43 Shennan, S., Gardiner, J. and Oake, M., *Experiments in the Collection and Analysis of Archaeological Survey Data: The East Hampshire Survey* (Sheffield: Department of Archaeology and Prehistory, 1985).

44 Lawson, A., 'The Horning Hoard', *Norfolk Archaeology*, 37, pp.333–8, 1980; Licence, T., 'Suneman and Wulfric: Two Forgotten Saints of St Benedict's Abbey at Holme in Norfolk', *Analecta Bollandia*, 122, 2, pp.361–72, 2004; Licence, T., 'The Origins of the Monastic Communities of St Benedict at Holme and Bury St Edmunds', *Revue Benedictine*, 116, 1 pp.42–61, 2006; and Pestell, T., *St Benet's Abbey: A Guide and History* (Norwich: Norfolk Archaeology Trust, 2008).

45 Henderson, C., 'Ecclesiastical Antiquities of 109 Parishes of West Cornwall: Lelizzick', *Journal of the Royal Institution of Cornwall*, 1955, p.377.

46 Grundy, G., 'The Saxon Land Charters of Wiltshire (First Series)', *The Archaeological Journal*, 76, pp.143–301, 1919, p.214; Fox, C., Palmer, W. and Duckworth, W., 'Excavations in the Cambridgeshire Dykes: V: Bran or Heydon Ditch, First Report', *Proceedings of the Cambridge Antiquarian Society*, 27, pp.16–42, 1924–5; Lethbridge, T. and Palmer, W., 'Excavations in the Cambridgeshire Dykes: VI: Bran Ditch Second Report', *Proceedings of the Cambridge Antiquarian Society*, 30, pp.78–96, 1927–8; Gray, A., 'The Massacre at the Bran Ditch, A.D. 1010', *Proceedings of the Cambridge Antiquarian Society*, 31, pp.77–87, 1928–30; and Reynolds, A., *Anglo-Saxon Deviant Burial Customs* (Oxford: Oxford University Press, 2009), pp.57 and 106–8.

47 Hinchcliffe, J., 'Excavations at Grim's Ditch, Mongewell', 1974, *Oxoniensia*, 40, pp.122–35, 1975, pp.126–8; Reynolds (2009), *op. cit.* in note 46, pp.130–31; Semple, S., 'Burials

and Political Boundaries in the Avebury Region, North Wiltshire', *Anglo-Saxon Studies in Archaeology and History*, 12, pp.72–91, 2003; and Sauer, E., *Linear Earthwork, Tribal Boundary and Ritual Beheading: Aves Ditch from the Iron Age to the Early Middle Ages* (Oxford: Archaeopress, 2005), pp.47–57.

48 Jenkins, D., *The Law of Hywel Dda* (Llandysul: Gomer Press, 1986), p.116.

49 Hart, C., *The North Derbyshire Archaeological Survey to A.D. 1500* (Chesterfield: The North Derbyshire Archaeological Trust, 1981), pp.111 and 116; and Barnatt, J. and Smith, K., *English Heritage Book of the Peak District: Landscapes Through Time* (London: Batsford/English Heritage, 1997), pp.53–4.

50 Brotherton, P., 'Celtic Place Names and Archaeology in Derbyshire', *Derbyshire Archaeological Journal*, 125, pp.100–37, 2005.

51 White, R., *The Yorkshire Dales Landscapes Through Time* (London: Batsford, 1997), p.46.

52 Fleming, A., 'Swadal, Swar (and Erechwydd?): Early Medieval Polities in Upper Swaledale', *Landscape History*, 16, pp.17–30, 1994.

53 Hunn, J., 'Kingston Bagpuize with Southmoor Bypass', *South Midlands Archaeology*, 22, pp.48–9, 1992.

54 Hankinson, R., *The Short Dykes of Mid and North-East Wales: CPAT Report Number 495* (CPAT: Welshpool, 2002); Hankinson, R., *The Short Dykes of Mid and North-East Wales: CPAT Report Number 592* (CPAT: Welshpool, 2003); and Hankinson, R. and Caseldine, A., 'Short Dykes of Powys and their Origins', *The Archaeological Journal*, 163, pp.264–9, 2006.

55 Macalister, R., 'The Ancient Inscriptions of the South of England', *Archaeologia Cambrensis*, 84, pp.179–96, 1929, p.188; Crawford (1936), *op. cit.* in note 23, p.174; Macalister, R., *Corpus Inscriptionum Insularum Celticarum* (Dublin: Dublin Stationery Office, 1949), pp.180–82; Holmes, J., *1,000 Cornish Place Names Explained* (Penryn: Truran, 1983), p.8; and Sims-Williams, P., *Celtic Inscriptions of Britain: Phonology and Chronology*, c. 400–1200 (Oxford: The Philological Society, 2003), p.210.

56 Blair, P., 'The Northumbrians and their Southern Frontier', *Archaeologia Aeliana*, 4.26, pp.98–126, 1955; and Higham, N., 'Northumbria's Southern Frontier: A Review', *Early Medieval Europe*, 14, 4, pp.391–418, 2006.

57 Fowler, P., 'Wansdyke in the Woods: An Unfinished Roman Military Earthwork for a Non-event', in Ellis, P. (ed.), *Roman Wiltshire and After: Papers in Honour of Ken Annable*, pp.179–98 (Devizes: Wiltshire Archaeological and Natural History Society, 2001); Reynolds (2006), *op. cit.* in note 33; Erskine, J., 'The West Wansdyke: An Appraisal of the Dating, Dimensions and Construction Techniques in the Light of Excavated Evidence', *The Archaeological Journal*, 164, pp.80–108, 2007; Webster, C., *South West Archaeological Research Framework* (Taunton: Somerset County Council, 2008), p.183; and Malim (2010), *op. cit.* in note 35, p.167.

58 Bapty, I., 'Look on My Works: Finding Offa', *British Archaeology*, 97, pp.20–5, 2007; and Ray, K. and Bapty I., *Offa's Dyke: Landscape and Hegemony in Eighth-Century Britain* (Oxford: Windgather Press, 2016).

59 Turner, F., *The Frontier in American History* (New York: H. Holt and Company, 1920).

60 Squatriti (2002), *op. cit.* in note 36, p.65; and Squatriti (2004), *op. cit.* in note 36.

61 Draper (2006), *op. cit.* in note 33, pp.59–60 and 75; and Reynolds and Langlands (2006), *op. cit.* in note 33, pp.31–4.

62 Green (1971), *op. cit.* in note 25, pp.132–3; Feryok, M., 'Offa's Dyke: The Anglo-Saxon Kingdom of Central England', in Zaluckyj, S. (ed.), *Mercia* (Almeley: Logaston Press,

2011), p.167; Hill and Worthington (2003), *op. cit.* in note 28, pp.54, 81 and 101; and Murrieta-Flores, P. and Williams, H., 'Placing the Pillar of Eliseg: Movement, Visibility and Memory in the Early Medieval Landscape', *Medieval Archaeology*, 61, 1, pp.69–103, 2017, pp.87–9.
63 An ankle-breaker is designed to force the attacker's foot to turn sideways, thus twisting or even breaking the ankle of an attacker. Attackers are also obliged to drop their weapon or shield to scramble out. However, it may also have served as a cleaning slot, a feature that either acts as a drainage point where debris collects, or one that is formed when a ditch is repeatedly cleared out.
64 Hill, D., 'The Construction of Offa's Dyke', *Antiquaries Journal*, 65, 1, pp.140–2, 1985; Hill and Worthington (2003), *op. cit.* in note 28, pp.113–19; and Tyler (2011), *op. cit.* in note 32, p.153.
65 Fox (1955), *op. cit.* in note 18, p.282.
66 Gerrard, J., 'How Late is Late? Pottery and the Fifth century in Southwest Britain', in Collins, R. and Gerrard, J. (eds), *Debating Late Antiquity in Britain AD300–700* (Oxford: Archaeopress, 2004), pp.65–75.
67 Dark, S., 'Palaeoecological Evidence for Landscape Continuity and Change in Britain ca A.D. 400–800', in Dark, K. (ed.), *External Contacts and the Economy of Late Roman and Post-Roman Britain* (Woodbridge: The Boydell Press, 1996), p.26.
68 Malim, Penn *et al.* (1996), *op. cit.* in note 26, pp.95–8.
69 Nurse, K., 'New Dating for Wat's Dyke', *History Today*, 49, 8, pp.3–4, 1999; Anon., 'Wat's Dyke Dated: Was it Coenwulf's Dyke?', *British Archaeology*, 97, 7, 2007; and Hayes and Malim (2008), *op. cit.* in note 35, p.149.
70 Alexander, D., 'An Oblong Fort at Finavon, Angus: An Example of the Over-reliance on the Application of Science?', in Smith, B. and Banks. I. (eds), *In the Shadows of the Brochs* (Stroud: Tempus, 2002), pp.45–54.
71 For example, Waldron, A., *The Great Wall of China: From History to Myth* (Cambridge: Cambridge University Press, 1990).
72 Jørgensen, A., 'Fortifications and the Control of Land and Sea Traffic in the Pre-Roman and Iron Age', in Jørgensen, L. and Storgaard, B. (eds), *The Spoils of Victory: The North in the Shadows of the Roman Empire* (Gylling: Denmark, Nationalmuseet, 2003), pp.194–210; and Hjardar, K. and Vike, V., *Vikings at War* (Oxford: Casemate, 2016), pp.120–24.

Chapter 2: The Archaeological Evidence
1 Hawkes, C., 'Britons, Romans and Saxons round Salisbury and in Cranborne Chase: Reviewing the Excavations of General Pitt-Rivers, *1881–1897*', *The Archaeological Journal*, CIV, pp.27–81, 1947, p.66.
2 Varley, W., 'Wat's Dyke at Mynydd Isa, Flintshire', *Flintshire Historical Society Journal*, 27, pp.129–37, 1975–6; Malim (2007), *op. cit.* in Ch.1 note 35, p.17; and Hayes and Malim (2008), *op. cit.* in Ch.1 note 35, p.149.
3 Reynolds (2009), *op. cit.* in Ch1 note 46, pp.220 and 249–50.
4 Morris, J., *The Age of Arthur* (London: Weidenfeld & Nicolson, 1973), pp.101–6.
5 Wenham, S. in Hawkes, S. (ed.), 'Anatomical Interpretations of Anglo-Saxon Weapon Injuries', *Weapons and Warfare in Anglo-Saxon England* (Oxford: Oxford University Committee for Archaeology Monograph, 1989), pp.123–40; and Reynolds (2009), *op. cit.* in Ch1 note 46, p.40.

6   Lethbridge, T., 'Anglo-Saxon Remains', in Salzman, L. (ed.), *The Victoria History of the County of Cambridgeshire and the Isle of Ely: Volume 1* (Oxford: Oxford University Press, 1938), p.309; Phillips, C., 'Ancient Earthworks', in Salzman (ed.), *The Victoria County History of Cambridgeshire and the Isle of Ely: Volume 2* (Oxford: Oxford University Press, 1948), p.9; Lethbridge, T., 'The Riddle of the Dykes', *Proceedings of the Cambridge Antiquarian Society*, LI, 51, 1957, pp.1–5; Biddle, M., 'Finds from the Fleam Dyke, Fen Ditton', *Proceedings of the Cambridge Antiquarian Society*, 56/57, pp.125–7, 1962–3; Royal Commission on the Historical Monuments of England (RCHME), *An Inventory of the Historical Monuments in the County of Cambridge, Volume 2* North-East Cambridgeshire (Worcester & London: Trinity Press, 1972), p.147; Webster, L., 'Cambridgeshire: Newmarket', *Medieval Archaeology*, 17, 138, 1973; Hope-Taylor, B., 'The Devil's Dyke Investigations, 1973', *Proceedings of the Cambridge Antiquarian Society*, 61, p.124, 1975–6; Reynolds (2009), *op. cit.* in Ch1 note 46, pp.46 and 217; and Taylor, A., 'Anglo-Saxon Cemeteries', Kirby, T. and Oosthuizen, S. (eds), *An Atlas of Cambridgeshire and Huntingdonshire History*, 25 (Cambridge: Centre for Regional Studies, Anglia Polytechnic, 2000).

7   Fox, Palmer et al. (1924–5), *op. cit.* in Ch1 note 46; Lethbridge and Palmer (1927–8), *op. cit.* in Ch1 note 46; Gray (1928–30), *op. cit.* in Ch1 note 46; Palmer, W., Leaf, C. and Lethbridge, T., 'Further Excavations at the Bran Ditch', *Proceedings of the Cambridge Antiquarian Society*, 32, pp.54–5, 1930–1; Reynolds (2009), *op. cit.* in Ch1 note 46, pp.57 and 106–8.

8   Hill, D., 'Bran Ditch – The Burials Reconsidered', *Proceedings of the Cambridge Antiquarian Society*, 66, pp.126–8, 1975–6.

9   RCHME, *An Inventory of Historical Monuments in the County of Dorset, Volume 3 Central Part 2* (London: RCHME, 1970), pp.313–14; and Youngs, S., 'Medieval Britain in 1980: Pre-Conquest', *Medieval Archaeology*, 25, pp.166–86, 1981, p.184.

10 Grundy (1919), *op. cit.* in Ch1 note 46, p.214, and Reynolds, A., *Later Anglo-Saxon England: Life and Landscape* (Stroud: Tempus, 1999), p.84.

11 Carver, M., *Sutton Hoo: A Seventh Century Princely Burial Ground and its Context* (London: British Museum Press, 2005), pp.347–8; Buckberry, J. and Hadley, D., 'An Anglo-Saxon Execution Cemetery at Walkington Wold, Yorkshire', *Oxford Journal of Archaeology*, 26, 3, pp.309–29, 2007; Reynolds (2009), *op. cit.* in Ch1 note 46, pp.51–2, 131–4 and 237–8; and Carver, M., *Sutton Hoo: Burial Ground of Kings?* (London: British Museum Press, 2014), pp.137–47.

12 Reynolds (2009), *op. cit.* in Ch1 note 46, pp.145–7.

13 Reynolds (2009), *op. cit.* in Ch1 note 46, pp.113–14.

14 Fox (1955), *op. cit.* in Ch1 note 18, pp.204–5; Feryok (2011), *op. cit.* in Ch1 note 62, p.188; Hill and Worthington (2003), *op. cit.* in Ch1 note 28, pp.152–3.

15 Clywd-Powys Archaeological Trust (CPAT), 'Buttington.' from http://www.cpat.org.uk/ycom/mont/buttington.pdf (2009).

16 Bray, W., *Sketch of a Tour into Derbyshire and Yorkshire* (London: B. White, 1783), p.206; Burne, A., 'Ancient Wiltshire Battlefields', *Wiltshire Archaeological and Natural History Magazine*, 53, p.403; and Reynolds (2009), *op. cit.* in Ch1 note 46, p.59.

17 Reynolds (2009), *op. cit.* in Ch1 note 46, p.48.

18 Clarke, R., 'The Fossditch – A Linear Earthwork in South-West Norfolk', *Norfolk Archaeology*, 31, pp.178–96, 1955.

19 Petch, J. and Davies, E., 'Excavations at Heronbridge', *Journal of the Chester and North Wales Archaeological and Historic Society*, 19, pp.46–8, 1932; Petch, D., 'The Roman

Period', in Elrington, C. (ed.), *The Victoria County History of Cheshire: Volume 1*, pp.115–236 (Oxford: Oxford University Press, 1987), p.189; Mason, D., 'The Heronbridge Archaeological Research Project: An Interim Report on the 2002 and 2003 Season of the Society's New Fieldwork Initiative', *Journal of the Chester and North Wales Archaeological and Historic Society*, 78, pp.49–106, 2003, p.56; and Mason, D., 'AD 616: The Battle of Chester', *Current Archaeology*, 202, pp.516–24, 2005.

20 Hinchcliffe (1975), *op. cit.* in Ch1 note 47, pp.126–8; and Reynolds (2009), *op. cit.* in Ch1 note 46, pp.130–31.

21 Sauer (2005), *op. cit.* in Ch1 note 47, pp.47–57.

22 Lucy, S., (1998), *The Early Anglo-Saxon Cemeteries of East Yorkshire: An Analysis and Reinterpretation* (Oxford: J. and E. Hedges, 1998), pp.85–6; and Semple (2003), *op. cit.* in Ch1 note 47.

23 Charles-Edwards, T., 'Boundaries in Irish Law', in Sawyer, S. (ed.), *Medieval Settlement: Continuity and Change*, pp.84–5 (London: Edward Arnold, 1976); and Reynolds, A., 'Burials, Boundaries and Charters in Anglo-Saxon England: A Reassessment', in Lucy, S. and Reynolds, A. (eds), *Burial in Early Medieval England and Wales* (London: The Society for Medieval Archaeology, 2002), pp.171–94.

24 Archaeological Services Durham University (ASDU), *High Harker Hill, Richmondshire, North Yorkshire: An Archaeological Excavation Report 3032* (Durham: Durham University, 2013).

25 Results from the table. **Becca Banks** radiocarbon dates: Wheelhouse, P. and Burgess, A., 'The Linear Earthworks', in Roberts, I., Burgess, A. and Berg, D. (eds), *A New Link to the Past: The Archaeological Landscape of the M1–A1 Link Road* (Exeter: Short Run Press, 2001), p.144; **Scot's Dyke** Optically Stimulated Luminescence dates: OAN, A66 (Package A) Road Improvement Scheme Greta Bridge to Scotch Corner: Archaeological Post-excavation Assessment, unpublished report, Oxford Archaeology North, 2008; **Clawdd Mawr, Llanfyllin** radiocarbon dates: Hankinson and Caseldine (2006), *op.cit.* in Ch1 note 54, p.266 and Malim (2007), *op. cit.* in Ch1 note 35, p.22; **Crugyn Bank** radiocarbon dates: Hankinson and Caseldine (2006), *op.cit.* in Ch1 note 54, p.266 and Malim (2007), *op. cit.* in Ch1 note 35, p.22; **Giant's Grave, Powys** radiocarbon dates: Hankinson (2003), *op.cit.* in Ch1 note 54, Hankinson and Caseldine (2006), *op.cit.* in Ch1 note 54, pp.266–8 and Malim (2007), *op. cit.* in Ch1 note 35, p.22; **Short Ditch, Powys** radiocarbon dates: Hankinson and Caseldine (2006), *op.cit.* in Ch1 note 54, pp.266–8 and Malim (2007), *op. cit.* in Ch1 note 35, p.22; **Offa's Dyke** radiocarbon dates unpublished study: http://us6.campaign-archive2.com/?u=5557bc147d34993782f185bde&id=b587d981eb&e=005096e2b1#mctoc8; **Upper Short Ditch** radiocarbon dates: Hankinson and Caseldine (2006), *op.cit.* in Ch1 note 54, pp.266–8 and Malim (2007), *op. cit.* in Ch1 note 35, p.22; **Wat's Dyke** radiocarbon dates: Fitzpatrick-Matthews, K. (2001), 'Wat's Dyke: A North Welsh Linear Boundary' from http://www.wansdyke21.org.uk/wansdyke/wanart/matthews1.htm pp.5–7 and Hayes and Malim (2008), *op. cit.* in Ch1 note 35, p.149; **Wat's Dyke** Optically Stimulated Luminescence dates: Malim (2007), *op. cit.* in Ch1 note 35, pp.20–21 and Hayes and Malim (2008), *op. cit.* in Ch1 note 35, pp.174–5; **Fleam Dyke** radiocarbon dates: Malim, Penn *et al.* (1996), *op. cit.* in Ch 1 note 26, pp.65–7 and 96; **Devil's Ditch, Garboldisham** Optically Stimulated Luminescence dates: Bates, S., Hoggett, R. and Schwenninger, J., 'An Archaeological Excavation at Devil's Ditch, Riddlesworth and Garboldisham, Norfolk', Unpublished excavation report 1436, BAU 1307 (Norwich:

Norfolk Archaeological Unit, 2008), p.17; **Harrow-Pinner Grim's Ditch** radiocarbon dates: Bowlt, C., 'A Possible Extension to Grim's Dyke', in Clark, J., Cotton, J., Hall, J. and Swain, H. (eds), *Londinium and Beyond: Essays on Roman London and its Hinterland for Harvey Sheldon* (York: Council for British Archaeology, 2008), p.111; **East Wansdyke** radiocarbon dates: Smith, P. and Cox, P., *The Past in the Pipeline: Archaeology of the Esso Midline* (Salisbury: Trust for Wessex Archaeology, 1986), pp.20–21 and Reynolds and Langlands (2006), *op. cit.* in Ch1 note 33, p.25.

26 Green (1971), *op. cit.* in Ch1 note 25, p.134; and Wilmott, T., 'Excavation and Survey on the Line of Grim's Ditch West Yorkshire 1977–83', *Yorkshire Archaeological Journal*, 65, pp.55–74, 1993.

27 Rippon, S., 'Landscape Change in the "Long Eighth Century"', in Higham, N. and Ryan, M. (eds), *The Landscape of Anglo-Saxon England* (Woodbridge: Boydell, 2010), pp.57–8.

28 Malim, Penn et al. (1996), *op. cit.* in Ch1 note 26, pp.78–95 ; and Squatriti (2004), *op. cit.* in Ch1 note 36.

29 Crampton (1966), *op. cit.* in Ch1 note 24.

30 Green (1971), *op. cit.* in Ch1 note 25, p.138; Astill, G. and Sheddon, K., 'Excavation at Grim's Bank, Aldermaston', *The Berkshire Archaeological Journal*, 70, pp.57–65, 1979–80; and Wheelhouse and Burgess (2001), *op. cit.* in note 24, p.141.

31 Erskine (2007), *op. cit.* in Ch1 note 57, pp.92–5.

32 Boldrini (1999a), *op. cit.* in Ch1 note 31, p.29; and Cronk, K., *Journey along the Roman Ridge: Exploring the Purpose of South West Yorkshire's Ancient Dykes* (Rotherham: Clifton and Wellgate Local History Group, 2004), pp.107, 184 and 188.

33 Wheelhouse and Burgess (2001), *op. cit.* in note 24, p.128.

34 Ford, S., 'Linear Earthworks on the Berkshire Downs', *Berkshire Archaeological Journal*, 71, pp.1–20, 1981–2; Ford, S., 'Fieldwork and Excavation on the Berkshire Grim's Ditch', *Oxoniensia*, 47, 1982, pp.32–5; and Mees, G. and Ford, S., 'A Molluscan Analysis from a Late Iron Age Ditch at Moulsford, South Oxfordshire', *Oxoneinsia*, 58, pp.305–8, 1993.

35 OAN (2008), *op. cit.* in note 24; and Dinn, J., Greig, J., Limbrey, S., Milln, J. and De Rouffignac, C., 'Three Long Mynd Earthworks: Excavation and Assessment of Environmental Potential', *Transactions of the Shropshire Archaeological and Historical Society*, 79, pp.65–88, 2004, p.75.

36 Dark (1996), *op. cit.* in Ch1 note 67; Straker, V., 'Early Medieval Environmental Background', in Webster. C. (ed.), *South West Archaeological Research Framework* (Taunton: Somerset County Council, 2008) pp.163–8; and Rippon (2010), *op. cit.* in note 27.

37 Arnold, C. and Davies, J., *Roman and Early Medieval Wales* (Stroud: Sutton Publishing, 2000), p.178.

38 Williams, G., *Early Anglo-Saxon Coins* (Botley: Shire Publications, 2008).

39 Williamson, T., 'The Environmental Contexts of Anglo-Saxon Settlement', in Higham, N. and Ryan. M. (eds), *The Landscape of Anglo-Saxon England* (Woodbridge: Boydell Press, 2010), p.148.

40 Green, B., Milligan, W. and West, S., 'The Illington/Lackford Workshop', in Evison, V. (ed.) *Angles, Saxons and Jutes* (Oxford: Clarendon Press, 1981), p.224; and Scull, C., 'Approaches to Material Culture and Social Dynamics of the Migration Period in Eastern England', in Bintliff J. and Hamerow, H. (eds), *Europe Between Late Antiquity and the Middle Ages* (Oxford: Tempus Reparatum, 1995), p.75.

41 West, S., *West Stow – The Anglo-Saxon Village* (Ipswich: Suffolk County Planning Department, 1985), p.170; and West, S., 'The Early Anglo-Saxon Period', in Dymond,

D. and Martins, E. (eds), *An Historical Atlas of Suffolk: Revised and Enlarged* (Ipswich: Suffolk County Council, 1988), pp.44–5.

42 Gilchrist, R., 'A Reappraisal of Dinas Powys: Local Exchange and Specialized Livestock Production in 5th to 7th Century Wales', *Medieval Archaeology*, 32, pp.50–62, 1988; and Arnold and Davies (2000), *op. cit.* in note 37, p.166.

43 Härke, H., 'Early Saxon Weapon Burials: Frequencies, Distributions and Weapon Combinations', in Hawkes. S. (ed.), *Weapons and Warfare in Anglo-Saxon England* (Oxford: Oxford University Committee for Archaeology Monograph,1989), pp.49–61; Underwood (1999), *op. cit.* in Ch1 note 13, pp.23–106; Lucy, S., *The Anglo-Saxon Way of Death: Burial Rites in Early England* (Stroud: Sutton Publishing, 2000); Lucy, S. and Reynolds, A., 'Burial in Early Medieval England and Wales: Past, Present and Future', in Lucy, S. and Reynolds, A. (eds), *Burial in Early Medieval England and Wales* (London: The Society of Medieval Archaeology, 2002), pp.1–23; and Härke, H., 'Anglo-Saxon Immigration and Ethnogenisis', *Medieval Archaeology*, 55, pp.1–28, 2011.

44 Wenham (1989), *op. cit.* in note 5; and Reynolds (2009), *op. cit.* in Ch1 note 46, pp.40–46.

45 Hines, J., 'The Military Context of the Adventus Saxonum: Some Continental evidence', in Hawkes, S. (ed.), *Weapons and Warfare in Anglo-Saxon England* (Oxford: Oxford University Committee for Archaeology Monograph, 1989), pp.35–9; Jøgensen, L. and Storgaard, B. (eds), *The Spoils of Victory: The North in the Shadow of the Roman Empire* (Gylling, Denmark: Nationalmuseet, 2003); and Bell (2012), *op. cit.* in Ch1 note 39, p.101.

Chapter 3: Analysing the Earthworks

1 Fitzpatrick-Matthews (2001), *op. cit.* in Ch2 note 24, p.10; and Lewis, P., *Wat's Dyke Way Heritage Trail* (Mold: Alyn Books, 2008), p.12.
2 Tyler (2011), *op. cit.* in Ch1 note 32, p.152.
3 Muir (1981), *op. cit.* in Ch1 note 10, p.160.
4 Ashbee, P. and Jewell, P., 'The Experimental Earthworks Revisited', *Antiquity*, 72, Issue 277, pp.485–504, 1998, p.491.
5 Wainwright, G. and Longworth, I., *Durrington Walls: Excavations 1966–1968* (London: Society of Antiquaries, 1971), p.196; Dames, M., *The Silbury Treasure* (London: Thames & Hudson, 1976); Foster, S., *Maeshowe and the Heart of Neolithic Orkney* (Edinburgh: Historic Scotland, 2006), p.16; and Leary, J. and Field, D., *The Story of Silbury Hill* (Swindon: English Heritage, 2011), p.75.
6 Simmons, B. and Cope-Faulkner, P., *The Car Dyke* (Sleaford: Heritage Trust of Lincolnshire, 2006).
7 Graham, F. and Embleton, R., *Hadrian's Wall in the Days of the Romans* (Newcastle-Upon-Tyne: Frank Graham, 1984), pp.14–19; Johnson, S., *Hadrian's Wall* (London: B.T. Batsford/English Heritage, 1989), pp.41–2; Woodside, R. and Crow, J., *Hadrian's Wall: A Historic Landscape* (London: National Trust, 1999), pp.36–7; and Breeze, D., *Roman Frontiers in Britain* (London: Bristol Classical Press, 2007), p.39.
8 Breeze, D. and Dobson, B., *Hadrian's Wall* (London: Penguin, 2000), p.82.
9 Hill, P., *The Construction of Hadrian's Wall* (Stroud: Tempus, 2006), pp.40 and 127.
10 Breeze (2007), *op. cit.* in note 7, pp.55–6.
11 Hanson, W. and Maxwell, G., *Rome's North West Frontier: The Antonine Wall* (Edinburgh: Edinburgh University Press, 1983), pp.132–3.

12 Higham, N., *Rome, Britain and the Anglo-Saxon* (London: Seaby, 1992), pp.94–5 and 149–52.
13 Breeze (2007), *op. cit.* in note 7, pp.49 and 62.
14 Morris, C., 'A Group of Early Medieval Spades', *Medieval Archaeology*, 24, pp.205–10 (1980a); and Ashbee and Jewell (1998), *op. cit.* in note 4, p.490.
15 British Library document: Cotton Julius A. vi and BL Cotton Tiberius B. v.
16 Wormald, P., 'The Age of Alcuin and Offa', in Campbell. J. (ed.), *The Anglo-Saxons* (Oxford: Phaidon, 1982), p.122.
17 Hayes and Malim (2008), *op. cit.* in Ch1 note 35, p.165.
18 Hill (1985), *op. cit.* in Ch 1 note 64, p.142; and Hill and Worthington (2003), *op. cit.* in Ch1 note 28, pp.113–19.
19 Reynolds and Langlands (2006), *op. cit.* in Ch1 note 33, p.410.
20 Tyler (2011), *op. cit.* in Ch1 note 32, p.152.
21 Jewell, P. (ed.), *The Experimental Earthwork on Overton Down, Wiltshire, 1960* (London: The British Association for the Advancement of Science, 1963); and Hutchinson, J. and Stuart, J., 'Analyses of the Morphological Changes with Time, through Denudation and Siltation, in Ditches of Trapezoidal and Triangular Section', *Journal of Archaeological Science*, 30, 7, pp.707–808, 2003.
22 Muir (1981), *op. cit.* in Ch1 note 10, p.160 ; Fowler (2001), *op. cit.* in Ch1 note 57, pp.192–3; Erskine (2007), *op. cit.* in Ch1 note 57, p.98; Lewis (2008), *op. cit.* in note 1, p.12; and Tyler (2011), *op. cit.* in Ch1 note 32, pp.152–3.
23 Atkinson, R., 'Neolithic Engineering', *Antiquity*, 35, pp.292–9, 1961; Wainwright (1971), *op. cit.* in note 5, pp.196–7; Hanson and Maxwell (1983), *op. cit.* in note 11, pp.132–3; Breeze and Dobson (2000), *op. cit.* in note 8, p.82; Hill (2006), *op. cit.* in note 9, pp.115–16 and 127; Pearson, M., *English Heritage: A Book of Bronze Age Britain* (London: Batsford, 1993), p.71; and Leary, J. and Field, D., *The Story of Silbury Hill* (Swindon: English Heritage, 2011), p.116.
24 Bachrach, B., 'Logistics in Pre-Crusade Europe', in Lynn, J. (ed.), *Feeding Mars: Logistics in Western Warfare from the Middle Ages to the Present* (Oxford: Westview Press, 1993), p.67.
25 Hanson and Maxwell (1983), *op. cit.* in note 11, p.132; and Breeze and Dobson (2000), *op. cit.* in note 8, p.82.
26 Dixon, P., 'The Anglo-Saxon Settlement at Mucking: An Interpretation', *Anglo-Saxon Studies in Archaeology and History*, 6, pp.125–47, 1993, p.147; and Lewis (2008), *op. cit.* in note 1, p.12.
27 *Royal Engineers Pocket Book* (Chatham: Royal Engineers, 2008 edition), 9-1-1.
28 Hill (2006), *op. cit.* in note 9, p.126.
29 Spain, B., *Spon's Estimating Costs Guide to Minor Works, Alterations and Repairs to Fire, Flood, Gale and Theft Damage* (London: Spon, 2001), p.5.
30 Waldron (1990), *op. cit.* in Ch1 note 71, p.26.
31 Millett, M., *Roman Britain* (London: B.T. Batsford/English Heritage, 1995), pp.14 and 78; and Breeze (2007), *op. cit.* in note 7, pp.22–4.
32 Crouch, D., *William Marshal: Knighthood, War and Chivalry, 1147–1219* (Harlow: Longman, 2002), p.203.
33 Clanchy, M., *England and its Rulers 1066–1307* (Oxford: Blackwell, 2006), p.295.
34 Bachrach (1993), *op. cit.* in note 24, p.65.
35 Bachrach (1993), *op. cit.* in note 24, p.67; and Squatriti (2002), *op. cit.* in Ch1 note 36, p.41.

36 Barber, J., Lawes-Martay, E. and Milln, J., 'The Linear Earthworks of Southern Scotland; Survey and Classification', *Transactions of the Dumfriesshire and Galloway Natural History and Antiquarian Society*, 73, pp.63–164, 1999.
37 Copeland, T., 'The North Oxfordshire Grim's Ditch: A Fieldwork Survey', *Oxoniensia*, 53, pp.277–92, 1988, pp.283–84; Bachrach (1993), *op. cit.* in note 24, p.67; Hill and Worthington (2003), *op. cit.* in Ch 1, note 28, p.126; and Tyler (2011), *op. cit.* in Ch1 note 32, p.149.
38 Crampton (1966), *op. cit.* in Ch1 note 24, p.376; Green (1971), *op. cit.* in Ch1 note 25, pp.136–41; Malim, Penn *et al.* (1996), *op. cit.* in note 26, pp.72–8 and 88–90; and Hayes and Malim (2008), *op. cit.* in note 35, p.156.
39 Green (1971), *op. cit.* in Ch1 note 25, pp.132–3.
40 Feryok (2011), *op. cit.* in Ch1 note 62, p.167; and Hill and Worthington (2003), *op. cit.* in Ch1 note 28, pp.54, 81 and 101.
41 Stanford, S., *The Archaeology of the Welsh Marches* (London: Collins, 1980), p.187; and Bapty (2016), *op. cit.* in Ch1 note 58, pp.191–2.
42 Feryok (2011), *op. cit.* in Ch1 note 62, p.167.

Chapter 4: Written Evidence
1 Dumville, D., 'The Tribal Hidage: An Introduction to its Texts and their History', in *The Origins of Anglo-Saxon Kingdoms* (Leicester: Leicester University Press, 1989), pp.225–30; and Zaluckyj (2011), *op. cit.* in Ch1 note 62, pp.17–21.
2 Brooks, N., *Communities and Warfare 700–1400* (London: Hambledon Press, 2000), p.33; and Halsall, G., *Warfare and Society in the Barbarian West, 450–900* (London: Routledge, 2003), p.103.
3 Hill, D. and Rumble, A. (eds), *The Defence of Wessex: The Burghal Hidage and the Anglo-Saxon Fortifications* (Manchester: Manchester University Press, 1996); Brooks (2000), *op. cit.* note 2, pp.114–37; and Reynolds and Langlands (2006), *op. cit.* in Ch1 note 33, pp.39–40.
4 Whitelock, D. (ed.), *English Historical Documents c.500–1042*, English Historical Documents (London: Eyre and Spottiswoode, 1955), pp.357–72; Griffiths, B., *An Introduction to Early English Law* (Hockwold-cum-Wilton: Anglo-Saxon Books, 1995); and Oliver, L., *The Beginnings of English Law* (Toronto: University of Toronto Press, 2002), pp.14–20.
5 Whitelock (1955), *op. cit.* note 4, p.366.
6 Whitelock (1955), *op. cit.* note 4, pp.361–2 and 366; and Curta (2011), *op. cit.* in Ch1 note 30, pp.29–30.
7 Whitelock (1955), *op. cit.* note 4, pp.363–8 and 369; Pelteret, D., 'Slave Raiding and Slave Trading in Early England', *Anglo-Saxon England*, 9, pp.99–114, 1981; and Griffiths (1995), *op. cit.* note 4, p.42.
8 Carr, A. and Jenkins, D., *A Look at Hywel's Law* (Hendy-gwyn ar daf: Cymdeithas Genedlaethol Hywel Dda, 1985); and Jenkins (1986), *op. cit.* in Ch1 note 48.
9 Jenkins (1986), *op. cit.* in Ch1 note 48, pp.9, 114–19 and 164–6; and Iverson, S., *Anglo-Welsh Wars 1050–1300* (Wrexham: Bridge Books, 2001), p.11.
10 Márkus, G., *Adomnáin's 'Law of the Innocents'* (Kilmartin: Kilmartin House Trust, 2008).
11 Jackson, K., 'The Britons in Southern Scotland', *Antiquity*, 29, 114, pp.77–88, 1955; and Wormald, P., 'Anglo-Saxon Law and Scots Law', *Scottish Historical Review*, 88, 2, pp.192–206, 2009.

12 Sawyer, P., *Anglo-Saxon Charters: An Annotated List and Bibliography* (London: Offices of the Royal Historical Society, 1968).
13 Fleming (1994), *op. cit.* in Ch1 note 52, pp.18 and 28.
14 Whitelock (1955), *op. cit.* note 4, pp.440–41.
15 Barker, J., 'Old English Fæsten', in Padel O., and Parsons. D. (eds), *A Commodity of Good Names: Essays in Honour of Margaret Gelling* (Donnington: Shaun Tyas, 2008), pp.333–44.
16 Grundy (1919), *op. cit.* in Ch1 note 46, p.214; and Reynolds (1999), *op. cit.* in Ch2 note 10, p.84.
17 Fox (1955), *op. cit.* in Ch 1, note 18, pp.216–18 and Feryok (2011), p.189.
18 Aldsworth, H., *Towards a Pre-Domesday Geography of Hampshire: A Review of the Evidence*, Southampton B.A. (1973).
19 Gresham, C., 'The Aberconwy Charter: Further Consideration', *Bulletin of the Board of Celtic Studies*, 30, Parts 3 & 4, pp.311–47, 1982.
20 Evans, J. and Rhys, J., *The Text of the Book of Llan Dav* (Oxford: J. Evans, 1893); and Davies, W., *An Early Welsh Microcosm: Studies in the Llandaff Charters* (London: Royal Historical Society, 1978).
21 Whitelock (1955), *op. cit.* note 4, pp.516–17; Brooks (2000), *op. cit.* note 2, pp.32–47; and Zaluckyj (2011), *op. cit.* in Ch1 note 62, p.208.
22 Douglas, D. and Greenaway, G. (eds), *English Historical Documents 1042–1189* (London: Eyre & Methuen, 1981), pp.875–7.
23 Squatriti (2002), *op. cit.* in Ch1 note 36, p.151.
24 Whitelock (1955), *op. cit.* note 4, p.197; Wormald (1982), *op. cit.* in Ch3 note 16, p.101; and Kelly, S., 'Trading Privileges from Eighth-century England', *Early Medieval Europe*, 1, 1, pp.3–28, 1992.
25 Colgrave, B., *The Life of Bishop Wilfrid by Eddius Stephanus* (Cambridge: Cambridge University Press, 1927), p.37; Colgrave, B., *Felix's Life of St Guthlac* (Cambridge: Cambridge University Press, 1956), pp.80–81 and 108–11; Hood, A., *St. Patrick: His Writings and Muirchu's Life* (Chichester: Phillimore & Co., 1978), pp.24 and 43; Morris, J., *Nennius: British History and the Welsh Annals* (London & Chichester: Phillimore, 1980b), pp.1, 37 and 78; Pelteret (1981), *op. cit.* in note 7, pp.109–10; MacQueen, J., *St Nynia* (Edinburgh: John Donald, 2005), p.94; Zaluckyj (2011), op. cit. in Ch1 note 62, p.84; and Thompson, I., *Felix, St Guthlac and the Early History of Crowland* (Scunthorpe: Bluestone Books, 2008), p.2.
26 Colgrave, B. and Mynors, R., *Bede's Ecclesiastical History of the English People* (Oxford: Clarendon Press, 1969); Sherley-Price, L. and Latham, R. (eds), *Bede: A History of the English Church and People* (London: Penguin, 1955); Higham, N., *An English Empire: Bede and the Early Anglo-Saxon kings* (Manchester: Manchester University Press, 1995); and Higham, N., *(Re-)Reading Bede: The Ecclesiastical History in Context* (Abingdon: Routledge, 2006).
27 Swanton, M. (ed.), *The Anglo-Saxon Chronicles* (London: Phoenix Press, 2000); Zaluckyj (2011), *op. cit.* in Ch1 note 62, p.xi; Jørgensen, A., *Reading the Anglo-Saxon Chronicle: Language, Literature, History* (Turnhout: Brepols, 2010); Higham, N. and Ryan, M., *The Anglo-Saxon World* (Newhaven, CT and London: Yale University Press, 2013), pp.271–6; and Brooks, N., 'Why is the Anglo-Saxon Chronicle about Kings?', *Anglo-Saxon England*, 39, pp.43–70, 2010.
28 White, S., 'Kinship and Lordship in Early Medieval England: The Story of Cynewulf and Cyneheard', *Viator*, 20, pp.1–18, 1989.

29 Sherley-Price (1955), *op. cit.* in note 26, p.103; Morris (1980b), *op. cit.* in note 25, pp.46 and 86; and Swanton (2000), *op. cit.* in note 27, pp.22–3.
30 For example: Fox and Fox (1958), *op. cit.* in Ch1 note 20, pp.42–4; Draper (2006), *op. cit.* in Ch1 note 33, pp.59–60; and Storr (2016), *op. cit.* in Ch1 note 38, p.206.
31 Morris (1980b), *op. cit.* in note 25, pp.44–9 and 85–91; Dumville, D., *Annales Cambriae, A.D. 682–954: Texts A–C in Parallel* (Cambridge: Department of Anglo-Saxon, Norse and Celtic, University of Cambridge, (2002); and Grigg, E., '"Mole Rain" and Other Natural Phenomena in the Welsh Annals', *Welsh History Review*, 24, 4, pp.1–40, 2009.
32 Griscom, A., The 'Book of Basingwerk' and MS. Cotton Cleopatra, B.V., *Y Cymmrodor*, 35, pp.49–109, 1925, p.106.
33 Morris (1980b), *op. cit.* in note 25.
34 Keynes and Lapidge (1983), *op. cit.* in Ch1 note 4; Smyth, A., *King Alfred the Great* (Oxford: Oxford University Press, 1995); Asser and Smyth, A., *The Medieval Life of King Alfred the Great: A Translation and Commentary on the Text Attributed to Asser* (Basingstoke: Palgrave, 2002); and Tyler (2002), *op. cit.* in Ch1 note 32, pp.192–4.
35 Winterbottom, M., *Gildas: The Ruin of Britain and Other Documents. Arthurian Period Sources Volume 7* (Chichester: Phillimore, 1978); and McKee, I., 'Gildas: Lessons from History', *Cambrian Medieval Celtic Studies*, 51, pp.1–36, 2006.
36 Bachrach (1993), *op. cit.* in Ch 3 note 24, p.64; and Bennett, M., Bradbury, J., DeVries, K., Dickie, I. and Jestice, P., *Fighting Techniques of the Medieval World AD 500– AD 1500* (Staplehurst: Spellmount, 2005), p.175.
37 Malone, K., *Widsith* (Copenhagen: Rosenkilde & Bagger, 1962); and Niles, J., 'Widsith and the Anthropology of the Past', *Philological Quarterly*, 78, 1/2, pp.171–213, 1999.
38 Wrenn, C. and Bolton, W., *Beowulf* (Exeter: Exeter University Press, 1996).
39 Crossley-Holland, K., *The Anglo-Saxon World: An Anthology* (Oxford: Oxford University Press, 1982), pp.304–6.
40 Griffiths, B., *The Battle of Maldon: Text and Translation* (Swaffham: Anglo-Saxon Books, 2000).
41 Evans, J., *Poems from the Books of Taliesin* (Llanberog: Tremvan, 1915), pp.113–14; Pennar, M., *Taliesín Poems* (Lampeter: Llanerch Enterprises, 1988), p.70; and Fleming, A., *Swaledale: Valley of the Wild River* (Edinburgh: Edinburgh University Press, 1998), p.29.
42 Williams, I., *Canu Llywarch Hen* (Cardiff: University of Wales Press, 1935), pp.3 and 42; and Ford, P., 'Llywarch, Ancestor of Welsh Princes', *Speculum*, 45, 3, pp.442–50, 1970.
43 Kirby, D., 'Welsh Bards and the Border', in Dornier, A. (ed.), *Mercian Studies*, pp.31–42 (Leicester: Leicester University Press, 1977), p.32.
44 Jarman, A., *Aneirin: Y Gododdin* (Llandysul: Gomer Press, 1988); Cessford, C., 'Northern England and the Gododdin poem', *Northern History*, 33, pp.218–22, 1997; and Lowe, C., *Angles, Fools and Tyrants: Britons and Anglo-Saxons in Southern Scotland* (Edinburgh: Canongate Books, 1999), pp.12–16.
45 OAN (2008), *op. cit.* in Ch2 note 24; and Elizabeth Huckerby of OAN personal communication.
46 Fleming (1994), *op. cit.* in Ch1 note 52, p.27; Koch, J., *The Gododdin of Aneirin* (Cardiff: University of Wales Press, 1997); Padel, O., 'A New Study of Gododdin', *Cambrian Medieval Celtic Studies*, 35, pp.45–55, 1998; and Lowe (1999), *op. cit.* in note 44, pp.13–16.
47 Gantz, J., *Early Irish Myths and Sagas* (London: Penguin, 1981).
48 MacQueen (2005), *op. cit.* in note 25.

49 Colgrave (1927), *op. cit.* in note 25; and Webb, J., *The Age of Bede* (London: Penguin, 1998), pp.105–84.
50 Hood (1978), *op. cit.* in note 25.
51 Ritchie, A., *Picts* (Edinburgh: HMSO, 1989), pp.22–7; and Lowe (1999), *op. cit.* in note 44, p.11.
52 Hill, D., 'Offa's Dyke: Pattern and Purpose', *Antiquaries Journal*, 80, pp.195–206, 2000; Hill and Worthington (2003), *op. cit.* in Ch 1 note 28, pp.108–10 and 178–80; Jones, O., 'Hereditas Pouoisi: The Pillar of Eliseg and the History of Early Powys', *The Welsh History Review*, 24, 4, pp.41–80, 2009; Tyler (2011), *op. cit.* in Ch1 note 32, p.156; and Murrieta-Flores and Williams (2017), *op. cit.* in Ch1 note 62.
53 Swanton, M., *The Two Lives of Offa* (Crediton: Medieval Press, 2010).
54 Vaughan, R., *Chronicles of Matthew Paris* (Gloucester: Alan Sutton, 1986), pp.169–72.
55 Pálsson, H. and Edwards, P., *Orkneyinga Saga: The History of the Earls of Orkney* (London: Penguin, 1978), pp.123–4 and 131–2; and Hill, D. and Sharp, S., 'An Anglo-Saxon Beacon System', in Rumble, A. and Mills, A. (eds), *Names, People and Places: An Onomastic Miscellany in Memory of John McNeal Dodgson* (Stamford: Paul Watkins, 1997), pp.157–65.
56 Winterbottom (1978), *op. cit.* in note 35, pp.22 and 94; and Erskine (2007), *op. cit.* in Ch1 note 57, p.98.
57 Fowler (2001), *op. cit.* in Ch1 note 57, p.197; and Erskine (2007), *op. cit.* in Ch1 note 57, pp.98–105.
58 Sumner, H., 'Combs Ditch and Bokerly Dyke, Reviewed', *Proceedings of the Dorset Natural History and Archaeological Society*, 52, pp.59–74, 1931, p.59; Forsberg, R., *A Contribution to a Dictionary of Old English Place-names* (Upsalla: Almqvist & Wiksells Boktryckeri AB, 1950), pp.204–5; Crawford, O., 'Place-names: A Review', *Antiquity*, XXV, 98, p.63, 1951; Mills, A., *The Place-Names of Dorset Part II* (Cambridge: University Press, 1980), pp.70–71; and Jackson, K., 'Gildas and the Names of the British Princes', *Cambridge Medieval Celtic Studies*, 3, p.30, 1982.
59 Griscom (1925), *op. cit.* in note 32, pp.98–9.

Chapter 5: Across the World: Raiding and Dykes from Other Periods and Places
1 Pryor, F., *Seahenge: A Quest for Life and Death in Bronze Age Britain* (London: Harper Collins, 2002), pp.213–14.
2 Pálsson and Edwards (1978), *op. cit.* in Ch4 note 55, pp.55, 123–4, 131–32 and 146.
3 Nunneley, J., *Tales from the East African Rifles* (London: Cassell & Co., 1998), pp.46–8.
4 Ashworth, T., *Trench Warfare 1914–1918: The Live and Let Live System* (London: Pan Books, 2000), pp.176–210.
5 Halsall, G., 'Anthropology and the Study of Pre-Conquest Warfare and Society: The Ritual War in Anglo-Saxon England', in Hawkes, S. (ed.), *Weapons and Warfare in Anglo-Saxon England* (Oxford: Oxford University Committee for Archaeology Monograph, 1989), pp.155–77.
6 Sauer (2005), *op. cit.* in Ch1 note 47, pp.30–45.
7 Breeze and Dobson (2000), *op. cit.* in Ch3 note 8; Hill (2006), *op. cit.* in Ch3 note 9; Breeze (2007), *op. cit.* in Ch3 note 7; and Breeze, D., *Hadrian's Wall* (London: English Heritage, 2011).
8 Keynes and Lapidge (1983), *op. cit.* in Ch1 note 4, p.78; and Harding, A. and Ostoja-Zagorski, J., 'Prehistoric and Early Medieval Activity on Danby Rigg, North Yorkshire', *The Archaeological Journal*, 151, pp.16–97, 1994.

9   For example: Hogg, A., *Hill-Forts of Britain* (London: Granada, 1975), pp.58–65; and Bassett, S., 'The Middle and Late Anglo-Saxon Defences of Western Mercian Towns', *Anglo-Saxon Studies in Archaeology and History*, 15, pp.180–239, 2008.
10 Crawford (1953), *op. cit.* in Ch1 note 21, pp.184–5; Collins, R., 'Before "the End": Hadrian's Wall in the 4th Century and After', in Collins, R. and Gerrard, J. (eds), *Debating Late Antiquity in Britain AD 300–700* (Oxford: Hadrian Books, 2004), pp.127–30; Sauer (2005), *op. cit.* in Ch1 note 47, pp.40–45; Mayor, J., García, R. and Pacheco, Y., 'A propósito de las fortificaciones lineales ástures de El Homón de Faro (La Carisa) y El Muro (La Mesa)', *Territorio, Sociedad y Poder*, 2, pp.53–64, 2007a; Mayor, J., García, R. and Pacheco, Y., 'Un sistema de fortificaciones lineales Astures en la Cordillera Cantábrica a finales del reino visigodo', *Boletín de arqueología medieval*, 13, pp.229–56, 2007b; Póo, M., Gancedo, M. and Martínez, A., 'Castellum (?) de Cotero Marojo y vallum duplex de Cotero del Medio (Luena y Molledo)', in Gancedo, M. and Martínez, A. (eds), *Castros y Castra en Cantabria. Fortificaciones desde los orígenes de la Edad del Hierro a las guerras con Roma* (Santander: ACANTO, 2010), pp.324–28; and Hjardar and Vike (2016), *op. cit.* in Ch1 note 72, pp.120–24.
11 Crawford (1953), *op. cit.* in Ch1 note 21, pp.121 and 184; Evans, E., *Prehistoric and Early Christian Ireland* (London: Batsford, 1966), pp.58–9 and 140–41; Muir (1981), *op. cit.* in Ch1 note 10, p.162; Waddell, J., *The Prehistoric Archaeology of Ireland* (Dublin: Galway University Press, 1998), pp.358–60; and Bell (2012), *op. cit.* in Ch1 note 39, pp.80–82.
12 Crawford (1953), *op. cit.* in Ch1 note 21, p.184; Wilson, D., *Civil and Military Engineering in Viking Age Scandinavia* (London: Trustees of the National Maritime Museum, 1978), pp.3–6; Squatriti (2002), *op. cit.* in Ch1 note 36, pp.15–16 and 20–29; Hill and Worthington (2003), *op. cit.* in Ch1 note 28, p.106; and Hjardar and Vike (2016), *op. cit.* in Ch1 note 72, pp.120–23.
13 Hines (1989), *op. cit.* in Ch2 note 45, p.34; Jørgensen (2003), *op. cit.* in Ch1 note 72; and Bell (2012), *op. cit.* in Ch1 note 39, pp.101–4.
14 Bury, J., 'The Bulgarian Treaty of A.D. 814, and the Great Fence of Thrace', *English Historical Review*, 25, 98, pp.16–23,1910; Squatriti (2002), *op. cit.* in Ch1 note 36, pp.15–16, 26–9 and 32–40; Rashev (2005), *op. cit.* in Ch1 note 37; Squatriti (2005), *op. cit.* in Ch1 note 36, pp.75–6; and Curta (2011), *op. cit.* in Ch1 note 30.
15 Waldron (1990), *op. cit.* in Ch1 note 7, pp.36–7 and 47.

Chapter 6: Raiding: The Epitome of Early Medieval Warfare
1   Curta (2011), *op. cit.* in Ch1 note 30, p.23, for example.
2   Keegan, J., *The Face of Battle: A Study of Agincourt, Waterloo and the Somme* (London: Pimlico, 2004), p.71; Crossley-Holland (1982), *op. cit.* in Ch4 note 39, p.297; Abels, R., *Lordship and Military Obligation in Anglo-Saxon England* (London: British Museum Publications, 1988), pp.35–6; and Bennett, Bradbury *et al.* (2005), *op. cit.* in Ch4 note 36, p.83.
3   Pàlsson and Edwards (1978), *op. cit.* in Ch4 note 55, pp.60–61 and 146–47.
4   Abels (1988), *op. cit.* in note 2, pp.11–37; and Iverson (2001), *op. cit.* in Ch4 note 9, pp.21–3.
5   Wrenn and Bolton (1996), *op. cit.* in Ch4 note 38, pp.155–6.
6   Pollington, S., *An Introduction to the Old English Language and its Literature* (Chippenham: Anglo-Saxon Books, 1994), p.53.

ENDNOTES

7   Keegan (2004), *op. cit.* in note 2, p.71; and Bennett, Bradbury *et al.* (2005), *op. cit.* in Ch4 note 36, p.83.
8   Davis, R., 'Did the Anglo-Saxons Have Warhorses?', in Hawkes, S. (ed.), *Weapons and Warfare in Anglo-Saxon England* (Oxford: Oxford University Committee for Archaeology, Monograph, 1989), pp.141–4; Iverson (2001), *op. cit.* in Ch4 note 9, pp.28–9; and Bennett, Bradbury *et al.* (2005), *op. cit.* in Ch4 note 36, pp.17–19 and 73–5.
9   Coleman, J., 'Rape in Anglo-Saxon England', in Halsall G. (ed.), *Violence and Society in the Early Medieval West* (Woodbridge: Boydell Press, 1998), pp.193–204.
10 Carroll, J., Harrison, S. and Williams, G., *The Vikings in Britain and Ireland* (London: British Museum Press, 2014), p.22.
11 Crawford (1953), *op. cit.* in Ch1 note 21, p.93; and Bowen, H., *The Archaeology of Bokerley Dyke* (London: Royal Commission on Historical Monuments, 1990), pp.52–7, 67–73 and 94–5.
12 Carroll, Harrison *et al.* (2014), *op. cit.* in note 10, p.35.
13 Wrenn and Bolton (1996), *op. cit.* in Ch4 note 38, p.196.
14 Winterbottom (1978), *op. cit.* in Ch4 note 35, pp.22–3 and 94–5; Ritchie (1989), *op. cit.* in Ch4 note 51, pp.22–7; and Lowe (1999), *op. cit.* in Ch4 note 44, p.11.
15 Wenham (1989), *op. cit.* in Ch2 note 5; Underwood (1999), *op. cit.* in Ch1 note 13, p.62; Mason (2003), *op. cit.* in Ch2 note 19, p.56; and Reynolds (2009), *op. cit.* in Ch1 note 46, pp.40–46.
16 Bone, P., 'The Development of Anglo-Saxon Swords from the Fifth to the Eleventh Century', in Hawkes, S. (ed.), *Weapons and Warfare in Anglo-Saxon England* (Oxford: Oxford University Committee for Archaeology Monograph, 1989), pp.63–70; Lang, J. and Ager, B., 'A Radiographic Study of Swords', in Hawkes, S. (ed.), *Weapons and Warfare in Anglo-Saxon England* (Oxford: Oxford University Committee for Archaeology, Monograph, 1989), pp.85–122; and Underwood (1999), *op. cit.* in Ch1 note 13, p.50.
17 Burne, A., 'Offa's Dyke – Boundary or Barrier?', *Journal of the Chester and North Wales Archaeological and Historic Society*, 46, pp.25–32, 1959.
18 Morris (1980b), *op. cit.* in Ch4 note 25, pp.47 and 88.
19 Muir (1981), *op. cit.* in Ch1 note 10, pp.158–9.
20 Allcroft, A., *Earthwork of England* (London: Macmillan, 1908), p.507.
21 Noble and Gelling (1983), *op. cit.* in Ch1 note 27, pp.49, 58 and 60; and Hill and Worthington (2003), *op. cit.* in Ch 1 note 28, pp.113–28.
22 Bell (2012), *op. cit.* in Ch1 note 39, p.110.
23 Abels (1988), *op. cit.* in note 2, pp.11–37; and Iverson (2001), *op. cit.* in Ch4 note 9, pp.21–3.
24 Bachrach, B., *Early Carolingian Warfare: Prelude to Empire* (Pennsylvania: University of Pennsylvania, 2001), p.ix.
25 Halsall (1998), *op. cit.* in Ch1 note 12, pp.15 and 26.
26 Arnold, T. (ed.), *Symeonis Monachi Opera Omnia: Volume 1, Roll Series* (London: Longman, 1882), pp.338–9.
27 Ottaway, P., *Romans on the Yorkshire Coast* (York: Yorkshire Archaeological Trust and English Heritage, 1996).
28 Fulford, M., 'Byzantium and Britain: A Mediterranean Perspective on Post-Roman Mediterranean Imports in Western Britain and Ireland', *Medieval Archaeology*, 33, pp.1–6, 1989.

29 Fleming (1994), *op. cit.* in Ch1 note 52, pp.26–7; White (1997), *op. cit.* in Ch1 note 51, p.46; Fleming (1998), *op. cit.* in Ch4 note 41, pp.18–32; and Higham, M., 'Names on the Edge: Hills and Boundaries', *Nomina*, 22, pp.60–74, 1999.
30 Squatriti (2002), *op. cit.* in Ch1 note 36, pp.43–6.
31 Halsall (1998), *op. cit.* in Ch1 note 12, p.20.
32 Pálsson and Edwards (1978), *op. cit.* in Ch4 note 55, pp.123–4 and 131–2; Hill and Sharp (1997), *op. cit.* in Ch4 note 55; Finlay, A., *Fagrskinna, A Catalogue of the Kings of Norway* (Leiden: Brill, 2004), pp.63–4; and Breeze (2011), *op. cit.* in Ch5 note 7, pp.142 and 220.
33 Hill and Worthington (2003), *op. cit.* in Ch 1 note 28, pp.4, 99, 121 and 127.
34 Spain, G., 'The Black Dyke in Northumberland: An Account of the Earthwork', *Archaeologia Aeliana*, 19, 3, p.155, 1922.
35 Fox and Fox (1958), *op. cit.* in Ch1 note 20, pp.26 and 37; and Reynolds and Langlands (2006), *op. cit.* in Ch1 note 33, p.16.
36 Hill and Sharp (1997), *op. cit.* in Ch4 note 55.
37 Reynolds, A., 'Avebury: A Late Anglo-Saxon Burh?', *Antiquity*, 75, 287, pp.29–30, 2001; and Reynolds, A., 'From Pagus to Parish: Territory and Settlement in the Avebury Region from the Late Roman Period to the Domesday Survey', in Brown, G., Field G. and McOmish, D. (eds), *The Avebury Landscape* (Oxford: Oxbow Books, 2005), pp.164–80.
38 Bothamley, C., 'Ancient Earthworks', in Page, W. (ed.), *The Victoria County History of Somerset: Volume 2* (London: Dawsons, 1911), pp.490–91; and Burrow, I., *Hillfort and Hill-Top Settlement in Somerset in the First to Eighth Centuries A.D.* (Oxford: BAR, 1981), p.214.
39 Mitchell, S., 'On the Southern Frontier Defences of the Brigantes and Northumbrians', in Bowman, W. (ed.), *Reliquiæ Antiquæ Eboracenses; or Remains of Antiquity, Relating to the County of York* (Leeds: Cooke and Clark, 1855), pp.73–4; and Armitage, E. and Montgomerie, D., 'Ancient Earthworks', in Page, W. (ed.), *The Victoria County History of Yorkshire: Volume 2* (London: Dawsons, 1974), pp.26–9.
40 Hornsby, W. and Laverick, J., 'The Roman Signal Station at Goldsborough near Whitby', *The Archaeological Journal*, 89, pp.203–19, 1932.
41 Nicholson, K., *Beacons of East Yorkshire* (Driffield: T. Holderness, 1887), pp.34–7; and Purdy, J., 'Flamborough', in Allison, K. (ed.), *The Victoria County History of Yorkshire East Riding: Volume 2* (London: Dawsons, 1974), p.153.
42 Laycock (2006), *op. cit.* in Ch1 note 34.
43 Brookes, S., 'Mapping Anglo-Saxon Civil Defence', in Baker, J., Brookes, S. and Reynolds, A. (eds), *Landscapes of Defence in the Viking Age: Anglo-Saxon England and Comparative Perspectives* (Turnhout: Brepols, 2013), pp.39–63.

INDEX

Aberbechan Dyke, Powys 39, 147, 151, 168
Aberconwy Charter 92
Aberford Dykes, Yorkshire 38, 48, 158–9
Aberlemno, Angus 103, 120
Abernaint Dyke, Powys 39, 147, 151, 168
Adomnáin 87, 133
Aelfrith's Dyke, Oxfordshire 28–9, 31, 34, 41, 53, 67, 75, 89–90, 113, 127–8, 145, 189
Aethelfrith (King) 95
Alfred (King) 11
Aneirin 101
Angevins 76
Anglesey, Gwynedd 76
Anglo-Saxon Chronicle 12, 32–3, 52, 94–7, 106, 113, 125, 135
Annales Cambriae 95–6, 133
Antonine Wall 65–8, 71, 109
Arthur (King) 10, 97
Asser 9, 13, 18, 32, 97–8, 106, 110
Avebury, Wiltshire 71, 130
Aves Ditch, Oxfordshire 26, 41, 53, 108, 152, 189

Bank Slack, Yorkshire 20, 39, 146, 159
Bar Dyke, Yorkshire 39, 131, 146, 159
Bardon Mill Dyke, Northumberland 38, 130, 146, 156
Battery Banks, Dorset 42, 149, 197
Beachley Bank, Gloucestershire 40, 48, 52, 89, 91, 148, 151, 175
Becca Banks, Yorkshire 38, 55, 57, 67, 74–5, 79, 144, 158–9
Bedd Eiddil Dyke, Glamorgan 39, 57, 64, 147, 168
Bede 60, 93–5, 98, 109, 133

Bedwyn Dyke, Wiltshire 42, 48, 52, 89, 114, 148, 193
Beowulf 99, 117, 120
Berkshire Downs Grim's Ditch 41, 57–8, 89, 152, 189
Berlin Wall 26, 109
Bernicia 53
Berry's Wood, Herefordshire 176
Bica's Dyke, Oxfordshire 29, 31, 37, 41, 67, 75, 89–90, 113, 127–8, 145, 190
Bichamditch, Norfolk 36, 41, 89–90, 114, 132, 151, 183
Bishopstone, Herefordshire 176
Black Book of Carmarthen 100
Black Ditch (Snelsmore Common), Berkshire 41, 56, 148, 190
Black Ditches, Suffolk 36, 41, 60, 151, 185–7
Black Dyke, Northumberland 38, 130, 153, 157
Black Pig's Dyke, Ireland 110
Bodmin Moor, Cornwall 58
Bokerley Dyke, Dorset 10, 24, 36, 38, 42, 44, 47–8, 52, 59, 67, 75, 78–9, 82–3, 89, 103, 114, 119, 124, 127, 143, 145, 198
Bolster Bank, Cornwall 37, 42, 129, 126, 148, 194
Book of Llandaff 92
Bowland (Forest of), Lancashire 58
Bran Ditch, Cambridgeshire 12, 26, 38, 41, 48–53, 57, 67–8, 75, 79–81, 114, 143–4, 180
Brent Ditch, Cambridgeshire 24, 34, 41, 49, 180
Broomhead Dyke, Yorkshire 20, 39, 131, 146, 151, 160
Brycheiniog 122

Buckinghamshire–Hertfordshire Grim's Ditch 41, 57, 152, 188
Bulgaria 19
Bunn's Bank, Norfolk 41, 56, 148, 183
Burghal Hidage 43, 85
Burpham, Sussex 37
Bury's Bank, Berkshire 41, 67, 75, 81, 145, 190
Buttington, Powys 48, 52, 130
Bwlch Aeddan, Powys 23, 34, 39, 169
Bwlch Garw Dyke, Glamorgan *see* Clawdd Mawr Glyncorrwg
Bwlch y Cibau, Powys 39, 147, 153, 169
Bwlch y Clawdd, Glamorgan 27, 39, 147, 151, 169
Bwlch yr Afan, Powys 29, 39, 57, 113, 147, 151, 170

Cadbury, Somerset 135
Cadwallon (King) 97, 101, 112
Calver Dyke, Derbyshire 29, 39, 146, 151, 166
Camborne, Cornwall 126
Camps Tops (Morebattle), Scottish Borders 65
Cantref 22
Car Dyke, Lincolnshire 66–7
Catrail, Scottish Borders 23, 38, 146, 151, 157
Catreath (Battle of) 101
Cefn Eglwysilan, Glamorgan 39, 147, 170
Cefn Morfydd, Glamorgan 27, 39, 147, 170
Cefn-y-Crug, Powys 39, 147, 151, 170
Charlemagne (King) 72, 74, 92
charters 88–93, 114
Chester (Battle of) 53, 96, 173, 106
Chevin, Derbyshire 27
China (walls) 46, 75, 111–2

Cissbury Rings, Sussex 83
Clawdd Llesg, Powys 39, 103, 128, 147, 151, 170
Clawdd Mawr, Dyfed 27, 39, 147, 151, 170
Clawdd Mawr (Foel), Powys 39, 147, 151, 170
Clawdd Mawr (Llanfyllin), Powys 36, 40, 55, 67, 75, 144, 151, 171
Clawdd Mawr Glyncorrwg (Bwlch Garw Dyke), Glamorgan 39, 57, 147, 171
Clawdd Seri, Gwynedd 29, 31, 40, 92, 113, 147, 171
Clwyd-Powys Archaeological Trust (CPAT) 29
Combs Ditch, Dorset 36, 42, 51, 83, 87, 89, 91, 105, 150, 198
Concenn (King) 103
Coombe Bank (Reading), Berkshire 24, 37, 41, 54, 125, 154, 190
Cornwall (kingdom/people) 28, 138
Cottam, Yorkshire 24
Cowlod Dyke, Powys 40, 142, 147, 151, 171
Cranborne Chase Grim's Ditch 57, 89, 152
Craven, Yorkshire 27–8
Crich, Derbyshire 27
Crookham Common, Berkshire 35, 38, 41, 81, 91, 125, 148, 190
Crugyn Bank, Powys 36, 40, 55, 67, 75, 81, 144, 171–2
Crungoed, Powys 130
Cumbria 27
Cyneheard (King) 95
Cynewulf (King) 95, 118

Danby Rigg, Yorkshire 54, 110
Danes Cast, Ireland 110
Danes Dyke, Yorkshire 16, 25, 37, 39, 43, 115, 125–6, 146, 160
Danevirke 14, 19, 110
Danube (River) 72, 76
Dee (River) 30, 103, 177

Deil's Dyke, Dumfries and Galloway 23, 38, 154, 157
Deira 94
dendrochronology 44
Devil's Ditch (Andover), Hampshire 42, 89, 149, 198
Devil's Ditch (Garboldisham), Norfolk 36, 41, 55, 114, 150, 183
Devil's Ditch, Cambridgeshire 32, 35, 38, 41, 48–9, 64–5, 67–8, 70–1, 74–5, 78–80, 114, 121, 134, 143–4, 181
Devil's Mouth Ditch, Shropshire 40, 58, 152, 178
Dinas Powys, Glamorgan 61
Dodman, Cornwall 37, 42, 148, 194
Dole's Wood, Hampshire 42, 199
Domesday Book 27, 87, 105, 127
Dorset Cursus 67
Dorsey, Ireland 110
Dundon Hill, Somerset 130–1
Durrington Walls, Wiltshire 65, 67, 71
Dyrham (Battle of) 94

East Anglia (kingdom) 36, 132
East Hampshire Dykes 42, 114, 142, 149, 199–200
East Tisted–Colemore Dyke, Hampshire 42, 149, 200
East Wixna 84
Eccles, Kent 48, 120
Edward I (King) 76
Edwin (King) 101
Egbert (King) 126
Eliseg (King) 103, 128
Epitoma Rei Militaris 72, 98, 104
Esjbøl-North 62, 199

Faesten Dyke, Kent 42, 60, 89, 91, 129, 149, 151, 201
Festaen Dic (Hartley Witney), Hampshire 42, 89, 91, 149, 201

Ffos Toncenglau, Glamorgan 40, 57, 147, 172
Filey, Yorkshire 131
Flamborough Head, Yorkshire 131
Flamingdice, Cambridgeshire 87
Fleam Dyke, Cambridgeshire 36, 38, 41, 44, 55, 67–8, 74–5, 79–80, 87, 89, 95, 143–4, 181
Fossditch, Norfolk 36, 38, 41, 53, 67, 75, 79, 144, 184
Fron Hill Dyke, Powys 40, 147, 172
Froxfield Dykes, Hampshire 23, 42, 149, 200
Fullinga Dyke, Surrey 29, 31, 42, 89–90, 129, 149, 202

geophysics 56, 139
Giant's Grave, Cornwall 16, 29, 36–7, 42, 148, 194
Giant's Grave, Powys 40, 55, 67, 75, 81, 104, 115, 144, 172
Giant's Hedge, Cornwall 23, 29, 37, 42, 83, 115, 126, 128, 130, 148, 195
Gildas 98, 102, 104, 109, 113, 120, 123, 133, 137
Gilling Wood Dyke, Yorkshire 16, 39, 94, 146, 160–1
Glastonbury Tor 130–1
Glastonbury, Somerset 25
Glywysing 122
Godfred (King) 110
Goldsborough, Yorkshire 131
Great Ridge Grim's Dyke, Wiltshire 89
Grey Ditch, Derbyshire 29–30, 36, 39, 48, 52, 67, 75, 81, 122, 130, 144, 166
Grim's Bank (Padworth), Berkshire 41, 57, 148, 190
Grim's Ditch (Leeds), Yorkshire 38, 56–7, 152, 158–9
Gwynedd (kingdom) 125